A LIFE IN THE GARDEN

A LIFE IN THE GARDEN

Tales and Tips for Growing Food in Every Season

BARBARA DAMROSCH

Timber Press
Portland, OR

Timber Press
Workman Publishing
Hachette Book Group, Inc.
1290 Avenue of the Americas
New York, New York 10104
timberpress.com

Timber Press is an imprint of Workman Publishing, a division of Hachette Book Group, Inc. The Timber Press name and logo are registered trademarks of Hachette Book Group, Inc.

Printed in China on responsibly sourced paper
Text and cover design by Leigh Thomas

The publisher is not responsible for websites (or their content) that are not owned by the publisher.

The Hachette Speakers Bureau provides a wide range of authors for speaking events. To find out more, go to HachetteSpeakersBureau.com or email HachetteSpeakers@hbgusa.com.

ISBN 978-1-64326-181-2

Catalog records for this book are available from the Library of Congress.

CONTENTS

144
PART FOUR: SHARING THE GARDEN

188
PART FIVE: WHAT TO GROW

WHY I GROW FOOD

PART ONE

CHAPTER 1

The Seeds Are Sown

To get to our own personal Garden of Eden took three days. Our mother would pack us into a cab—my sister Eloise, my sister Anne, and me, city kids all—and head for New York's Grand Central Station, where we boarded a train. On it we four travelled due north up the Hudson River to Troy, along the famous "Water Level Route," but at some point during the night, asleep in cozy bunks lit by tiny blue lights, we switched direction and headed west. The next day we changed trains in St. Louis and made our way toward the Deep South, sleeping through the Ozark Mountains, and finally, on day three, pulling into Texarkana, a town named for the spot where Texas and Arkansas railroads met, a bit north of Louisiana. Then down into Louisiana we went by car, to the small town of Haynesville, where our mother, Eleanor, was born.

Our grandparents Lucille and Asa ("Cile" and "Pop") both grew up on farms and never gave up the habit of growing their own food. The land on which their house sat was a green paradise. Flower gardens exploded with color. Tall pecan trees yielded a huge harvest of the nuts that are still essential to my cooking. Other trees, such as persimmons, grew fruits I'd neither seen nor tasted up north. And, of course, there was a large

Corn planted in hills

vegetable garden. There Pop taught me how to thump melons and listen for the resonant sound that signaled ripeness. Sometimes he took us to a nearby lake where we caught fish for supper. In his younger days he had raised and cured his own hogs, and the family ate storage crops from the root cellar in wintertime. Cile made home-canned mayhaw jelly (from the fruit of native hawthorn trees), tomato relish, watermelon pickles, and other condiments for the winter table.

Cile ran a busy household. The oldest of twelve children, she had numerous relatives and friends who lived nearby and often came and visited. I will always think of visiting—which meant just sitting and talking—as a major feature of southern life. Sometimes, as we sat together, we shelled homegrown peas, the creamy little "lady peas" that Cile preferred.

Back in New York we received shipments of Cile's preserves and other treats: winter-blooming camellias that barely survived the trip, and a box full of sugarcane that Mother taught us to chew on, to extract the sweet juice. Another shipment caused a brief panic. "Mrs. Damrosch, Mrs. Damrosch!" cried the elevator man, pounding on our door, next to a pile of heavy, lumpy muslin bags labeled "Dallas National Bank." "Don't worry," Mother said, "It's only pecans." We all set about with our little picks and nutcrackers to extract the meats. To us they were more valuable than gold doubloons.

We talked about our grandparents' home as if it were heaven. At the hospital where our father practiced pediatrics, his colleagues would ask him: "What is this place your children go to, where the streets are paved with gold?" We begged to be taken to Louisiana. Once, at summer's end, we were seated on the train that was to take us home, three little girls in a row in our sandals and summer dresses, crying our hearts out. The porter pleaded with Mother, "Why are you taking these children up north? Can't you see they don't want to go?"

Was it just the food? Not entirely. One thing that made Cile and Pop's home so special for us was the way we were treated. Grown-ups acted as if the only thing that mattered in life was to keep children happy, and, short

of anything that might harm us, we were given the run of the property and the freedom to do whatever we liked. If I wanted to pick armloads of flowers from Cile's gardens, pile them onto the dining room table, and try to recreate arrangements she made for the Baptist church, well, that was fine with her, no matter how much of a mess I made. We were welcome in the kitchen too, and we were never forced to eat anything that we didn't like.

But it was all delicious! There was homemade bread at every meal, not just loaf bread but also biscuits, corn pone, and muffins. Growing, cooking, and eating the best possible food was a matter of such importance that it remains a part of my core values to this day and is one of my foremost pursuits. It was among the most precious things that Mother brought to her marriage. In addition to her natural kindness, her skill and generosity in the kitchen seemed like a miracle to our father, raised by a pious, rigid mother who seemed to frown on pleasure of any kind. Much

Sisters on a mule, with me up front, then Eloise, then Anne.

That's me with the mattock, planting pine trees with my dad.

to our delight, the southern passion for good food rubbed off on him, and he started cooking too. We became a cooking family.

When I was ten, we acquired a small cottage in the Connecticut woods. Our father needed a place to escape on weekends, after making house calls day and night all over New York. And that's where we became gardeners as well. Mother filled the yard with flowers. Daddy planted a kitchen garden on a sunny slope and felled trees to get a big asparagus patch going. Each daughter had her own tiny plot, mostly succulents such as hen-and-chicks, nestled among rock outcroppings. But, as the oldest, I wanted something more ambitious, and nagged Daddy to till me up some sod so that I could oversee a real garden. Time passed. One day while he was socializing indoors with some friends, one of them looked out the window and said, "Doug, do you know that Barbara is out there hacking up the lawn?"

I've been hacking up lawns and planting gardens ever since. For a considerable stretch—graduate school at Columbia University, teaching jobs at four colleges, and several years as a freelance writer in New

York—gardening was impossible, although I did grow a few tomatoes in Vermont while teaching at Middlebury College. But during my thirties, I read Helen and Scott Nearing's classic bible of self-sufficiency, *Living the Good Life*, and, like so many others, I became obsessed with the way the Nearings lived. Whenever I needed to think of something pleasant (such as when I was in a dentist's chair), I imagined myself walking between rows of tall, trellised tomatoes, smelling that tomatoey smell and gathering the red, sun-warmed globes.

Helen Nearing in her greenhouse

Eliot Coleman transplanting seedlings

I was right in step with many in my generation, questioning the value of modern, commercialized life. But I was luckier than most of my city friends. Because of Louisiana, I had grown up with a direct personal link to food of the pre-industrial past.

In 1976, a house suddenly became available to me next to the Connecticut place, where my parents had retired. Single again, after a short marriage, I moved there with my nine-year-old son, Christopher, with the goal of growing food. Without the money to buy farmland, I planted a 40-by-60-foot vegetable garden. Thanks to its success, I landed a job at a nearby organic farm and nursery. Subsequently, I made a living as a landscaper and then as a landscape designer. I still wrote, but now my main subject was gardening.

In May 1991, my father passed away, and in the months to come I made trips to Maine to see my mother, who was living alone in the town of Blue Hill. Amazingly, it turned out that she was friendly with Helen Nearing, who lived half an hour away in the stone house she had built with Scott, who had died in 1983. I paid Helen a visit, as so many of her followers had done before me. She was tying up tomato plants inside the small lean-to greenhouse that was part of her bounteous stone-walled food garden. Assisting her was Eliot Coleman, a fellow author, who owned a vegetable farm next door on land he had bought from Helen and Scott in 1968. That encounter changed everything.

Eliot showed me around Helen's garden, then his own extensive plot, where he was resurrecting his farm after a nine-year absence. He asked me out for pizza. He followed me to Connecticut. I followed him back to Maine, and we began growing vegetables together, both at the farm and at a large home plot. On December 15, 1991, we were married. We are still here.

So this is a love story. But it's also about the ways our lives have been enhanced by working with the natural world. I'd like to share some of the knowledge that has made growing food such a pleasure for me—not just the techniques I've learned but also the mindset that it takes to learn them. It's about giving up some control, and letting natural forces do much of the labor.

Because I live in a particular region of the United States, midcoast Maine, my climate may not be very much like yours. In some cases the plant varieties I've had the best luck with may not be the ones for you, and may not even be in the catalogs where I originally found them. So I may be on the prowl for the best new ones. Good gardening always requires a measure of flexibility. It is not a struggle, either mental or physical. It is an art of adaptation, contemplation, and an expansion of the mind. Many find it addicting.

For me and for Eliot, growing our own food is a given, an act that is essential to our well-being. Many of our friends and neighbors think about it the same way. But it's interesting to look back on our nation's history and see how such attitudes, over the years, have changed.

Summer fields at
Four Season Farm

CHAPTER 2

Kitchen Gardens in America

There was a time in our country when growing food was the most important thing you could do. When Thomas Jefferson referred to the United States as "a nation of farmers," he included the citizenry as a whole, which had gardens and was capable of ensuring its own food supply. Those gardens were tidy rectangular plots, models of clarity and designed for high yields. Their rows ran crosswise, like lines on a page, each sown to a different crop. Jefferson's own garden at Monticello was a thousand feet long, but a more typical family could be fed with a plot of a modest 50 by 100 feet.

By the 1970s, less than half of U.S. families grew any vegetables at all. As the baby boomers came of age, food gardening continued to dwindle. People were busy, had jobs, shopped at the supermarket, ate out. But that was just one point in time. If you look at the twentieth century as a whole, a pattern emerges:

- **World War I.** An army of American gardeners took up the shovel and the hoe to compensate for food shortages, send provisions abroad, and help ensure the nation's self-sufficiency. Daylight saving time was instituted to give people an extra hour after work

for growing peas, broccoli, and other crops in what were called "War Gardens."

Eliot and me in our first garden together

- **The stock market crash of 1929 and the Great Depression.** People picked up their shovels and hoes again, driven by economic uncertainty and need.

- **World War II.** People planted War Gardens again, which were renamed "Victory Gardens." Between home gardens and the community gardens that sprang up in vacant city lots, citizens were producing almost 40 percent of the nation's vegetables.

The gardeners of World War II

- **The Arab oil embargo, 1973–1974.** Home gardens sprang up again, in a time of scary economics.

- **The mortgage meltdown and Great Recession of 2007–2008.** This crisis led to the same result, with a big spike in sales of vegetable seeds.

- **The COVID-19 pandemic, 2020 and forward.** Home gardens are popular again, with vegetable seed sales higher than ever.

In some ways this is a reassuring tale. The urge to take control of our own food supply is a sane one in times of insecurity, especially if we can do it in our own backyards. It was Henry Ford who said, "No unemployment insurance can be compared to an alliance between man and a plot of land."

I have sometimes read about creatures that are inherently savvy about imminent danger, like the wild animals that race inland and upland when they sense from far away that a tsunami is coming, or dogs that can tell if you're about to have an epileptic fit. I like to think that we too have some innate scrap of good sense that tells us, when the outlook is dark, to head for the nearest piece of earth and make it bountiful. Given the complexity of the national food supply, a chain with many weak links, the reaction is a natural one.

The discouraging part is that in between these crises the interest in food gardening declines. After World War II the U.S. food supply became even more centralized. Farms were consolidated and relied heavily on fossil fuels, not only to drive farm machinery and transport the food, but also to manufacture the petrochemical-based nitrogen fertilizers that emerged from the cauldrons of the wartime gunpowder factories. There was also a growing capability gap. Before the war, most Americans probably knew enough about gardening to plant their Victory Gardens with some degree of confidence and success. But that changed to the point where we no longer have a familiarity with gardening to draw upon when the need or desire for homegrown food arises.

The contrast between having that knowledge and not having it was made clear to me in January and February of 1995. Eliot and I decided to take a trip in which we followed the 44th parallel—the line of latitude on which we live—through France and then Italy. Every point along that line naturally had the same day length we had at home, but in a climate made milder than ours by the Gulf Stream. Eliot had pioneered season-extending techniques that created milder microclimates than we had naturally in Maine, so we wanted to know what European farmers and gardeners were growing in their winter months. Much the same ones that we were, as it turned out—vegetables that did best in the cold season. But as we drove through both the towns and the countryside, we were surprised that so many homes had gardens. We glimpsed the blue-green foliage of leeks and other winter greens, sometimes protected by low, homemade tunnels of plastic stretched over wire hoops, or even small homemade greenhouses. It seemed that France and Italy not only embraced a tradition of eating a seasonal diet, they had also maintained a gardening culture, whereas ours had largely been lost in the distractions of modern life. And what a shame, given the fact that most of our country has a strong advantage in our longer day length and stronger winter sun.

I found it even more disheartening to open, in 2005, a book called *Hungry Planet: What the World Eats,* a splendid effort from writer Faith D'Aluisio and photographer Peter Menzel. That couple took a much more ambitious trip than ours, visiting thirty households in twenty-four countries and documenting their culinary lives. Menzel photographed each family amid the food it consumed during the course of a typical week.

The text celebrated whatever beauty, creativity, and pleasure were still inherent in the way these people ate. It was, as D'Aluisio put it, a "freeze-frame snapshot of a fast-moving target." Yet the overall picture was clear: The rest of the world was adopting America's worst eating trends. In most portraits, the people were surrounded by factory-made food, packaged in plastic wrap, bottles, cans, plastic foam trays, and cardboard boxes. Rows of large Coke and Pepsi bottles standing at attention in frame after frame spoke for themselves. And contributions by other

Vegetables grown by
chef Jean Bardet in
Tours, France

writers included in the book ensured that the message would not be
missed. Michael Pollan described the dark side of factory meat farms;
Dr. Francine R. Kaufman commented on rising diabetes rates worldwide;
and Marion Nestle noted that "today, except in the very poorest countries, more people are overweight than underweight." Maybe I shouldn't
have been surprised that only five of those thirty families were raising
any significant amount of their own food. Many admitted that they were
getting less exercise and eating less nutritious food but had opted for
convenience.

Menzel's portraits are fascinating cultural artifacts, and in years to come
they will illustrate a transitional time, one in which people were often
confused about food. What I see right now at home is a wave of food anxiety,
almost a fear of food. Many people I know want a healthy diet but they
believe that, by avoiding meat, fat, carbs, dairy, yeast, gluten, or some other
single input, their lives will change for the better. Yet they're still spending
a lot of money on manufactured foods and nutritional supplements.

I think the solution is much simpler. If you are lost in the woods, you try to retrace your steps to where you turned off the original path and then continue on from there. How about we just go back to the garden and find a way to make it mesh with our busy lives? It's such a perfect touchstone. Food grown at home or at a local farm and then processed at home is fresh. It's real. It tastes better. We need to hang onto those tastes as a point of reference, lest we forget.

Will we continue to see a pattern where spikes of unease alternate with valleys of complacency? I see the future as more of a downward slide, in which we experience a state of perpetual calamity for both our own health and the fate of human life on Earth—unless we face certain realities. The rest of the world may go its own way, but we can at least set a better example than we do now.

CHAPTER 3

You Can Do It

There are always some people who grow food at home, even in relatively secure times. Take the placid 1950s, for example, when my parents laid out their Connecticut plot. What made them exceptions to the rule? The examples of Cile and Pop for sure. But they were also ardent conservationists, and I find that those who stick with their gardens in good times and bad, who enjoy them and succeed with them, tend to have a positive view of the natural world. They understand that when you embrace that world, harness its power, and follow its rules, it will feed you. Working with it will invigorate you, get you out into the fresh air, and help keep you fit. At the end of a gardening day, you will feel what I call "the good kind of tired," the kind that gives you a healthy appetite for dinner and a sound sleep.

My own kitchen garden helps keep me in sync with a natural flow of life. The more I learn from working with the flora and fauna in my modest plot, the more centered, secure, and empowered I feel—not just in terms of ensuring my food supply, but in somehow tapping into the generosity of life on Earth.

It's hard to argue with that. But I so often hear that what I do is impossible for most people in the modern world. I'm told that few have the time, money, space, knowledge, or degree of fitness needed to have a garden. Yes, those limitations are sometimes real, but they don't always have to stop you in your tracks. Let's take a look.

Money

The idea that growing food is just a hobby of the privileged is a comical one. Before the industrial revolution, those who worked the soil were considered the bottom of the social ladder. Earning money to buy your food was seen as the first step up out of the dirty, mucky depths of the peasant class. In fact, anything store-bought was considered better than something homemade, whether clothing, furniture, or chocolate cake. But as the quantity of most purchased goods has grown and their quality has declined, the whole equation has been turned upside down.

Often the same skeptics who trivialize gardening are the ones who rage about the price of local organic food and the farmers' markets that sell it, because it's out of the price range of many customers. But real, wholesome, safe food is not expensive. It honestly reflects the cost to the people who grow it. Rather, the highly processed, additive-laden food sold by multinational corporations is artificially cheap, thanks to government subsidies and the underpayment of those who do most of the physical work of feeding the nation.

But while we're waiting for the government and the agricultural industry to end the policy of bad food for all and start to guarantee good, healthy food for everyone, let's make an end run around that dilemma and see if the obstacles facing would-be growers are as mighty as the pessimists claim.

Let's start with the easiest one: money. You can turn gardening into an expensive hobby, or you can spend almost nothing. A collection of basic hand tools such as rakes, shovels, and trowels can be picked up at garage sales dirt cheap. Pun intended. Big noisy tools such as rototillers and leaf shredders can be shared by a group of neighbors, but you can also garden without them. I do.

Purchased fertilizers cost money but homemade compost is free food for your garden, so once you get your system going you might never have to spend a dime on fertility. When I started that first 40-by-60-foot garden, I had nothing to fertilize it with, so I carried around a bunch of old empty feed bags and a shovel in the back of my car. Whenever I passed a horse stable or other likely spot to mooch from, I stopped and asked the owner if they had an old pile of well-rotted manure I could relieve them of. Often they did.

Packets of seeds you buy often contain enough for several seasons. Better yet, seeds produced by open-pollinated varieties, as opposed to patented F^1 hybrids, can be saved from the plants you grow and resemble their parents—unlike the hybrids that must be purchased repeatedly from the patent holder. And look at nature's math: one tomato contains enough seeds to grow a very long row of plants, each of which can produce a bucketload of tomatoes. Once established, your plot will more than earn its keep, since even a small harvest represents dollars not spent at the store.

These seeds were saved from an heirloom kale variety.

Time

Finding time for an ambitious garden might involve a drastic step, such as one family member quitting their job, cutting back on work hours, or working at home to avoid a long commute. Or it might involve more minor adjustments in the way you spend your time, such as limiting social media involvement, swapping aerobics class for gardening, or weeding on weekends instead of watching football. There are also ways to garden more efficiently, usually by letting natural forces do some of the work. Choosing the right tools can make a big difference. And so, oddly, is extending the season. Growing cool weather vegetables, while protecting them from severe cold (more about that in Chapter 12), allows me to spread both the work and the harvest out over the year instead of cramming it into a frenzied summer, followed by a canning-and-freezing marathon at summer's end. I've also swapped the convenience of finding

Front yard vegetables steal the show in this productive little garden.

anything I want at the supermarket, any day in the year, for the special pleasures of eating with the seasons. And, as with most skills, the more I garden, the better I do it and the less time it takes.

Space

Obviously, it helps to have a yard. Ideally, it's a backyard, but a well-tended vegetable garden in front of the house, with plants of different colors in tidy rows, can be as pretty as a perennial border and more interesting than a row of pruned shrubs. Ideally, the spot for a garden gets six hours of sun a day, but it's worth trying even with just four, especially if most of the crops are leafy ones such as lettuce and stem crops such as celery, as opposed to fruiting ones like tomatoes and squash. A bit of pruning or even deforesting may be in order to let in more sun. It's great if the yard already has good soil, but soil can always be improved or even created from scratch. Even a yard or patio that's all concrete can host a garden if you build raised beds on top of it. If a planting area is very small, there are many ways to make the most of the space by choosing the most productive crops and a planting scheme that ensures continuous harvests.

When landscaping, why not choose fruit-bearing shrubs, trees, and vines that add beauty and bounty at the same time? Sometimes you have to sacrifice the lawn—or at least part of it. Lawns do have their virtues. They are often the center of family activities. Visually, they make a tidy scenic frame for the other features in a home landscape. But if you're tired of endless mowing, it might be fun to pick tomatoes instead.

No yard at all? Try the buddy system. If you can find a neighbor who has a suitable space and would love to have a regular supply of fresh produce but lacks the initiative, make a deal that gives you a garden site in return for a share of the harvest. Or perhaps you have the yard, but the neighbor contributes the time and muscle. Or you share it together.

Obviously, the more urban the setting, the less personal garden space may be available. That's where community gardens come in. This is a concept dear to my heart. Some of these shared plots are grassroots efforts in places called "food deserts" where sources of good fresh produce and the money to buy it are both in short supply. Often it starts when one energetic person, or a group, takes over a vacant lot, and soon there's a band of folks working their plots and sharing knowledge. Sometimes the instigators have immigrated from countries where gardening is still a birthright. Other community gardens are more institutional ones, where you can rent a plot for the duration of the growing season. There are certain rules to obey ("Always shut the gate" and "Don't let your squash vines wander") but the benefits of shared space outweigh any inconvenience. Friendly competition spurs gardeners on. New varieties to try are on display all around you and you can usually beg a taste. If you need to take a break, you might swap weed duty for food or repay the favor with help later on. Pride in the community garden can sometimes turn a neighborhood around, as the spirit of cooperation overflows into other projects or causes.

Vegetables and
flowers share a
community garden
plot in Burlington,
Vermont.

Community gardening is not new. During the Middle Ages, individual plots encircled the towns, outside the walls. A more modern version had its beginnings during the industrial revolution, when people flocked to the cities but still wanted access to fresh, homegrown food. My friend Pauline recalls her childhood in London, when her grandfather loaded her into a wheelbarrow and wheeled her down the street to a garden where there were seventy family plots. Many had little toolsheds, chicken coops, and rabbit hutches. When Pauline went back to visit, she was happy to see these gardens still being tended. Europe still has these "allotment" gardens, usually grouped together. The individual plots tend to be larger than American ones—the size of a doubles tennis court would not be unusual. The community gardening movement here is alive and well. Look to the American Community Gardening Association (communitygarden.org) to find out about ones in your area or to inspire you to start your own.

We need more urban land specifically targeted for growing food. Finding it is a great exercise of the imagination. Think of civic spaces that might have a bit of land that they can spare, such as parks, hospitals, churches, universities, prisons, libraries, apartment complexes, retirement villages, factories, office buildings, and, best of all, schools. Any available school land not used for sports might well be tilled up to let oats, peas, beans, and barley grow, as the old song goes—plus the most important harvest: knowledge.

Garden Literacy

A while back I interviewed a number of restaurant chefs who had created food gardens on their properties, partly to supply their kitchens with the freshest produce and partly to give their patrons a close look at the food-to-table connection. One used to send his diners on a pre-meal tour of the garden, with wine glasses in their hands. He recalled one woman's puzzlement when she saw a red pepper on a plant. "You mean, that's the same thing that you buy at the store and eat?" she asked. Sometimes the disconnect is astonishing.

Without family mentors, how can we expose our children to the idea and science of growing real food? Some life skills, such as riding a bicycle, are just picked up along the way. But the best way to guarantee a nation-wide garden literacy is to teach it in school.

Future chroniclers of our nation's culture will note a particularly dismal interval during the twenty-first century when public schools sold junk food to students, despite mounting evidence of its link to obesity and ill health. Administrators, dodging the issues of contracts with fast-food chains and vending machines, offered the defeatist line that if the kids didn't eat it at school, they'd eat it elsewhere. Installing machines with healthier options did not always help, since the items in there were rarely fresh and lost out to worse choices if those were in there too.

But every now and then one sees an intractable problem solved by people who are simply determined to make it happen. One day about ten years ago, while visiting a public school in Deer Isle, Maine, I noticed a piece of paper tacked up in the school kitchen, with a list of healthy snacks, such as fruit, nuts, carrot sticks, and cheese, that could be made available to sustain everybody's energy level without doing harm. Whatever the hurdles may have been, that school was trying to clear them.

Back in 2005, Eliot and I saw another powerful example of making the impossible happen. We got a hope-inspiring tour of the famous Edible Schoolyard Project at the Martin Luther King Jr. Middle School in Berkeley, California. An urban school with few resources, it didn't have a lunch program. Ten years before, it had drawn the attention of author and restaurateur Alice Waters. Then, fortunately, its principal Neil Smith caught Waters's visionary spark. With help from many donors and volunteers, Waters and the school replaced an asphalt parking lot with a one-acre school garden, and then a kitchen classroom. The project is now the model for a nationwide movement to put gardening and cooking in schools.

The day we visited, edible calendula and borage flowers were in bloom. The children had planted some veggies in straight rows, others in free-form beds with meandering paths. They had painted beautiful colored signs that identified crops in various languages (more than two dozen native tongues were represented at the school). Saplings had been formed into arches, teepees, and fans that supported the taller crops. Two giant bay trees framed the entrance, and fruit trees were espaliered on the back fence. A magnificent homemade stone baking oven had pride of place, and a central ramada, built of logs and clothed with vines, served as a rainproof classroom. There was even a henhouse, and a toolshed.

As we arrived, thirty jeans-clad students began their ninety-minute class in the garden. They looked about twelve years old. With no horsing around, they settled into an attentive circle, sitting on straw bales inside the ramada, where a teacher and two aides launched the day's discussion.

As the kids chose their work details, one bunch headed off to build a sapling fence. A large jovial group, mostly girls, sat down to design creative seed packets at a long table under a tree. The third squad, devoted stewards of the compost, raked up leaves, spent crops, and chicken manure to put on the compost piles. The chickens had their own devoted little cadre. One small boy approached me, holding a brown hen against his chest. "I can feel her heart beating," he said.

Meanwhile, inside the kitchen bungalow, thirty younger children were making wonton soup. They simmered the noodle wrappers to soften them, then stuffed them with a filling made from the garden's vegetables. These were then added to a broth along with bright green scallions and some cut-up bok choy, also from the garden. It was a beautiful dish that would not have looked out of place at Waters' famed Chez Panisse, and the children ate it with gusto. These were conscientious little cooks who had mastered knife safety and kitchen cleanup. And they were enjoying something still rare in today's world—a homemade meal served up with lively conversation at a communal table.

The Brooksville Elementary School Garden in Brooksville, Maine

Alice Waters founded the Edible Schoolyard with broad goals. As their consulting farmer Wendy Johnson told me, "People always ask if we're changing the way the children eat, but what we're doing is changing their lives." They were learning responsibility, good work habits, respect for the natural world and for each other. They studied world food culture, seasonal eating, the cycle of nutrients from earth to table and back to the earth. The whole school faculty was using the garden as a resource, tying it into everything from biology to history to math. Parents and the local community were drawn in too, through festivals, or by volunteering. And a new school cafeteria was being built, for which the garden would soon contribute something to each meal.

Waters went on to initiate a city-wide program called the School Lunch Initiative, a partnership between the Chez Panisse Foundation and the Berkeley Board of Education. Its goal was to "treat lunch as an academic subject" with the goal of "transforming public education by using food traditions to teach, nurture and empower young people."

Since that time, her initial efforts have had a profound influence on people in this country, including Michelle Obama, who brought local school kids to her White House garden. I wish I could say that every

American school now has a garden, but thousands of them do, and the idea no longer surprises people. It's spreading because it has its own logic and its own appeal. Sometimes the cooking connection is there, sometimes not.

The K-through-8 public school in my town, Brooksville, Maine, has only about fifty students. But it's equipped with a garden and a small greenhouse, as are a number of other schools in Hancock County. Ours has a gardening summer day camp, a garden club for students, and a paid gardening teacher named Justine. It gives me hope for the future.

Never Too Old

I've noticed that few people who garden ever retire from it. In recent years more of the young and fit have taken it up, thanks to a growing focus on eating a more wholesome diet and treating the planet more kindly. But it's still often portrayed as an old person's game, one you play after a career in something more profitable—gardening and digging weeds as the Beatles sang in "When I'm Sixty-Four." Many oldsters are far more active in their gardens now than they were when they lived behind their desks. Maybe that's why they've made it so far, their joints greased with raking and hoeing, their bones strengthened by hoisting bags of peat moss into their SUVs, their weight stabilized by the endless dragging of hoses, their nervous systems calmed by the rhythm of weeding, and their diets fortified by homegrown carrots and beets.

My favorite exemplars are the Nearings, whose books still lure readers back to the land, or at least to the veggie plot. Scott Nearing, who died at age one hundred in 1983, was a personal mentor to Eliot. He recalls how Scott worked regularly in his garden until he was ninety-nine. I was lucky to know Helen, who was still tending a kitchen garden in her nineties, until a car accident took her life. She pushed laden wheelbarrows, made compost, and ate almost nothing she didn't grow herself.

Helen once told me that gardening was her tennis, her golf, and her fitness routine. I follow that example. Why tussle with a Nautilus machine when I can walk outside, spend some time in the fresh air, and come in with an armload of beautiful fresh food?

Becoming wiser is one of the oft-touted benefits of age, and old gardeners who keep on going have learned to lift things with their backs straight and their knees bent, and to vary their chores throughout the day to avoid repetitive stress. They pause to stretch a bit, drink lots of water, watch for ticks, and wear hats.

People who view gardening as backbreaking are probably using their backs when they should use their brains. It helps to vary the position as well as the task. If you're weeding, kneel on one knee, then the other, then sit, crouch, or squat. It's easy to get caught up in the project and ignore what it's doing to your body—until the next morning when you try to get out of bed. It helps to divide big jobs into small units. Deadlines are, well, deadly. Eliot and I learned this the hard way when we had to— almost overnight—create an entire set for *Gardening Naturally*, the TV series we hosted for The Learning Channel. It took a shiatsu practitioner to untie all the knots in our crippled little bodies.

I get my weight-bearing exercise from carrying bales of mulch hay, my resistance training when I pull out stubborn roots and stumps, and my heart/lung workout when I break up sod to make a new bed. I may not know my gluteus maximus from my latissimus dorsi (weren't they Roman emperors?) but I'm sure they both get well used.

However, you have to know your limitations. This has been a hard lesson for me to learn, because the harm that we do to our bodies does not always show up right away, or even give us a warning. When I was doing landscaping work in my thirties and forties, I felt that I was indomitable. No hole was too deep for me to dig and no tree was too big for me to plant. I loved the work, and my body gave me no hint that I was asking too much from it. It didn't deliver that message until I reached my seventies and my shoulder joints showed evidence of too much wear and tear. Since there is often no sure way to predict outcomes like that, it pays to practice moderation.

Eliot's battle scars owe more to sports than farming, though he did clear his own land by hand with an axe and a bow saw. In fact, I was surprised to learn, when I started farming with him, that the work was easier than landscaping could ever be. Early on, he introduced me to its gentle rhythm. One evening, when darkness was falling and I was still crouched in a path, weeding carrots, he came over and scooped me up as if I were a laying hen, carried me down the path, and set me on the grass. "Quitting time," he said.

Moderation. Write the word down.

Weathering It

There's only one thing wrong with gardeners: They're always talking about the weather. Everybody uses conversational gambits such as "Nice day" or "Hot enough for you?" But with the weather-obsessed that's just the opening pitch. They have to tell you how low the thermometer went last night at their place, evaluate the likelihood of rain, and then produce statistics on how deep the frost was last winter as compared with the winter before that. It'll take the whole nine innings to wrap it all up. But better them than the West Coast friends with news of their daffodils in February, when I'm tempted to screen all California numbers with caller ID.

When the weather does something really spectacular, it's a different story. Everyone wants to know, from one minute to the next, at what speed the latest hurricane is revolving, and its likely path. These events are so mythopoeic in their power that we give them proper names. But to a gardener concerned about her beans, local conditions can loom just as large. Maybe if we named these as well, more people would take notice. Would ears perk up if I described my tussle with Two Week Drizzle Frances? Would drivers brake to read the bumper sticker: "I survived Microburst Paul"?

It's not that weather isn't fascinating. I love hearing something I didn't know already, such as the fact that raindrops don't fall faster than 18 miles per hour, whereas hailstones might nail your corn at 100 mph. And that hailstones are formed when updrafts lift raindrops into a zone of frigid air, bouncing them around like Ping Pong balls until they are so heavy that they plummet to Earth.

I'd like to get better at reading the weather reports that the clouds write so eloquently across the sky. The sweeps of mares' tails and the puffs of mackerel skies mean a warm front is coming. With a stretch of damp weather ahead, that's a good time to sow seeds. I might get that same report online—or maybe not. If you spend time outdoors, you get a very real sense of the weather. It's touching your skin, it's entering your body. Some people say they can smell weather, and I'm sure this is true. After all, air currents pass over various landforms on their way, bringing a resinous scent from spruce forests, a briny one from the sea.

The weather report can become an obsession. Leafing through a catalog that sells gadgets for home prognosticators, I found one that could project the present temperature on my bedroom ceiling so as to be the first thing I saw when I opened my eyes. Surely, some mornings I would never get out of bed, but just stay in my burrow for six more weeks, until spring.

If I were going out in a boat or up in a plane, I'd like to know if thunderstorms were on the agenda. But on a gardening day, I'd rather just feel a sudden stir in the air and look up to see a magnificent cumulous cloud bearing down on me, with just enough time to take the laundry off the line.

There's an old joke that goes, "Everybody talks about the weather, but nobody does anything about it." While gardeners may often wish they could "turn the winds around," as Steve Martin's weatherman did in the film *L.A. Story,* their best course is to prepare for whatever the sky throws at them. You need a good slicker, a sun hat, and plenty of good spongy organic matter in your garden's soil to both absorb and release rain. A simple cold frame will do something about winter's ice and snow. A row of fluffy white pine trees will absorb strong winds.

Eliot tells a story about his car going off the road during a soggy Vermont snowstorm, and the farmer who stopped and helped him dig out. Old Vermonters are notoriously laconic, and while the two were shoveling there wasn't much conversation. "Wet, isn't it?" Eliot finally remarked. The farmer replied, "Wet? I couldn't be wetter 'less'n I was bigger." And that about summed it up.

WHERE TO START

PART TWO

CHAPTER 4

Horticulture: The Humble Science

I hadn't read much about growing food before I sunk my spade into the soil of that first large Connecticut plot. I'd pick the brain of the produce guy of the local grocery store, a former farmer, and he was helpful. I picked up tips from my industrious father, but not always the right ones. For example, he once mentioned to me that "if you can wiggle a large rock with a crowbar, you will be able to remove it with a come-along." Now that happens to be true, but I heard it as "you *have* to remove it." The soil in northwestern Connecticut is notoriously rocky, and any rock you remove has another rock underneath it. So what I ended up with was a 40-by-60-foot sunken garden, with massive boulders all around the sides.

If I'd known more about how nature gardens, I would have understood that soil is formed from the top down. I would have removed only the rocks close to the surface, then added as much organic matter as I could find, until I had a rich, loamy plot.

Here are some more of the things I've discovered about gardening over the intervening years. It helps to get a handle on how things work out there, beneath your feet.

The Living Soil

I learned the most about plant science on my hands and knees, working the soil, and there was a point in my nineteenth year when I might have had a great head start. As a freshman at Wheaton College in Norton, Massachusetts, in an invertebrate zoology class, I began a research project on soil organisms. Kneeling in the forest, brushing away the rough upper layer of dead leaves, followed by the increasingly crumbly layers of duff, I inspected the successive strata of the soil. I found worms, ants, grubs, beetles, and the sleeping pupae of insects that would emerge with wings in summer. I looked forward to repeating this sampling at various other locations in the Wheaton woods, and spending hours at the microscope in the lab, discovering other soil communities that were invisible to the naked eye. As ill luck would have it, my research was stopped dead at the upper leaf layer, a layer composed largely of the species *Toxicodendron radicans*, otherwise known as poison ivy.

After I got out of the infirmary, I rerouted my study toward a fruitless search for intestinal parasites in the goldfish of Wheaton's pond. Had I persevered with my first topic I'd have learned sooner rather than later the most important lesson for any gardener—that the soil is alive, more alive than you can possibly imagine.

It's very busy down there. Entire civilizations are trading, cooperating, battling, and building structures. While some ants are herding aphids aboveground and milking them for their sweet secretions, others are tending fungus gardens down below. Soil creatures are highly specialized, doing particular tasks at different levels in the soil, under specific conditions, and most of them are buried, operating in the dark, and much too small to see. In Fritz-Martin Engel's 1961 book *Creatures of the Earth's Crust*, he described the diverse species of microscopic, bacteria-munching rotifers, also called "wheel animals," each with a unique set of jaws. He writes that each "turns out to be a biological prototype for seizing, holding, cutting, pricking, or grinding. We meet forms which might serve

Chewing mechanisms of various wheel animals (*Rotifera*), from the simplest to the most perfectly constructed type.

Microscopic rotifers or "wheel animals"

as patterns for hammer and anvil, awl, knife, shears, file, pincers, and dozens of other such tools."

The top six inches or so of soil teem with populations of microscopic bacteria, fungi, algae, protozoa, and slightly larger nematodes and mites, to name just a few. Because of their numbers, and importance, soil microbes make life on Earth possible. Most of this happens in the rhizosphere, the area where a plant's roots partner with microbial teams. The plants actually select the appropriate microbial communities that will not only feed them but also fend off harmful forms of bacteria and fungi. The suitability of a plant's chosen range of microbes, acting in concert, has been referred to as a "second genome."

How does this work? Plants' roots exude carbon sugars that feed microbes, which return the favor by breaking down nutritious organic wastes—plant and animal matter—into forms that plant roots can absorb and use. Without them, no plants will grow, and no animals will exist. Humus, the end result of decomposition, could not be there to give the soil structure and tilth, with plenty of air spaces between soil particles so that plant roots can breathe. There could be none of the sponginess that makes soil both able to hold water when needed and release it when not. We can thank certain soil fungi for creating a gummy protein called glomalin that causes soil particles to clump together into that wonderful chocolate cake structure that gardeners prize.

Soil scientists are still uncovering the mysteries of how these microbial communities operate and how similar exchanges take place in the human gut, with enormous implications for the health of our bodies. Now that's humbling. It's like finding out that the guys in the mailroom are running the company.

Nothing in my subsequent academic studies led me back into that inspiring underground world, certainly not my senior thesis on Chaucer's sense of humor, or my never-completed doctoral dissertation on his pagan goddesses, fun as those topics were. Yet I have tried to read as much as I can to make up for lost time. Other sources about soil life I recommend are the works of Selman A. Waksman and, more recently, David R. Montgomery. His book *The Hidden Half of Nature: The Microbial Roots of Life and Health*, coauthored with his wife, Anne Bicklé, is a fine introduction to the subject. Another is *Teaming with Microbes: The Organic Gardener's Guide to the Soil Food Web* by Jeff Lowenfels and Wayne Lewis.

Who's in Charge?

Aboveground, in our own fields and gardens, we humans are newcomers, and clumsy ones. We clomp about with our boots and bulldozers, compacting the soil and crushing all the magnificent worm burrows and the airshafts of ground-dwelling native bees. Too often we fail to consider the life of the soil—and any other part of nature that we touch—as an endlessly complex set of interrelationships. Faced with a cloth of many patterns, we pull it apart and isolate single threads, appropriating them out of context. Our short-term gains are sometimes spectacular, but our long-term results are not. Our minds are as clumsy as our feet.

The "Green Revolution" that followed on the heels of the Second World War did not, I believe, take agriculture down a path of long-term success. It reduced soil fertility to a few basic elements that plants need, notably nitrogen, potassium, and phosphorus. This approach resulted in crops with fast growth and high yields that were less nutrient dense, less flavorful, and less resistant to pests and diseases. An increase in the use of toxic pesticides naturally followed.

Even when more close attention is paid to essential trace minerals, the problem still persists when the complexity of naturally fertile soil is not considered. We might analyze healthy, living soil and try to list all of its ingredients, including organic ones, but even if we were to round up everything on that list in the right proportions and put them all in a bucket, we'd only be setting the stage for living soil, not creating it. Garden soil isn't a thing, it's a process by which the residues of once-alive organisms are regenerated into new ones. It involves complex biochemical reactions among animals, vegetables, and minerals—including, no doubt, many "X" factors that are not on anyone's list yet. We may study these X factors, try to understand their roles, pay homage to them, and find ways to better allow them to work. But that does not mean extracting them, simulating them, synthesizing them, and selling them for profit. That simply does not work. It does not get us better food.

The same reductive policy is at work in the dwindling number of crops being grown: The great cornucopia of plant germplasm that exists on Earth, that has evolved partly through humans' efforts, has been reduced to a handful of varieties adapted to industrial methods of growing, harvesting, storing, shipping, and consumption. The whole industry has become so consolidated that most rural farming communities no longer exist. Most food no longer has any local flavor. It's grown in vast monoculture wastelands, devoid of plant and animal diversity. Worst of all, these practices are being spread throughout the entire globe so that the planet's vast wealth of ancient or traditional gardening and farming lore is ignored and in danger of being lost forever.

Food nutrition is approached in the same reductive way—breaking food down into key components to be isolated, fabricated, and sold. Just the way fertile soil is a complete package of nutrients that benefit plants in complex, synergistic ways, so the foods that humans have evolved with are complete packages too.

We do learn. Let's take the provitamin beta-carotene, present in a large number of food plants, which the body turns into vitamin A. Riding the crest of publicity about its properties as an antioxidant and potential cancer fighter, it was packaged as a dietary supplement. But studies have shown that the supplement could actually cause cancer instead. Better to

It's all connected: The yolks of these eggs are bright orange thanks to the nutrient-rich dandelions our chickens eat. The two together make a superhealthy dish.

get your carotene from carrots, or orange-fleshed squash, or dark leafy greens that deliver it in synergy with other elements, in a setting our bodies are used to.

The same thing happened with folate. Eating folate-rich foods such as legumes and leafy greens seems to lower the risk of colon cancer. But according to the American Institute for Cancer Research, folate taken alone in supplement form increases the incidence of precancerous colon polyps. The more stories like this I hear, the more I feel that eating well is very simple. Get your nutrients from eating a balanced diet of real food.

Every time a new miracle of nature is brought to light, it is turned into a product. Research into the allelopathic chemicals with which plants fight pests might lead to repellents made from those compounds, or even crops engineered to contain them. Is that a good idea? It sounds risky. I'd rather try to grow healthy, vigorous plants more likely to resist those predators. As for the insane idea of putting a fish gene in a tomato to make it more cold tolerant, the whole point of eating a tomato is to do it in summertime when it has been sun ripened, carries a good nutritional package, and tastes good.

Cold weather is for dishes such as roast pork, but even this one has been hideously tampered with. In January 2002 it was announced that Japanese scientists had produced two generations of leaner pigs by the insertion of a spinach gene. This is an insult to the noble pig, whose flesh is leaner and healthier when it leads the athletic life it was designed to lead, foraging for acorns in the woods, not gorging on corn in a pen. It's also an insult to you, an intelligent animal quite capable of eating a smaller slice of pork, or a bigger dish of spinach.

You Have the Power

Scientific advances in farming and gardening are needed, but let's discover more about how Nature does things, then direct our gentle efforts in ways that observe its laws, or if you object to the word "laws," then its patterns of cause and effect.

Leaves fall from the trees. Earthworms and other creatures chew them up and drag them down into the soil where the underground labor force digests them, along with manure and other excretions. Creatures above and below die, and the earth receives them. Nature recycles organic wastes and produces plants from them. Imitating this process is a gardener's work. It's the principle to which all the fine-tuning you do in the garden always returns. The soil's fertility gives you your food, and the organic matter you return to the soil keeps the cycle going. It's amazing how many problems can be solved by just improving soil the way nature has always done it—by adding what organic materials you have at hand.

Home gardeners operate well below the radar of agribusiness. We're invisible, like those wheel animals that Fritz-Martin Engel wrote about, with their tiny tools. But our numbers are growing, and we are part of an alternative universe of small farmers, shoppers at local farmers' markets, and old-fashioned, make-it-from-scratch home cooks who think that real

whole food, not processed food, is important. And the opportunity is there for you to march out onto a patch of earth with a spade and grow it. Maybe you think that our industrial food system is just fine. But be aware that there is another path.

So here's my advice: be humble before Nature. Don't poison your garden with biocides. Set the stage with plenty of organic matter, then stand back and let it do the work. But if you walk into the kitchen carrying a basket of beautiful food that you have grown? Be proud.

CHAPTER 5

Feeding the Soil

Among gardeners, soil envy abounds.

"Try living on a glacial moraine," one will grumble. "Millions of years ago, a receding glacier casually dropped rocks all over my yard, leaving me to dig them up and haul them away. No sooner do I do that than evil forces push up more from below."

"You think you have troubles," whines another. "My soil is sandy, so it doesn't hold water and nutrients well. The corn is as high as an elephant's toenail in summers if we don't get rain."

"That's nothing," wails a third. "Job had better soil than mine. Have you ever tried to till gumbo clay? When it's too wet, it's like glue. When it's too dry, it can form an impenetrable crust, cracked like the surface of an inhospitable planet and I need a jackhammer to dig the parsnips."

The fact is, though, that every type of soil texture, based on the size of its mineral particles, has its virtues. Sandy soil, which is made of mineral particles 0.05 to 2.0 mm, warms up fast in spring, is easy to dig, and drains well after rain. Carrots love it. Clay, with its smaller particles (less than 0.002 mm), tends to be fertile, holding onto moisture and soluble nutrients in times of drought, to the delight of peas and beans. Silt, whose particles are 0.002 to 0.05 mm, is in between. Even soil with lots of

A hand tiller is useful for removing small stones.

visible rocks in it has its good points. Once I followed my friend Deborah's pigs through some oak woods while she showed me their foraging habits. "There," she said, pointing to a favorite, stony patch. "Stones hold the sun's heat well, producing tasty roots, and luring worms and other soil life that the pigs love." Maybe that explains how my own granite-strewn garden produces hardy crops so well in late fall. You must make the best of your soil's texture—the size of its particles, that is. But its structure is a different matter. And that's where organic matter comes in.

What Is Loam?

The word "loam" has long confused gardeners. In rural areas I have often heard it used as a synonym for topsoil, sometimes pronounced "loom," as in "I can bring you a truckload of loom." But topsoil is a much more general term than loam. It's the soil on the earth's natural surface—as opposed to subsoil, which lies below. It's darker and more fertile, because it's the layer in which plants grow, fertilized by decaying plant and animal matter.

Otherwise, it would be just like the subsoil, which is only good for filling up an inconvenient swale or pit—as in "I can bring you a truckload of fill."

True loam is not just any old topsoil. Technically, it has a certain texture, based on a balanced combination of particles, with the water- and nutrient-holding capacity that clay provides and the good drainage and aeration offered by sand. The ideal loam is said to be 40 percent sand, 40 percent silt, and 20 percent clay.

More importantly, loam is not loam unless it contains organic matter from decaying root fibers, microbes, worm castings, and all the other ingredients found in a living soil. Organic material is the best remedy to any imbalance in particle size. Rarely would you correct clay soil by adding sand, or sandy soil by adding clay, even if it were easy to do. Organic matter buffers both by helping clay to drain and sand to retain. It buffers the soil's pH too, compensating for the effects of either a soil that is too acidic or too alkaline. It also ensures that there are oxygen-filled air spaces between the soil particles, giving the soil the structure of a squeezed-out sponge. It's been said that the most important fertilizer in the soil is air.

We're used to adding organic matter in the form of compost, leaf mold, peat moss, or some similar amendment to make the soil loamier, but in older times a pasture was often the source. The most fertile loam you can find is in a pasture of grasses mixed with legumes such as clover and grazed by livestock. Smart farmers know that if you set arable land aside and put it into such a pasture for a stretch of time, then, after tilling it up, plant crops again, those crops will thrive mightily.

On a domestic scale, a home gardener might till up a grassy area or section of lawn, cut it into blocks of turf with a spade, and turn them grassy-side down, then spread manure over them. Fall is a great time to do that, so that the grass will decompose and mellow into the soil over wintertime. Come spring, plant vegetables in this new garden plot and sow last year's plot in grass and clover to improve its fertility. Turn over that plot the following year. Then alternate between growing soil-improving crops on one site and growing vegetables on the other, for a two-year rotation.

Another trick is to take cut blocks of turf turned upside down and layer them in a stack. Once rotted down and mature, you'll have a material perfect for use as a potting mix or as a top-dressing for the garden. And if someone ever offers to bring you a truckload of that, adopt them, marry them, or at the very least get their cell number, as it's the finest loam you'll ever come by.

The Nutrients in Your Soil

You don't need a chemistry course to take up gardening, a practice at least nine thousand years older than the periodic table of elements. But some of the elements in that table do find their way into a gardener's vocabulary.

If you've ever bought a bag of fertilizer labelled with the letters N, P, and K in percentage amounts, you know how much nitrogen (N), phosphorus (P), and potassium (K) that fertilizer contains. Those three soil elements are the ones plants most need for growth. Others they require are calcium, sulfur, magnesium, and (in trace amounts) the micronutrients iron, boron, molybdenum, copper, chlorine, manganese, and zinc. A soil test from your local USDA Cooperative Extension Service will alert you to any deficiencies your garden soil may have. Then what?

There are certain natural soil amendments you can buy that address specific needs. Dried blood, cottonseed meal, and fish fertilizer all produce quick, nitrogen-fueled growth. Bonemeal and rock phosphate provide phosphorus for healthy roots. Seaweed fertilizers made from sustainably harvested North Atlantic seaweed contain a wealth of soil minerals. Dehydrated alfalfa meal gives a nitrogen boost but is balanced with phosphorous and potassium as well. Garden lime (pulverized limestone) is a staple for raising the pH of your soil if it is too acidic as measured by the pH scale. That scale ranges from 0 (the most acidic) to 14 (the most alkaline, also described as basic). Seven on the scale is described as neutral, and the ideal for most plants is considered 6.5 to 7. One ounce of lime per square foot of soil will raise the pH by 1.0. Conversely, amendments such as elemental sulfur are sometimes used to increase the soil's acidity. All of these and other additions can address specific soil deficiencies. But if you keep a compost pile you may never need any of them at all.

The idea of gathering together organic materials to fertilize a garden certainly dates back to prehistoric humans, who noticed that plants grew more vigorously in midden heaps (places where domestic waste has been deposited) or in spots where animals had pooped. Ancient farm communities all over the world followed this obvious train of thought, gathering not only animal excrement but also straw, spent crops, dead fish, and any other plant or animal material that improved the soil and nourished growth. This was simply a given until, in the mid-nineteenth century, scientists such as Germany's Justus von Liebig proved that plants could be grown by feeding them a chemical solution of N, P, and K without the aid of a fertile, humus-rich soil. This discovery fueled the development of modern chemical agriculture and was followed by the organic movement that arose in opposition to it.

What Is "Organic"?

It's important to know that "organic" does not only describe the avoidance of biocides such as pesticides and herbicides. Its name comes from the practice of growing plants in a living soil into which organic matter is continually recycled. Growing organically was never a new thing to be "invented." It came about as a defense of the way food had traditionally been grown all over the world, long before the chemical system fostered by industrial farmers.

There have been many founders and many heroes of that movement, but credit for the enshrinement of the compost pile as the focus of organic gardening is usually assigned to Albert Howard, a British agronomist whose primary work was done in India. Howard's work inspired the American author J. I. Rodale to part the chemical sea that had flooded agriculture after World War II and to lead many of our gardeners and farmers to the organic way.

Howard's research and writing culminated in two books, *An Agricultural Testament* (1940) and *The Soil and Health* (1945). His lasting message was a defense of nature's Law of Return—that anything taken from the soil should be returned to it. The most potent symbol of that return, especially for the home gardener, is compost.

The word *compost* simply means "mixture." For gardeners it's our duplication of the way diverse plant and animal residues collect on the ground and, after a long process of decay, are transformed by soil organisms into a rich, dark, fertile humus. Stacking these materials in a pile speeds up the action because it provides a feast for aerobic bacteria, that is, bacteria that work in the presence of oxygen. The work of those bacteria fires up a cauldron, so to speak, in the center. Fungi also play a role, breaking down the woodier materials in the mix. So do worms, beetles, and other small organisms that help with aeration. In short, what happens in a compost pile is just like what happens to the organic material on the ground in a forest or field, except that you collect a big pile of it, further enriched, matured, and ready for your garden—the best fertilizer and soil conditioner you can find. It works as a multivitamin, introducing elements that your soil may be lacking, neutralizing the pH and aerating the soil. And it's free.

When the compost is "done," it is dark, crumbly, and odorless, like the most fertile soil you've ever seen. You can buy compost in bags but its quality is often poor. Even if you've bought it in bulk locally, you can never be sure of what has gone into it. It is rarely as good as the "black gold" you make at home from scratch.

Making Compost

I've heard people speak of a compost heap as if it were some sort of garbage dump, abuzz with flies, hidden in a far corner of the yard. But a well-managed one is a clean, efficient operation that deserves pride of place—near the garden so that it can be fed with weeds and spent crops and can then feed the garden in return. Ours is fairly near the house as

Plant debris added to
a compost bin made
of trap wire

well, the better to accept kitchen scraps. Everything in it was once alive
and will live again in the form of the plants it feeds, which in turn will
feed us.

To make compost you need two kinds of ingredients: high-nitrogen
substances and high-carbon ones. High-nitrogen materials tend to be soft,
moist, and green. They include fresh grass clippings, weeds, carrot tops,
coffee grounds, potato peels, rotting apples and other fruits. High-carbon
ones tend to be crisp, dry, and brown. They include dead peavines, dry
plant stems, straw, and hay. Some ingredients, such as manure from farm
animals bedded on straw, are a combination of both. In terms of volume,
you need more of the brown stuff than the green, but the green is essential. Think of it as the spark that lights a fire.

Eliot and I alternate green and brown matter in our compost pile as
much as we can. If we've added a lot of brown stuff, we look around for
a nitrogen source such as newly mowed grass, rotting tomatoes, or the
shells from a big lobster feast, and spread it around in an even layer. If
we thrust a digging fork into the middle of the pile and it feels warm
when we pull it out, that tells us it's working. (Long-stemmed compost
thermometers are also available.)

Sprinkling the pile with a hose in dry weather will help keep it active.
If the pile is too wet, with too little air, there will be an ammonia-like

smell, telling you that it is time to add some dry matter. It helps to sprinkle a little soil over the pile from time to time to inoculate it with microbes, worms, and other creatures that keep the action going; however, these do tend to come in on their own, and some soil is added every time we add sod or weeds that have soil on their roots.

As heat builds in the center of the pile, turning it from time to time can also speed things along. It's best done when the center has reached its maximum temperature and has started to cool. The idea is to exchange the cooler outer parts with the hot center, so they get a chance to bake. This can be done by redistributing the materials into an adjacent container, or by shoveling and forking them into two separate piles on the ground and putting them back in reverse positions, with the least decomposed matter in the middle. You're also introducing air into the mix, which keeps the aerobic bacteria on the job. Some people do this repeatedly, but it's hard work.

An easier method is to have a row of several piles going at the same time: one that's being added to, one or more that are just sitting there cooking, and a final one where the compost is finished and ready to use. The best compost setup I've ever seen belonged to Helen and Scott Nearing. It involved just such a progression, with twelve square piles in a row. Never one to let anything go to waste, Scott built his piles with spruce and fir saplings he acquired while cutting firewood—too slender for most purposes. He stacked them, log cabin style, so there was plenty of space between them to let in air. He even placed a bundle of saplings on the ground to start the pile, and a vertical clump of them standing upright in the center—all in the interest of letting in more air. After a year, the material in the first pile was ready to spread on the garden, and the saplings reused to build a new pile. As the famous bumper sticker says, "Compost Happens." With no turning required.

My favorite way to make a compost pile is to use bales of hay or straw for the walls, stacking them like building blocks. Their own gradual decomposition lends heat, fertility, and moisture. Afterward they become fodder for the next pile to be built.

As Eliot and I add materials, bulky ones seem to fill up the pile quickly, only to settle over time. Nevertheless, it's important not to make the pile become so tall that we can't work it comfortably. About four feet is my limit. We also don't want it so wide that air can't reach into the center. To enlarge it, it is best to make it a longer rectangle, or have multiple piles.

We know the compost is "done" when the original ingredients cannot be identified. If it is needed a bit sooner, it can be added to the garden as "rough compost." Worms and other soil creatures will set right to the task of distributing it and helping it break down. If a few extra-tough items have retained their form, we just toss them into the next pile we make, for another go.

Organic materials that should never be added include dog and cat manure, plastic and any other nonorganic material, coal and charcoal ashes, weeds at the seed-dropping stage, weeds with highly invasive root systems (unless you have laid them out and dried them thoroughly in the sun), highly toxic plants such as poison ivy, or plants that have been sprayed with poisons, including weed killers. Twigs much thicker than your finger will break down too slowly, and twigs from trees that chemically inhibit other plants' growth, such as cedar and black walnut, are best avoided. Autumn leaves are fine in small amounts, especially if they are crinkly ones like oak leaves, which don't mat down the way maple and other flat ones do. Leaves that have been chopped up by your lawn mower are okay too. But the best use of tree leaves is to let them slowly decompose in their own separate pile. The result will be a rich, light, fluffy substance known as leaf mold. It takes a long time to mature but is excellent both as a soil amendment and a mulch. You can even use it as a medium for potting up plants or germinating seeds.

Whether to ban scraps from meat and fish is an individual choice. The common fear that they will attract rodents, including rats, is not unfounded. But vegetable scraps may sometimes attract those as well. In a country setting like our place, that's not a big deal. In an urban one it can be, but there are solutions.

Compost Contained

In a setting where a pile of miscellaneous organic matter can just sit there and rot without offending anybody, a pile can simply be a pile. In fact, it's easier to turn that way if you're into turning. But urban and suburban gardeners do have to consider their neighbors. Some may not be as reverent about the natural cycle of growth and decay if it is happening right up against their fence.

A compost container can be built out of wooden planks, as long as you leave spaces between them for aeration. It could be a wooden frame with rodent-proof ¼-inch hardware cloth stretched across each panel, including a lid. We often make compost in connected panels of trap wire, a black plastic–covered metal mesh used to make lobster traps in Maine.

All sorts of ready-made bins are available but beware of shoddy ones. Eliot and I once bought an economical black plastic stacked unit that was promptly torn apart by a bear. I know, that's not a very common problem, but does cheap plastic ever come to a good end?

Barrel-shaped composters that are turned with a hand crank are popular with some gardeners. The turning speeds up the composting process, but the more material you put in these, the harder they are to turn. They're kept well off the ground by metal stands that no rodent can climb. But neither can the earthworms, microbes, and other creatures that enrich the final product. Contact with the soil is always beneficial, so if you have a choice between a pile on the ground or a pile on pavement, choose the ground.

Covering your compost is a good idea, whether with an engineered lid or just a tarp. Remove it to let in needed rain, close it against excess rain. Cover it in winter to keep it warm in a cold climate. A cover hides it from crows, and keeps them from making their noisy raids, although this can also be accomplished by burying tasty scraps you've just added in the pile. I sometimes keep a bale of hay at hand for this purpose, using a fistful for a quick covering.

If you are collecting kitchen scraps indoors for compost, a tidy receptacle is a must. "It's your turn to take out the compost," whether said peevishly or as a gentle reminder, is a remark heard even in households that are joyful about their compost bucket and the idea of returning corncobs and melon rinds to the earth from whence they came.

Choose a container that simplifies the job, like a well-made stainless steel pail that's easy to wash and small enough to encourage frequent trips. Two quarts is about right. One learns to put the old bread in first, then pour the spoiled milk over it, to be absorbed. I found a way to keep the pail handy and invisible at the same time, by having a hole cut in the countertop, next to the sink. In a drawer beneath sits the pail, for easy removal. Using a lid might seem tidier, but cutting off air promotes anaerobic decomposition, which is smellier than the aerobic kind.

So I'm at peace with my pail, as are most of our neighbors with theirs. But we still laugh about a winter potluck we all attended some years back, lit by flickering candles and rollicking good cheer, with a bounty of home-cooked dishes lined up on our host's kitchen counter.

My compost pail setup

"Who brought this?" someone asked at the table, in a voice edged with anxiety. "And what is it?" It was some compost she had spooned from a tasteful, locally made crock, placed a little too close to the potluck buffet. Sometimes a lid does come in handy.

Spreading the Wealth

There are other ways to add fertility to the soil besides making compost. You can sow a cover crop such as buckwheat, oats, or a legume in a garden or an individual bed as a placeholder to keep weeds from taking hold. You will need to cut it down before it goes to seed, then till it under or turn it under with a mattock or spade. At that point it becomes a green manure—a plant incorporated to add nutrients. If that takes too much effort, or is best done with equipment you don't have, you will do better to rake or pull it out and put it on a compost pile instead, or leave it lying on the ground as mulch.

That was the course taken by Ruth Stout, an independent-minded woman who took up gardening at the age of forty-four, and had a large, conventional garden, which was plowed up every year by a man with a tractor. After fourteen years, tired of always waiting for him to show up and do it, she went ahead and sowed her seeds among the previous year's debris. When she brushed it aside, the soil was moist and easy to make furrows in, and the plants thrived.

Each year she brought in more organic materials to mulch with: "Any vegetable matter which rots," she wrote in her book *How to Have a Green Thumb Without an Aching Back.* To sow or transplant her vegetables, she just pulled some mulch aside, then put it back when the plants were big enough that they wouldn't be smothered. Aside from a little lime and cottonseed meal, the garden needed no fertilizer other than the decaying mulch, and as that became part of the soil, she mulched some more. When she died at ninety-six, she was still mulching.

For a glimpse of that I watched Arthur Mokin's twenty-minute documentary, *Ruth Stout's Garden.* You see her at ninety-two, wearing a

housewifey dress and cardigan, planting potatoes she has just brought up from winter storage, with white sprouts. She rakes away the mulch, tosses the spuds on the ground, and rakes the mulch back. Done.

My approach to feeding the garden is not as radical as Ruth's, but for the most part I rely on the soil's own army of tiny tillers to do most of the work for me. I spread compost or well-rotted manure and only rake it in shallowly before planting, then I aerate the soil with a broadfork if needed. Even compost or manure that isn't quite mature can be applied in fall and be worked in over the winter by the earth's own action. I count on the soil to freeze and thaw, causing fissures that open to receive what I've spread. And every year it does.

Mulching the beds and paths in this greenhouse with straw keeps them nearly weed-free.

CHAPTER 6

Getting the Most from Your Garden

"How much space do you need to grow vegetables?" There are no absolute answers. Any food garden is worthwhile, even if it's just a whiskey barrel with one paste tomato plant encircled by oregano and basil. Hey—that's all you need to top a pizza, from a space not much bigger than the pizza itself.

Today, many home lots aren't big enough for the gardens that people once planted. Their style was based on the nineteenth-century farm model, where a gardener left enough space between rows for horse (and later tractor) cultivation. It also assumed that the garden's goal was food self-sufficiency. That topic is certainly on many minds these days, but some people simply want better-tasting produce than what they can buy. Their focus might be a summer of salads, or crops such as tomatoes and corn that are much better tasting if eaten freshly picked and homegrown.

In any case, the important question to ask is "How much food can I grow in the space I've got, and with the time I have to grow it?" There is no formula for that either, because it depends partly on how well you manage your soil's aeration and fertility, and how you manage weeds.

Fortunately, there are ways that you can plan your garden to affect its yield. These result in many efficiencies—less time weeding, less time watering, and fewer inputs such as fertilizers and mulches. Space efficiency can turn your little plot into the old circus act where a tiny car appears and out jump twenty clowns.

Thinking Small

Gardeners without gardens have a rich fantasy life. They dream of tomatoes on the vine and a kitchen table heaped with fragrant, just-picked melons. I, on the other hand, have land to spare for my country garden.

Sometimes, though, I fantasize about what I'd grow in a yard with concrete underfoot. I don't actually want that garden, hooked as I am on daily abundance, but just like those tiny houses that people find so fascinating, a tiny garden is an idea I occasionally try on for size, so to speak.

My imaginary mini-plot will grow in planters, surrounding a table where I eat alfresco, close enough to the one cherry tomato plant—trained to one stem and tied to a sturdy pole stuck into the center of its pot—to eat its fruits right off the vine. There will be another pot with a beefsteak tomato, if there's room. Nearby I will have a whiskey half-barrel in which a few bean vines climb a teepee made of bamboo poles. Picking regularly, I will enjoy snap beans for most of the summer. Another pot will hold an eggplant or two, a variety such as Orient Express with smallish, slender fruits. Or peppers—little hot Serranos. One summer squash plant will be plenty.

I will want fresh salads, so I'll fill a few wooden planters from a local garden center with cut-and-come-again greens that regrow after picking. They are mixed lettuces sown two inches apart and cut at baby-leaf size, along with arugula, spinach, claytonia, and little curly endives. I will want a few larger greens for cooking too, such as ruby chard with its glowing scarlet stems, and fountain-shaped Tuscan kale with its gorgeous blue-green foliage. With those plants, as I harvest the outer leaves, new ones will keep emerging from the center all summer long.

Of course, there will be herbs. Annuals including basil, cilantro, and parsley will share a pot or box, but perennials such as tarragon and sage, with their more substantial root systems, would need their own.

Little carrots, sown and thinned to two inches apart, French Breakfast radishes, plus beets and Hakurei turnips, both picked small, and scallions for sure, might all have their place in this garden. I might even try the potato barrel trick: Plant a single potato in a whiskey half-barrel (about twenty-six inches in diameter) of fertile soil, and it will fill the soil with roots—and potatoes. I once proved this point accidentally. While turning a compost pile I discovered that it was chock-full of perfectly edible potatoes, grown from some I'd thrown on the heap with other kitchen wastes.

Just like the tiny house I'll never move into, this imaginary pocket garden will remain a dream, but the basic idea of it translates into any home garden, planted in soil, of any size. The use of cut-and-come-again salads and cooking greens that keep producing new growth at the center are just two examples of making the most of the space you have.

What Should You Plant?

With all due respect, vegetables grown in containers are the pampered pets of horticulture. No tree roots can encroach on plants thus enthroned. Each can be given its own favorite combination of soil, sun, water, and nutrients. Pests don't find them easily, and weeds are quickly spotted and removed. Their gardeners are pampered too. Their work can be a few steps away from the back door. After a busy day, all they need to do is water the pots, pluck off a dead leaf or two, and harvest a salad or the makings of a stir-fry.

Move the operation down to earth level and you have the luxury of more space, and along with it the freedom to bite off more than what you can—quite literally—chew. It helps to ask some important questions first, starting with "What does my household actually like to eat?" Take a poll on that, because there's no point in growing twenty feet of kohlrabi if it's going to be unpopular. After the votes come in, you'll then need to assess them according to how much space certain favorites will take up, and whether you are going for superstars like tomatoes, or a general mix that brings you closer to the elusive goal of a balanced diet. Especially if space is limited, you'll need to take your choices, crop by crop, and grade them on their productivity.

Greens, both salad ones and cooking greens, are always a good idea, especially those I've mentioned, which regrow after cutting. Fruiting crops that grow on relatively small plants, such as peppers and eggplant, are fairly productive and easy to fit in. Ones such as cucumbers, pole beans, and tomatoes that grow on rampant vines over a long period of time are very productive in relation to their footprint (the space their roots take up in the soil) but only if you trellis and train them vertically. Summer squash such as zucchini can be a trap. Even though they are large, space-hogging plants, they are extremely productive. But if you don't pick them every day or two, they give birth to giant green torpedoes that are too big to be practical, and the growth of new fruits slows down. By picking regularly, I once fed three families from one zucchini plant.

Root crops like radishes, carrots, turnips, and beets can be planted close together and picked small, or thinned as they grow by picking every other one and letting the ones left grow big. That works for onions, scallions, and leeks as well. Turnips and beets are also dual purpose because you can judiciously steal some of the leaves to cook as greens without impeding growth of the orbs below. Swiss chard and bok choy come with a bonus too: the mild-tasting leaves might go into one dish, saving the thick, crisp stems and central ribs to be sautéed in another.

Some vegetables, on the other hand, are just not ideal for a very small garden because their yield per square foot is hard to justify. These include potatoes, cabbages, cauliflower, and Brussels sprouts. Broccoli too, unless you choose a variety with good side shoot production after the center head has been harvested.

Crops that are best suited to large gardens, alas, include some delicious ones. Most sweet corn varieties rarely produce more than one ear per plant. The wandering vines of melons and winter squash are uncontainable in a small space. Artichokes are wonderful but grow on large plants that sit there for many months before bearing. Asparagus, which is perennial, needs its own separate plot and is only picked for six weeks a year. Admittedly, I can think of an excellent reason to grow every single one of these great crops. So, in order to fit any of them in, gardeners employ a few magic tricks to make the whole plot act bigger than it actually is.

Less Space, Bigger Harvest

The tomato plants were magnificent—a foot tall in their pots and ready to go into the ground. But there was no ground left, and no needy friends were standing by to adopt them. Eliot and I found a spot for them, though, in a bed already planted with two rows of young lettuce. We just dug holes down the center of the bed, between the lettuces, and installed the tomatoes, which already towered over the lettuces like trees above the forest floor. Tomatoes are hungry, thirsty plants that normally don't like competition, but these were young enough not to mind. The lettuce, in turn, benefited from a bit of shade from the tomatoes, and in any case would be picked and eaten long before the tomato plants reached full size.

Doubling up two crops in a bed is called intercropping or interplanting and it can greatly increase a garden's yield. Here's another example: you have a bed with a single row of young Brussels sprouts down the middle.

Eventually they'll become quite large plants, but they will need most of the season to finally yield those firm little cabbage-like balls on one single stem. While you're waiting for that to happen you could easily plant some quick crops on either side: radishes, carrots, scallions, and even some little hot peppers.

Another great space saver, succession planting, is even simpler. The strategy is "Whenever there is a space in the garden, plant something in it." To make this work, you have to give up any idea that in spring the garden is "put in," and all you need to do after that is weed, water, and pick. After the last of the early peas have been harvested and pulled out, in goes something heat-loving, such as cucumbers, or, after a brief wait, a fall crop such as kale. Early carrots might be followed by broccoli, and early spinach might be followed by late beets. Early beets could be followed by escarole.

It's like a board game in which perseverance pays off, and the only rules are the limits that weather and climate put in your way. You plant a cool weather crop when cool weather is imminent, so the midsummer

Vertical crops such as peas and tomatoes on trellises and beans on bamboo teepees increase space in our garden.

planting of fall vegetables like kale, spinach, and carrots (even if you've had early plantings of them) is an important moment.

Succession planting gives you a chance to pop in particular favorites ("arugula, anyone?") whenever a space opens up, to ensure a good supply. Some people are very organized about this, drawing up charts and schedules in advance. I tend to just watch for the reminder that bare soil gives me and ask "Hey, what could go here?"

Sometimes the way to increase a small garden's footprint is to go vertical. Just as a street of high-rise buildings can house more people than a street of single-family houses, a row of long peavines supported by a tall trellis produces more peas than a row of short ones. But you do have to weigh this strategy against others. A row of vining tomatoes or beans held aloft on strings that they can climb won't necessarily outyield bush varieties that produce a big crop early on and then stop. Which you grow depends on whether you want a long season of munching or a bounty to harvest all at once and preserve for winter eating. Another thing to consider: "bush," "compact," or "container" version of plants such as tomatoes, cucumbers, and squash, though often recommended for small gardens, are sometimes quite sprawling. Also, these fruiting crops are sometimes healthier when held aloft, above the reach of nibbling mammals and soilborne diseases.

There are other space-increasing options to consider. Sometimes these involve stepping outside the perimeter of your plot.

Planting Outside the Box

"Half the city … stands in a regular forest of old trees, which shade all the streets," wrote the Swiss psychiatrist Carl Jung, describing Worcester, Massachusetts, in a letter to his wife. It is a style Americans take for granted. We love our forested towns, leafy suburbs, and shaded yards. The trees next to our homes provide stately beauty, a sense of protected seclusion, and relief from summer heat.

A gardener hell-bent on growing food might have to make a painful choice between beloved trees and a perfect plot near the kitchen door. Signing up for space in a community garden may be the solution, but another might be to broaden the idea of what a kitchen garden looks like, and where it might be placed. Take a close look at the yard and see what unexpected sites are suitable.

Trees with an open canopy and a lacy leaf pattern, like birch, shadblow, honey locust, and crab apple, cast a filtered sunlight that is kind to gardens. It's a dancing light, never lingering long enough on tender lettuce plants to scorch them, nor shading them altogether. In fact, most leafy crops tolerate and sometimes even prefer dappled shade, or shade during the afternoon when sun is strongest. Lettuce and spinach are less apt to go to seed if shaded. Arugula in cooling shade tastes milder. Kale, cabbage, endive, and most other greens—both salad ones and cooking ones—will be content. Root crops like carrots, stem crops like celery, and bud crops like broccoli are somewhat shade tolerant as well.

Letting go of the idea that the garden has to be in a single spot will open up many choices. Put part of it in front of the house and another part in the back. One bed in bright sun, one in part shade. Beans where it's hot.

This boundary fence keeps out deer and provides growing space for small winter squash.

Blueberries where it's damp. Try food crops in places where ornamental ones normally go. Make some of your trees fruit trees, and some of your shrubs fruit bushes. For a foundation planting, choose a row of asparagus plants with their mighty ferns, green in summer and gold in fall. Instead of covering the arbor over your patio with wisteria, plant grapes.

A boundary fence is one of the best places for vegetables that grow on vines—whether it marks the edge of the yard or the edge of the garden. I have used six-foot-tall open-lattice fences to grow beans, cucumbers, tomatoes, and even small pumpkins and squash. Inspired by gardeners who get melons to climb fences, cradling the heavy fruits with little netted hammocks (and even large brassieres!), I once tried some hefty winter squash of a brilliant red-orange color. They were too heavy to climb, but one vine ducked under the fence, headed toward the house, and came to rest among the hydrangeas in all its red-fruited glory. From the kitchen window, it seemed to have found the perfect spot.

CHAPTER 7

Garden Geometry

Every gardener has a few absolutely essential tools. One of mine is a pad of graph paper, sometimes called a "quad pad." Each page is a grid of horizontal and vertical blue lines that make up ¼-inch squares. When each square is made to represent one square foot in real outdoor life, it is easy to draw up a plan for the garden—its boundaries, its paths, its beds, its rows, and even the spot where you intend to put each plant. Such plans tend to go through countless modifications, so a pencil and a large, nonsmudgy eraser are essential accessories. A handy wastebasket to catch false starts and discarded goals is also useful, but I find that a "final" plan that represents as nearly as possible what actually got planted should be carefully filed away to jog my memory the next year at planning time. A camera is helpful too.

It is possible to be more creative with garden shapes, from circles to paisley swirls, but I'd reserve those for ornamental beds. They are drawn on graph paper too, but I find the art of kitchen gardening essentially rectangular.

Make a Plan

There is a wise motto used by civil engineers: "Roads first." Whatever the work may be, you can't begin it until you get there. It is no different for a garden. A path leads you in and allows you to work there productively and comfortably.

Someone with land to spare might plan a garden with single rows, separated by wide paths. An intensive gardener might do the opposite, broadcasting seeds of leafy greens and other crops so that they form thick carpets. My father, inspired by author Dick Raymond in the 1960s, used to sow bush peas that way in a large patch, with no paths at all. He harvested them by moving a little stool around the plot to sit on while he picked all the pods, ready to shell and freeze.

The garden I plant and tend with Eliot is designed like a small green city. A four-foot-wide path runs down the center, like a four-lane avenue. Foot-wide paths lead out from it on both sides, like one-way streets. Between these are thirty-inch-wide beds like city blocks. The beds are not subdivided with paths because we never, ever put our feet in them. Our system rests on the fact that the paths are trodden, but the beds are always full of loosely textured, uncompacted soil.

A good layout, scaled to your body, is often the difference between a garden you avoid and one you enter eagerly, trowel in hand. You need room to set down your weed bucket or harvest basket—and your butt. I find that those thirty-inch beds are the maximum width I can reach into the center for comfortably picking and weeding, without stressing my back. It's also the maximum width a 5-foot-2-inch person like me can leap over without a running start. (People with very large feet sometimes find our twelve-inch-wide paths awkward.) For Eliot, thirty inches is the width he can straddle with ease.

This is the exact same bed layout we use at our farm. Even though overall we measure the farm in acres rather than square feet, and not all of the work is handwork, it's important for us to have growing areas that are scaled to the human body, not just the tractor.

Choosing materials for paths is a balance between looks and practicality. Stone or brick paths are handsome features that tie the garden together visually and set off the colors and textures of the plants, but they're expensive and time-consuming to install. They lock you into a fixed scheme and location. It's hard to pry weeds from the cracks between them. I have had gardens with gravel paths between the beds, edged with wooden planks. They looked great, but soil and compost from the beds tended to trickle into the gravel, and weeds adored this combination of excellent drainage and a fertile top dressing. Grass and clover paths had a downside too. Even if mowed to prevent seeding, they crept into beds. I've come to feel that plain old dirt paths are hard to beat. On a dry day it takes only minutes to march down them with a wheel hoe, slicing weeds just below the surface and leaving the weeds to bake and shrivel in the sun. When available, I have sometimes used finely chipped up tree branches on the wide central path. These smother weeds very well until they start to break down and more must be added.

Once, many years ago, inspired by the little household plots I saw at Plimoth Patuxet's historical reenactment of colonial life in Plymouth,

Massachusetts, I tried growing vegetables in raised beds made of naturally rot-resistant cedar planks, filled with soil. Schemes based on these tidy, bottomless boxes, which are once again very popular, are valuable in places where the existing soil is poorly drained, rocky, compacted, heavy with clay, devoid of organic matter, or simply nonexistent. They warm up quickly in spring, a boost in cold climates, but they lose moisture too quickly in dry ones and ones with sandy soil. Creative gardeners sometimes attach add-ons to them, such as cold frames and permanent trellises. Sometimes I think that one main purpose of raised beds is psychological, helping a gardener to focus and to exert control over nature's enthusiasm when needed. Nothing wrong with that!

Raised beds are a little too permanent for my gardening habits, though, and finding enough soil to fill all those boxes can be daunting.

We get a similar effect by achieving luxurious, fluffy, and well-oxygenated soil in our beds, so that they actually look raised, in contrast to our flattened paths. There is no mistaking where a bed begins and ends, and the impression of order is welcoming.

Crop Rotation, Yes or No?

Any garden book will tell you that crop rotation is a good idea. The principle is simple: Don't plant anything in the same place it grew last year and, ideally, the year before that.

Rotating results in healthier crops and better yields, partly because specific pests and diseases plague specific plants or plant families. Relocating a crop as an evasive tactic can disrupt a pest's life cycle by removing its host—or at least making the host harder to find.

Also, garden plants affect the soil in different ways. Corn feeds deeply and hungrily, consuming lots of nutrients but bringing minerals up from below as well. Legumes such as peas and beans help turn atmospheric nitrogen into a form that plants can use, which benefits the crop that follows them. Their root systems also leave lots of organic residues in the soil, stimulating biological activity. Big smothery crops such as squash deter weeds, but skinny onion plantings may leave many weeds in their wake.

For a farmer, or someone with a large garden, rotation is common practice, and common sense. It's a game in which you divide your vegetables into teams based on family relationships:

- Brassicas, such as cabbage, kale, broccoli, mustard, and turnips

- Legumes, such as peas, beans, and certain cover crops such as clover

- Cucurbits, such as squash, melons, cucumbers, and pumpkins

- Solanaceous vegetables, such as tomatoes, potatoes, peppers, and eggplants

- Apiaceae, with their umbrella-shaped flowers, such as carrots, parsnips, fennel, and dill

- Grains, including corn

- The beet group, which includes spinach and Swiss chard

- Asteraceae like lettuce, artichokes and chicories

- Alliums, including onions, garlic, leeks, and scallions

The object of the game is to see how long you can go without repeating a crop, or its relatives, in the same place. Here are two basic plans you might follow, based on two dances: the square dance and the Virginia reel.

For the square dance you divide a rectangular garden into four equal quadrants, assigning each to one major family—usually the first four listed above—and either rotate the whole scheme a quarter turn each year or switch the diagonal opposites. You'd leave some spaces in the quadrants for members of the other families, many of which make good fill-in crops.

In the reel-type rotation, the whole garden is laid out in parallel beds, like books lined up on a shelf. You still group plants by family, with a crop assigned to each bed, and the whole thing marches in family groups to the right each year, with the last jumping back to the opposite end, just like the lead couple in a reel dance.

The game can become more complicated the more you practice other maneuvers at the same time, such as interplanting, successions, and using tall crops like corn or trellised tomatoes to shield leafy green crops from the midday sun. If at this point you find your sheet of graph paper worn through with erasures and your brain as tangled as spaghetti squash, you are probably ready for Plan B.

Plan B is to follow the idea less strictly, using rotations only when needed—when a specific pest (yes, you, potato beetle) tends to move in on a spot, defying eviction, or a reluctant crop needs the aid of a previous booster crop, such as beans. You might bear in mind a few other rotation maxims, such as "Brassicas like to follow alliums" or "Greedy corn likes to follow generous peas." One gardener I know rotates by having two alternate garden sites, putting one into a soil-enriching green manure every other year for a beneficial cleanse.

In a small garden, all the crops are so close to one another that rotation may not be of much benefit. And if you have grown your plants well, with plenty of organic matter in the soil, you might have just as much success without it.

Spacing Is Adjustable

Garden math must follow nature's rules, but it sometimes seems like using MapQuest to find Nirvana, especially with plant spacing. Just as I'd rather cook without a recipe, I'd rather pay close attention to vegetable varieties' individual growth habits and how I expect to use the harvest. With today's smaller gardens, tighter spacing is often practiced, for better yields. As a friend of mine huffed, "If I planted vegetables as far apart as tradition demands, they'd be in my neighbor's yard."

Wide and tight spacing each have their virtues. Yields sometimes diminish, rather than increase, with crowded plants, but it depends on each vegetable's habits. A carrot needs only four square inches of soil to grow well, so it's fine to sow them two inches apart in rows spaced two inches apart. Miniature head lettuces such as "Tom Thumb" can be set out as transplants six inches apart. Standard-sized heads will need a square foot.

Beets might need two to six inches each way, depending on whether you want baby size, medium, or huge. We set them out as transplants, but it's more common to sow them directly, then thin them, using the thinnings in salads. You can also pull small beets as needed, leaving the others to grow large for storage.

Cooks with small families can plant cabbages closely, to get more compact heads. Broccoli spaced widely gives you big heads (good for freezing). Broccoli spaced closely yields smaller heads followed by many side

In this 30-inch bed, lettuce is given three rows but the smaller Mei Qing Choi is given four.

shoots. Closely spaced leeks are more numerous but thinner. Tight spacing of celery yields heads that are more blanched but have narrow stalks.

Peas and beans do well with close spacing, yielding more when planted thickly. Close planting also creates a living mulch. The thick canopy of leaves shades the ground, keeps it moist, and discourages weeds. That's especially important with peas because the delicate seedlings are easily disturbed by weeding.

As you can see, it's a balancing act, and you must always be alert to the points at which close planting fails to pay off. One is where it begins to foster disease because air can't circulate and moisture can't evaporate. Another is the point where close planting blocks sunlight from parts of the plant that need it: Picture a wall of tomato vines in which fruits hidden among the leaves have trouble ripening and developing good flavor. Worst of all is the point at which crowded plants exclude not just the sun but also the gardener. A bean jungle will never be properly harvested. A prickly chaparral of zucchini foliage is as enticing as the evil forest in *The Lord of the Rings*.

No, wait. The worst point of all is where the great wall of tomatoes or the great wall of beans is so massive that the whole thing comes tumbling down, splat, in a storm.

"I wish plants could tell me how they want to be planted," my friend complains. But they do. If only the last plant in the row is, in your estimation, up to size, that means that the rest are too close together. That's garden math I can believe in.

CHAPTER 8

Tools

One of the things I love about gardening is its material simplicity. It's about seeds, soil, and compost, not gear. You do need some basic tools but after a while you've collected enough of them so that new purchases are rare. They should be well made and just right for your own use—sturdy but not so heavy that you come to hate them. Strong, well-attached handles are a must.

I'm all for ingenuity but I can easily live without the many garden gadgets I've seen in catalogs: linking plant supports that don't stay linked, butterfly houses with no tenants, plastic landscape fabric that disintegrates into hard-to-remove shreds. Do I need to buy a "giant nectar-filled flower" (in blue or purple) that "attracts butterflies by the dozens" when I can grow the real thing, full of nectar compounded in the flower's own lab? Are you considering a device that tells you whether the soil in a pot is dry? You have one: It's your finger.

It's bad enough to see garden gizmos ending up in landfills along with all the other cracked, faded plastic objects that litter our lives, but the problem is even more universal. Much of the smog that hangs over our populated areas is caused by gasoline-powered machinery such as lawn mowers, weed whackers, leaf blowers, hedge trimmers, rototillers, and shredders. The musical hum of bees on a summer day is drowned out by their engines, and I'm told that the volume of accidental spills from filling their little fuel tanks, over the course of a year, exceeds the one from the *Exxon Valdez*.

I've used some of these machines. In my thirties, ashamed that the only pull-start cord mechanism I'd ever mastered was the lettuce spinner, I forced myself to improve my skills, and even took a power tool maintenance course at the local school. The one piece of information I remember learning is that a lawn mower contains a long blade, coiled within and as sharp as a rapier, which can remove your fingers if handled carelessly. Now I don't even consider home repair.

How pure you want to be is a personal choice. I have been lectured by cooks who only dry salad greens by gently pressing them between cloth towels. But I must be a tool-crazed American. I'll stick with my lettuce spinner, thank you.

Basic tools mounted on a tool wall are easy to grab when needed.

Small Hand Tools

All garden tools are extensions of our bodies, fulfilling our need to be stronger, faster, and protected in our dealings with soil and stones. With small hand tools this is true in an intimate way. Holding a claw weeder, our fingers gain the power of an eagle's talon. Just picking one up sends a charge of confidence down the muscle of a forearm. Such tools are personal. We select them according to the job we're going to do, but also to how our hand is going to feel doing it.

Trowels, for instance: A big, heavy scooped one, a bit like a miniature wheelbarrow with a handle but no wheels, is helpful for transporting soil amendments and mixing them in a pot. I can make a good-sized hole with it when transplanting seedlings in spring. If the soil into which I'm placing the seedlings is very loose and fluffy, I'll just make holes in it with my hand, with a pawing motion, but I could also use a right-angle trowel to do this, jabbing it into the soil and pulling it toward me. The one I have is made in Switzerland, where its name is the Pflanzhand, translated as "plant hand."

If I were to have only one trowel, though, it would be a medium-sized wood-handled one with a slight bend in the shank that connects it to the slightly narrow, slightly scooped, pointed blade. The Gardener's Lifetime Trowel from Gardener's Supply is one example, but hardware stores sell similar versions. Something about that bend gives me just a bit more strength as I thrust the tool forward. The pointed tip makes it easy to plunge into the ground next to a weed with my right hand while pulling out the dislodged plant with my left. Stab and pull, stab and pull. For dandelions, this trowel doesn't go as deep as one of those long, skinny dandelion diggers with a notched end, but I find it's more accurate and frees up most of the root. It's also very easy to misplace. If I have to leave it alone even briefly, I stick it upright into the middle of a path, so it looks like a dog to which I've just said, "Sit!"

The other small tools you cannot do without are the ones that cut plant stems, and there is a range of them for stems of different thickness and firmness. The ordinary kitchen scissors that you take outside to cut twine for tying up a vine will also cut a daisy. The sharp little knife you peel apples with indoors is fine for cutting a zucchini of any size from its stem. But to pick an apple, pepper, tomato, or cluster of grapes, I reach for my needle-nose shears from Johnny's Selected Seeds, which have bright red handles that stand out even when they've been dropped onto a pile of snipped-off greenery. They are also good for pruning woody stems up to a certain size.

It's important to develop a keen sense of when a cutting tool is straining to do its job and you need to move up to a stronger one. When pruning woody stems, I'd move up to a basic hand pruner. It comes in two styles: an anvil pruner, which has one moving blade, and a bypass pruner, with two curved blades that move in two planes, the way scissors do. Which you use is a personal choice.

When that pruner starts to strain because the branch I'm cutting is too thick, I move on to loppers. These are much larger and more heavy duty, with handles a foot or two long. Some even have a gear system that multiplies their leverage, so that you don't have to work so hard. They can

This right-angle trowel is an efficient ergonomic tool for making holes for transplants.

deal with small branches of a fruit tree. When they strain, you reach for a pruning saw, then to a bow saw, a chain saw, and from there to a professional tree surgeon or lumberjack. Always good to have one on call.

The Perfect Shovel

Before days of mechanized garden tools, various countries had their specialties. The British had their fine spades, a different one for every task. The Dutch had an array of clever hoes. But Americans had shovels—great shovels, with the steel shank and blade made from one solid piece. Handles were cut from straight ash saplings. The bottom part, where the handle entered the shank and absorbed the most force, was made from the dense wood closest to the sapling's root. It was also steam-bent, so it extended all the way into the curved shank, for strength. There was a structural integrity to the entire tool, from handle to head. Now, only a few specialty businesses steam-bend their tool handles, and you're not likely to find a shovel made with one.

That might be a fine point, but fine points make the difference between good tools and merely adequate ones. Tiny variations in design make manual work easier, but with manual work in decline, the art of tool-making has declined too. It's a vicious circle: The harder tools are to work with, the less we want to use them.

We may think the shovel we use is perfectly okay but show us a better one and heaven help the gardener who borrows it and doesn't bring it back. The bond between a gardener and her tool is the result of the right tool for the gardener and the right tool for the job.

To begin with, let's call a spade a spade—and a shovel a shovel. A spade may be long-handled or short, its blade square at the bottom or curved, but the blade is always fairly flat. Usually there's only a two- or three-inch rise between the end of the blade and the ground when you lay it down. Driven by the power of your foot on the flat "step" of the blade, a spade digs by slicing through the soil, severing roots, edging beds, stripping off sod, or sculpting a root ball, the life-supporting orb of soil and root that allows you to transplant a shrub or tree. A spade will move soil too, but unless you are skimming it off shallowly, a shovel moves soil better.

A shovel is "shoved" into a pile of earth (or gravel, or compost, or mulch). If I need to excavate a large hole or trench, I use both tools—the spade to free up the material, and the shovel to move it. I'll use a round-point shovel, one with a good arc to the shank, so that the blade has a five- or six-inch lift. It gets into the corners of a hole or a wheelbarrow and allows me to scoop with the side of the blade. I like one with a deep, scooped blade that I can thrust into a pile of matted earth or heavy gravel and shake slightly, letting the material fall into it. But for scattering compost over a wide area, I need a shallower blade, better for flinging accurately. There are also square-pointed shovels for lifting material, which hold even more.

For most jobs, a shovel with a long handle is best because I need to stoop less, but when I'm working with very dense materials, a short D-handled shovel with a heavy blade gives me more push. From habit, I know exactly how hard I can force a familiar shovel when it is nudging loose a stubborn rock without breaking the handle.

One year, on impulse, I bought a shovel with a bright yellow fiberglass handle. It was suspiciously lightweight, and the angle of the lift was too shallow, but it cost $9.97. It wasn't all that popular on the farm, but someone borrowed it once and it came right back to me with the handle snapped off. Lesson learned. At the other extreme, I was once given a very heavy, expensive blacksmith-forged English spade. According to the label, it was a "lifetime tool." "Weighs a ton," was my opinion. A neighbor of mine agreed. "It would sure last a lifetime at my place," he said, "because I'd never take it out of the shed."

You can still buy some interesting shovels from A. M. Leonard, including a scary-looking sawtooth shovel with jagged teeth for slicing through compacted soil, roots, stones, and ice. They also have shovels on which the hollowed curve in the back of the blade is closed, so that heavy, sticky clay soil can't accumulate there. Leonard also sells replacement handles, which are hard to find. Eliot took the crappy yellow shovel to the local hardware store where I'd bought it and asked for a new handle that might fit. "We don't sell handles," they said. "Cheaper to buy a new shovel for ten bucks."

In the past there were hundreds of different shovel styles, many of them now extinct. I once saw a Web posting from the Nebraska State Historical Society, offering a bounty for a shovel with a very curved shank and a flat blade, used to skim the soil for archeological artifacts. They asked readers to scour used tool sales for this treasure.

The Right Fork

Reach for the wrong fork at a dinner party, and at the worst you might get a snooty glance. The wrong fork in the garden, on the other hand, makes for less-efficient work.

A garden fork might bring to mind the hayfork held by the dour farmer in the painting *American Gothic*. But that long-handled tool, though emblematic of farm life, has a special use: pitching loose hay onto a hay-stack or a wagon, which is not something you might do every day—or at all. Home gardeners rely on the spading fork, which is indispensable.

A spading fork's four tines are much heavier than those of a hayfork. If well-made, a spading fork is a rugged tool, having a midlength shaft with a D-handle, built to do battle with soil—and the rocks it contains— without bending. It pierces the ground more easily than does a shovel or a spade and is great for preloosening soil that you can then lift out with a shovel. It's good for breaking up heavy soil clumps so that amend-ments can be worked through them. Even the stubborn, matted roots of meadow grasses yield to it, and can then be yanked out intact, without leaving broken-off pieces behind to sprout anew. Dandelions can usually be pulled out unbroken too if a spading fork has probed around them.

The digging fork, a similar tool but with flattened tines, is the best one for harvesting potatoes or loosening root crops such as carrots without piercing them in the process.

A manure fork resembles a spading fork, but its tines are thinner and curved for scooping. It usually has four tines but may have as many as twelve. Though it's meant for cleaning out stalls and other farm chores, gardeners value it for lifting compost materials or for shifting mulch from pile to wheelbarrow to garden bed. More rugged than a hayfork, it is nevertheless a lifting-and-pitching tool. Confusingly, the name is often used interchangeably with bedding fork, ensilage fork, scoop fork, stall fork, and compost fork.

It's best to shop for this tool, and any tool, with the task in mind. Hay mulch or compost materials that have not decomposed much can be moved with a few tines, widely spaced. More crumbly compost and mulches such as shredded bark and wood chips require the type with many tines spaced close together, so that the material doesn't fall through. The widely spaced kind was designed to scoop lumps of solid manure from fine bedding material such as wood shavings, where you want the bedding to fall back into the stall.

The broadfork is a big step up from all these others. It's a wide, sturdily built tool made to aerate soil in place. Its heaviness is a good thing because gravity does most of the work. Holding its two handles upright, you press down on the crossbar with your foot, allowing the long tines to sink into the ground. I find I can even hop briefly onto the crossbar with that foot, using the mighty force of my 110-pound body to drive the tines in a little deeper. Pulling the handles toward and slightly past me causes the tines to lift upward just enough to loosen the soil, opening up air channels. I back up and repeat this action every six inches down the bed, and in minutes the job is done. This movement is so effective that it can replace tilling altogether. I love this tool. It's so easy to use that I don't even work up a sweat.

A broadfork is an investment, but cheaper than a rototiller. You can do the same kind of aerating with your trusty spading fork, but it will not aerate the soil quite as deeply, and it will take much more time. If your garden is a large one, a broadfork would be an excellent fork to reach for.

Eliot using a broad-fork

The Right Hoe

The Roman poet Horace wrote in his ode "To Maecenas" that "The man who joyfully cleaves his ancestral fields with the hoe … will never be persuaded … to cleave to the sea." During Horace's time, the first century BC, forged iron hoes were numerous and varied, from heavy, mattock-like tools to the more slender sarculum, with its straight, cupped, or pronged blade. They vary still.

Even prehistoric hoes took different forms, depending on their uses and the materials at hand. Stout sticks with angled roots or branches were used for scratching the soil. Implements were lashed to the working end—a sharpened stone or the shoulder blade of a deer for digging, and a turtle shell or clamshell for scooping. Early hoes imitated the work of human hands and were of first importance until the time when heavy-soled shoes made spades and shovels possible. Bare or moccasin-clad feet could not have pressed down on these to drive home the blade.

In the industrial era, hoes in hundreds of styles have passed through gardeners' hands, but in most minds a hoe is shaped like what we call the garden hoe or the common hoe, with a blade about six inches wide and four inches high, sharpened on the outside edge, and attached to the handle at an 80- to 90-degree angle. This is a chopping hoe, designed to sever large weeds below soil level or move soil, as when you are mounding earth around potato plants or making a furrow in which to sow seeds. You can find this type of hoe in any hardware store.

A few of the many versions of this hoe include the onion hoe, whose narrow blade (about seven by two inches) has the maneuverability needed to address weeds among closely planted onions and can better creep beneath leafy crops like tomatoes. There's also the southern hoe, with a heavy blade designed to work in dense clay soil, and the lightweight floral hoe, once called the ladies' hoe—back in the day when people underestimated female gardeners.

For cultivating the soil—dispatching weeds when they are tiny—you need a hoe that is parallel to the ground, so you can skim lightly beneath the soil surface and not bring up weed seeds from below. Some of these are push hoes, which have a blade sharpened in front so that the hoe is urged forward. I have a V-shaped version that is sturdy and excellent for cultivating crusted soil or weeding a gravel walk. Another is the collinear hoe, a draw hoe whose blade is a 6½-by-1-inch sliver. Collinear means that the blade is right in line with the handle, so you are scoring a bull's-eye. With little effort you pull the tool along as you stroll down the row. Wire weeders, which come in several styles and are even narrower, are almost like a surgeon's tools, wiggling among small, closely planted crops without harming them.

I also enjoy using scuffle hoes, which employ a push-pull motion and are great for slicing off firmly entrenched weeds just below the soil's surface. Some are flat, such as the one shaped like a diamond, sharpened on all four sides. Another is a corrugated strip, attached to the long handle at one of the strip's ends. One very popular variation is the stirrup hoe, shaped like a riding boot stirrup with a slightly curved blade, sharp at both edges. Some stirrup hoes are fixed in their attachment to the handle and others are called action hoes, oscillating hoes, or hula hoes. These swing back and forth as you pull or push them, cutting on both the forward and backward strokes, and can deal even with monster weeds in compacted soil.

Monster weeds? Sooner or later every garden has them, but if we can joyfully cleave to them any row will seem shorter. You can take this attitude to the next level if you add another great invention of ancient man, the wheel.

A stirrup hoe, left, and a collinear hoe, right

A Wheel Hoe

There's always a time in summer when busy days are whizzing by as fast as sprouting pigweed. The garden could use an eight-hour spa day, but all I can give it is a quick manicure. So I reach for the wheel hoe.

A few generations ago, wheel hoes were standard equipment for market gardeners and for home gardeners who grew much of their own food.

Clara Coleman using a wheel hoe to weed the blueberries

An octogenarian neighbor who was raised on a vegetable farm recalled to me how twenty workers would show up each morning and reach for one. It was a tool by which large areas could be managed even without a horse or tractor.

A wheel hoe is simply a hoe blade supported by one small wheel with an inflatable tire. The wheel is there to lessen the work of moving the blade along, to keep it a consistent depth in the soil, and lend force to its cutting action. There are a number of attachments you can put on this tool, but the one I always use is an oscillating stirrup hoe, mounted just behind the wheel. Grasping the tool's two 4-foot-long wooden handlebars, I push it forward, allowing the blade to slice under any weeds in its way so that none can regrow. At times I can simply walk along at a steady pace, weeding close to crops planted in straight rows, or destroying weeds in the paths between beds. If the weeds are especially stubborn or the earth compacted, as it is in the paths, I can take advantage of the back-and-forth motion that an oscillating hoe provides. In fact, the job it does on paths, normally the most annoying areas to weed, is reason enough to own it. The weeds can either be raked up afterward or left to wilt in the sun. I have also used the wheel hoe to clear out an entire bed, or ready a new area for planting. It works something like a tiller, but without pulverizing the soil.

In recent years wheel hoes have become something of a cult, partly because of their long unavailability. Enthusiasts became fanatical collectors of old versions with wooden or steel wheels, made during the period of its widespread use. They turned up rich material about the tool's history and how it became a symbol of a saner way to grow food. Its inventor was Jethro Tull—no, not the English rock group, but the English agricultural engineer who developed the first mechanical seed drill in 1701, of which the wheel hoe was a spinoff. In the United States, Tull's hoes were quickly adopted, and in the late nineteenth century the firm S. L. Allen and Co. supplied farms and households with horse-drawn versions in its successful Planet Jr. line. As horses gave way to tractors, the company pioneered a motorized version, but always favoring home gardeners and small farmers, despite the pressure on farmers to go large scale.

Hand-pushed versions were offered as well and became increasingly popular. Many of the attachments were ingenious, such as a seeder that opened a furrow, dropped in seeds from a canister, covered the seeds with soil, tamped the soil, and marked it for the next furrow.

There are online sites where wheel hoe devotees share information. It's hard not to like a tool that does away with the need for herbicides and fossil fuels and is well adapted to the layout of home gardens and small farms, with their intensively planted beds and narrow paths. It's perfect for a greenhouse, where even a small rototiller is difficult to use. As a great timesaver, it contradicts the often-voiced dismissal of small-scale growing as too labor intensive to be profitable or even worthwhile.

Currently, the wheel hoe cult seems farm centered. But in many ways, home gardens and small farms have more in common than do small farms and their large, industrialized counterparts. Understandably, if your garden is a small collection of raised beds with brick paths, a wheel hoe is not an obvious necessity. But try it once, and it might lead you to consider a modest—and more easily managed—expansion.

A Wheelbarrow

A lot of the work in gardening is getting stuff from one place to another, and the larger or more isolated the garden, the more moving around of stuff there will be. Tools, plants, weeds, compost, bags of lime, bark mulch, rocks, bricks, gravel, firewood, buckets of water, UPS packages, jugs of cider, and giant zucchini are all things I have trundled about with my trusty, sturdy metal contractor's wheelbarrow.

I also use a boxy, wooden two-wheeled cart, especially useful when a flat bottom is needed for carrying pots and seedlings, or bulky items like hay bales. But nothing beats a wheelbarrow for maneuverability. It can turn on a dime, negotiate the narrowest of paths, hold its load without spilling, and then dump tidily forward at its final destination. With a few extra trips, a wheelbarrow can do a cart's job, but not always vice versa.

Here are a few ways to get the most out of this ancient garden workhorse:

- When loading up, place the heaviest part of the load over the wheel for efficiency and stability.

- Keep the tire inflated with a bike pump or small compressor. Or get an airless "no flat" tire.

- Sand the handles occasionally to keep them free of splinters, then protect them with linseed oil.

- When moving out seedlings for transplanting them into the garden, pour a few inches of water in the bottom of the wheelbarrow and let them sit for a while to thoroughly moisten them from below. (You can also use a kid's toy wagon for this job.)

- Don't overload the wheelbarrow, especially on hilly ground. Going up, it will exhaust you. Going down, it can run away from you and tip over.

- To go up a step with a wheelbarrow, either set up a wide plank as a ramp, or turn the wheelbarrow around and pull it up the step backward.

When shopping for a wheelbarrow, go for a sturdy one with a decent capacity, even if your yard and garden are small. If your strength is limited, just fill it partly full. Sooner or later there will be something large, light, and fluffy to move, and a dinky little wheelbarrow will be useless. If cheaply made, it will have a dinky little lifespan too. Buy one with one wheel. Those with two may be more stable, but I find them more awkward to handle.

When not in use, stand the wheelbarrow up on its front edge and lean it against a wall. This will keep rainwater from collecting in the dish and rusting it out. This is not true of one with a plastic dish, but a plastic dish is more breakable, especially when someone, trying to help, flings firewood into it repeatedly. Collecting water will also breed mosquitoes. And keeping its unnecessary weight in the wheelbarrow for a long time will add pressure to the tire.

The mattock is a heavy-duty chopper and digger.

Opposite: A three-tine cultivator, on the job

No doubt, the wheelbarrow will be improved on in the future, though we may look to the past as well. European travelers during the Renaissance found the Chinese using ones with masts and sails. How's that for power assist?

Other Useful Tools

Meanwhile, if spring is coming and your garden isn't ready for planting, there are a couple of tools you might need.

The mattock is a heavy, long-handled tool that Eliot and I have nicknamed the "human rototiller." The heft of its blade allows you to hack up the ground, weeds, stones, and all, enough to turn it into a garden. It's hard work, but you may only have to do it once.

The three-tine cultivator also allows you to chew up the soil without motorized equipment, but it's much lighter and doesn't go as deep as a mattock. It's a good tool for mixing compost, lime, and other amendments into the soil.

Okay, now you're ready for spring.

THE GARDEN YEAR

PART THREE

CHAPTER 9

Spring

Spring is a season of beginnings: the first crocus, the first buds on the maples, the return of monarch butterflies from their winter homes. The tracking and studying of such events are part of a science called phenology. But they are also keenly noted by plain old gardeners, farmers, and other observers of the natural world.

According to the Aldo Leopold Foundation, the word "phenology" comes from the Greek *phaino*, which means "to show or appear." Leopold himself, a forester, writer, and conservation pioneer, described phenological data as a "record of the rates at which solar energy flows to and through living things." Practically speaking, the data has been especially useful because the events are in step with one another, so that if warm weather arrives earlier than usual in a given spring, all the things that the warm weather brings will happen at about the same time. As a result, gardeners can use these signals from nature's schedule to plan their work. "Sow your peas when daffodils bloom" is one of many common signposts, but some of us have our own markers as well. If I see the orange blaze of daylilies along the roadsides and I haven't set out long-term crops such as Brussels sprouts yet, I know I've blown it for the year, though I can still start quicker ones like broccoli for fall.

Sadly, the phenological world order is no longer as dependable as it once was. Aldo Leopold would cry to see how we have messed up the world's climate, and thereby disturbed the delicate balances and small windows on which its populations depend. A particular flower must open in time for its special bee to pollinate it, and in time to offer pollen or nectar to that bee. A migrating bird, flying over an island where it normally refuels, might find that a human-driven shift in the ocean's current (and therefore its temperature) has caused the caterpillars that the bird normally expects to find to have hatched out either too early or too late. Or that they have disappeared because their habitat has been altered.

As a species we will need to do better. But meanwhile we can celebrate what a friend once called "phenological holidays": the first ripe melon, the first ear of sweet corn. In our house we have our own ways of noting and enjoying a crop's birthday. For me and Eliot it's a chance to give one's spouse a little surprise, such as a few spears of the first asparagus, steamed and buttered on the plate. Often it's the "Open your mouth and close your eyes" game, followed by the taste of the first sun-ripened (not chemically ripened) strawberry.

At other times we're less solicitous of each other. He who notices the first green peas swelling in their pods might fill his mouth with them, hiding behind the dense vines. She who spots the first ripe Sungold tomato claims it as her own.

As gardeners we observe nature's annual clock, but of course we also have a few harmless ways of resetting it, such as starting transplants indoors for an earlier harvest. Or "chitting" seed potatoes: letting them sprout in a warm spot so that they're off and running when planted in the ground. And we like to brag about our garden's "firsts."

A small restaurant in our little town once held a friendly competition, offering a prize for the first gardener who brought in a pound of sugar snap peas. The winner was an old-timer who walked in proudly with his harvest to collect the prize, which was a free dinner for two. "I live alone," he said. "Can I come in twice?"

Seed Fever

The stack of mail is heavy with seed catalogs all through December and January. By February it's noisy with the swish and rattle of seeds. Seductive little envelopes whisper "plant me" to the winter-weary gardener.

Resist those voices. For most vegetables, at least in our climate, February is too early for spring planting, outdoors or in. Seedlings sown prematurely grow tall and spindly in their windowsill pots long before the earth is ready to receive them. Best to pay strict attention to the dates on the packages and count backward from the expected frost date in your area. If it says eight weeks, allow eight weeks. If it says four, allow four. With the exception of leeks, artichokes, perennial herbs, and any others that take longer to reach planting size, most crops must wait a bit.

Meanwhile, there is plenty for manic planters to do while they are biding their time. Here are a few occupational therapies for those in the grip of seed fever.

First, reach for the seed trays, but only to take inventory. Discard broken ones and clean up the rest.

Lay in a supply of starting mix, little wooden labels, and indelible marking pens (not red ones, which bleach out in the sun).

Make charts and maps of what you're going to plant, where, and when. I find it's best if I've kept notes on what varieties grew well last year, and how they tasted. If not, I make a note to myself to make notes.

Go through last year's seeds and decide which ones might be usable. Poor keepers such as parsley and dill will not be. Tomatoes will. When in doubt, you can test germination by sprinkling a pinch of seeds on a damp paper towel. Fold the towel and keep it in a plastic bag at room temperature. After a week or so, see if most of the seeds have sprouted. You can also check the quality of your potting mix by planting a few seeds in it but discard your test subjects. It's too early for them, remember?

There are always jobs that were left out of fall cleanup and will still be neglected once the spring scramble begins if you don't do them now.

Round up any stray tools and put them away in their properly designated, agreed-upon, permanent spots where they can always be found when needed. Good luck with that.

Put up a critter-proof garden fence tall enough to keep the deer out and, if necessary, a length of electrified wire at the top to deter raccoons. Make the gate impregnable.

Keep making compost from kitchen scraps, dead houseplants, and any stored root crops that are sprouting and decomposing. Tasks like this keep idle hands busy. If symptoms of planting mania persist, make a terrarium out of an old fish tank or goldfish bowl. If there is a wooded part of your property, dig up a few mosses and other tiny woodland plants and establish them in fertile, humus-rich soil. Place glass over the top to keep the soil moist and sniff it periodically to slake the desire to rush outside and dig. Even the weeds that sprout will seem interesting to you.

For me, the soggy days of mud season in late March and early April are the worst. One of the cardinal rules of gardening is that you must never work, till, dig, or even walk on wet soil. Any of these things will compact it and turn it into dense clods that are hard to break up later—not only by you, but by all the soil organisms that till it by tiny degrees, tunneling it and keeping it loose and easy for air to penetrate. Soil should be just as moist as a squeezed-out sponge. If yours feels more like porridge, let it be for now.

Instead, buy a potted jasmine plant, let it bloom, inhale the fragrance, then make jasmine tea from the dried blossoms. Next time the urge to sow tomatoes or form a bed overwhelms you, make a cup of this tea, sit back, and sip the perfumed brew. Remind yourself that soon you'll be too busy to stop and smell the flowers. Now's the time.

Waking the Seeds

Every seed is a little time bomb with its own complex settings. Inside each one is an embryo ready to burst forth at the precise moment when conditions favor its growth. Until then, a hard seed coat helps keep it dormant as long as it stays dry. (That's why seeds are properly stored in moisture-proof containers.) Water softens that coat and awakens the life-form within, activating its growth enzymes and allowing it to consume the little package of nutritious carbohydrates it has on board.

Triggers for germination vary from plant to plant. Some need light, others need darkness. Most have an optimum range of temperature for sprouting. But all need water. If seeds contain chemical substances that keep them from germinating too soon, water is needed to flush these away. With some slow-germinating seeds such as carrots (which are direct sown in the garden), the embryo inside has not fully formed and needs fairly cool, moist soil to complete the process. If that is halted by dryness, it can be impossible to restart. So with carrots it's go, go, go. We make sure we keep the soil surface from drying out as we wait for that hint of green.

People talk about seeds "coming up," but initially they go down. First to emerge is the radical, the first tiny root, followed by the hypocotyl— the first stem. The radical looks like a little green crochet stitch, taking a sudden bend deeper into the soil. After this point the seedling will still need ample water, but with the radical plunging into moister regions, the pressure on the sower eases a bit.

For centuries gardeners eager to give seeds a good start have improved on cold, soggy spring soil by starting them indoors in a lighter, better aerated, and more controllable medium. In the old days, vegetable growers stockpiled upside-down chunks of pasture loam, in which the roots of the grasses kept those blocks intact, aerated, and suitable for growing seedlings. Before peat became a popular ingredient, growers used mixes based on leaf mold—still an excellent, light medium—often with added nutrients such as bonemeal, blood meal, and lime. After that came the era when sterilization of your seed medium was thought necessary to prevent soilborne diseases, such as the "damping off" fungus. Gardeners started to cook their soil trays in the oven before sowing. But then Harry Hoitink, a professor at Ohio State University, showed us that well-made compost introduces disease-suppressing microflora into a starting mix, to better effect.

The young carrot plants in this bed were watered daily when first sown.

One of my best garden mentors, Lee Bristol in Sherman, Connecticut, used to start seeds in a very fine-textured finished compost, taken from the bottom of his magnificent compost piles. That taught me the value of sifted compost, a truly grade A material from which dense clods, sticks, stones, and bones are neatly removed. There are compost sifters for sale, but you can easily make your own. Yes, you! Cut four lengths of two-by-fours and screw them together to make a rectangular frame that fits the top edge of your wheelbarrow as closely as possible. Cut a rectangle of ½-inch hardware cloth (or ¼-inch for a finer texture). Screw 1-by-2-inch strips of wood to the top of the frame with the hardware cloth in between, to hold it in place.

To sift, place the frame over the wheelbarrow, drop a shovelful of compost on the frame, and shake it back and forth, with the two-by-fours sliding on the wheelbarrow's top edges, so that the material falls through the mesh. You can also use your hands, in thick rubber gloves, to work the compost through.

Sifted compost can be mixed with peat, soil, or be used just on its own for starting any seeds indoors. It's great as a potting mix when you're moving little tomato seedlings into larger pots so that you'll have nice big ones to go in when the soil temperature is at least 60 degrees Fahrenheit and mud season finally loosens its grip.

Tools for Planting Time

If you're spending a lot of money during seed-starting season, it may be the gadgetry that gets you: plastic cell trays that crack, blow away, and need replacing, peat pots you must purchase annually, heat pads, grow lights, and so forth. It pays to ask what devices you can do without, and which ones you can buy that will truly pay their way.

Early in my gardening life I found that I could put newly sown flats on top of my kitchen cabinets, where the air was the warmest, until they sprouted, checking daily for germination. When they had, I set them on the kitchen counter, below the fluorescent lights that were attached to the underside of the upper cabinets. When I moved to a home that didn't have those, I built a simple wooden frame set on the floor, from which I hung a couple of wide-spectrum fluorescent shop lights by means of chains, just above my seeded flats. These produced both light and heat to urge the plants along, and I raised the lights gradually, securing them with S-hooks, as the plants grew. I was—and am—a very primitive carpenter, so if I can build something like that, maybe you can too.

My disillusionment with peat pots came one fall when I pulled up some old fennel plants that had been started in them. Theoretically, peat pots decompose due to soil moisture, microbes, and plant roots breaking through as they grow. But these pots were still intact, and what few roots that had poked through had clearly struggled. In subsequent years I stripped off the pots' edges, removed their bottoms and slit their sides, but that seemed to defeat the purpose. I considered trying one of those tools that form old newspapers into pots, but if I were a root I wouldn't choose to tunnel through newsprint. Paper isn't delicate. It lasts a long time if you use layers of it for mulch.

Finally, Eliot introduced me to the perfect apparatus for seed-starting: the soil blocker. With this well-made, indestructible device, you can form moistened peat-based seed-starting mix into sturdy cubes. You do this by plunging the blocker into a flat-bottomed tray filled with the mix, rotating it while pressing down hard. You then tip it up a bit, lift it, and eject the blocks you've made onto a flat by means of a spring-loaded handle. (The flat needn't have sides: it could be just a piece of thin plywood or polycarbonate.) Making the blocks takes a little practice, but soon you're a pro. Sown in these surprisingly stable cubes, plants develop excellent root systems and, with transplant shock much reduced, take hold quickly in the garden. Johnny's Selected Seeds sells these and a number of other soil-block sizes, including stand-up models that are great if you are growing large numbers of plants.

The cleverest aspect of the blocker is its companion, a tiny miniblocker that makes twenty soil blocks filled with germination mix, each a ¾-inch cube with a slight indentation on top to receive the seeds.

The miniblocker makes ¾-inch cubes of potting mix, each of which holds one seed.

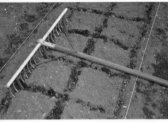

Top: After germination, the tiny cubes are dropped into ¾-inch holes made in a 2- or 3-inch block.

Middle: Marking out the bed for planting, with a bed rake

Bottom: Putting in the transplants

These save space, since you can discard any that don't germinate. You will need to buy the set of little snap-in cubic dibbles that fit inside the two-square-inch blocker. These allow it to make square holes in the top of the blocks exactly the right size to receive the miniblocks that have germinated. As soon as a speck of green life appears in our miniblocks, we move them on to the hole in the two-inch block, before they can form a long root. We drop each one gently into a square hole, and the seedlings soon fill those larger blocks with their roots, making them even more shatterproof.

While the seedlings are growing, the beds can be formed and made ready for planting. For that we use a bed rake. Eliot and I use three kinds of rakes: a standard plastic lawn rake; a traditional metal rake for grading soil, smoothing it, and picking up small stones and other surface debris; and the bed rake, which does pretty much what the metal rake does but is much wider—ideally as close as possible to the width of a thirty-inch-wide bed. It is lightweight, with curved tines. It can be instantly turned into a bed marker by sticking pieces of plumber's tubing on some of the tines at measured distances apart, to elongate them and mark the rows as we draw or push the rake down the length of the bed.

To mark the spacing we want the plants to have in the row, we set the tubes at that distance and draw the rake crosswise, thus forming a grid. We then transplant the seedlings at the intersections in the grid.

Many vegetables, such as lettuce and other greens, we transplant into the garden as two- or three-inch blocks, but for some others that are better planted in our climate at a more mature size—chiefly tomatoes, peppers, eggplants, cucumbers, and artichokes—we pot the blocks up in reusable plastic pots about five inches across at the top. Either square or round, these are often found kicking around a gardener's toolshed because so many nursery plants, especially perennials, are sold in them, and people are always looking for a way to pass them along to someone who can put them to use. If larger than needed, just fill them with less potting mix.

Holes for plants in these pots can easily be made with a shovel, but there is a tool that works even better: the posthole digger.

I love tools that can be used standing up, and that harness the force of gravity, and the posthole digger is one of them. It consists of two metal blades shaped like narrow, cupped, curved-bottomed spades, joined at the top by a hinged metal cuff and two long handles. Holding the tops of the handles close together, you plunge the tool downward into the soil, then spread the handles apart. This action causes the blades to come toward each other, trapping the earth between them and thereby leaving a hole. You pull up the tool, and bring the handles together again, above the spot where you want the soil to go, and let it drop there. Then do it again, if necessary, until the hole is the depth it needs to be. I find this much less tiring than using a shovel, and it makes a lovely round hole. It is perfect for digging holes for the actual posts you will need when the deer finally break you down and you put up a fence.

Dave makes holes for the artichokes with a posthole digger; Anna takes them out of the black pots and puts them in the ground.

Orphans

At the end of spring planting season I sometimes think of the poem by Louise Bogan titled "Women," which begins "Women have no wilderness in them. They are provident instead." It comes to mind because all the female gardeners in the neighborhood, myself included, have been busy finding homes for all our leftover seedlings. It seems intolerable to throw out partial flats of perfectly healthy tomato plants, even if they are a bit leggy. Surely somebody on our road needs them.

Eliot, the ever-practical farmer, can see no pathos in that, and it's true that being overprovident is often not worth the energy spent. It's not as if we were drowning kittens.

Nevertheless, there's something valuable in the instinct to conserve, and the belief that nothing should be wasted. This mentality, born of frugality, led Italians to create high-alcohol grappa out of grape skins after the juice was pressed from them to make wine, and the French to press the grapes' seeds into the rinds of cheeses to add flavor. It's part of a cook's genius to use by-products in a creative way.

Besides, this little flurry of plant swapping, as spring gives way to summer, is a pleasant exchange. Busy friends, behind in their planting, often welcome our handouts. Our former farm manager, Siri Beringer, when told to discard transplants, would arrange them carefully on top of the compost pile in hopes someone might come by and take them before they got buried, and they often did. Sometimes we sell them. Sometimes we put them on a table marked "Free." You could do that, next to your door. A nearby food co-op used to do that on its porch.

Some thrown-out plants refuse to die. I've accidentally raised squash and tomatoes from seedlings tossed on the compost pile. Of course. Why wouldn't a big pile of organic waste be the perfect place for them to grow?

So much about growing and eating is serendipity. Once I espied an old flat of basil tossed in a corner, and suddenly there was pesto for lunch. After being cut, it grew back and we had pesto again. Once I was making salad when a worker named Kennon Kaye walked in with a bowl of fennel plants, gleaned when she'd thinned a bed. They were tiny, just like spindly blades of grass, with a delightfully subtle fennel flavor, and all washed and ready to go into the salad bowl. Now, that's my kind of woman.

CHAPTER 10

Summer

Think a minute. Can you name a spring vegetable? Asparagus? Good. Can you name another? Um, sorrel? Fava beans?

The fact is, there aren't very many. Gardeners are busy planting lots of early crops, but, in my climate, harvest really begins in early summer. Meanwhile, what goes on our plates are the last remnants of the fall harvest, kept in storage. In the old days, this period was often called "the hungry gap" by those who relied on their gardens for survival. The saddest stories were about those who depended chiefly on grains. For them the hungry gap came in midsummer before the wheat, rye, and barley had been cut. Nothing separated rich from poor like the difference between having plenty of grain in the larder from the previous year as opposed to having it run out.

Early summer is the time for me to prowl around my garden and see what greens might have overwintered. (I thank myself for having permanent paths in place so that I needn't step in any beds.) Biennials like Swiss chard, kale, and beets may look battered by winter, but if the roots are intact, they may be sprouting new young leaves for spring salads before warmer weather comes and makes them go to seed. Sometimes

overwintered root crops such as carrots are also viable, especially parsnips, for which the spring dig is their whole reason for being.

The best strategy is to use protective devices such as cold frames so that we can grow tender little carrots, turnips, peas, lettuce, and other salad greens without having to deal with sudden freezes or soggy soil. I find that these gems taste even better in April and May than they will in June and July. Spinach is sweeter and less coarse. Arugula has less bite. Lettuce, beet greens, and Asian greens such as mizuna can be sown as cut-and-come-again crops and picked for a stretch before the weather turns hot and makes them go to seed. With a little forethought, we can turn the gap into a time of fresh flavors and the garden's rebirth. It's the time to take a deep breath, brace yourself, and get ready for the great party that is about to happen in the garden.

Off and Running

Of all the work gardeners do in summer, the hardest is picking, because we don't think of it as a job. Our vision is that we plant, we weed, we water, and then we reap the rewards. But reaping, for many vegetables, is a regular assignment that cannot wait. The image of the cornucopia, the horn of plenty full of food, should not be a static one. It should be played as a film on a device with no pause button.

With most fruiting crops we must keep up with the picking or the harvest will stop. Garden peas are picked when the pods are green and smooth with just-formed, tender peas inside. But any rough-skinned pods with hard peas must be picked at the same time or they will become stop signs for the plants, which declare the job is finished. The same thing happens with pole beans and cucumbers. If the central head of a broccoli plant is not cut while green but is left to make yellow flowers, we won't get as much side shoot production thereafter. Cut-and-come-again lettuce, if not cut, will not come again as tender leaves but will make tall, bitter-tasting towers. Summer squash plants left to make giant clubs will slow their production of the tasty small ones that must be picked about every other day.

I feel better about my excess food if I can find people who need it or would simply appreciate the gift. But it also helps to have a compost pile to give it to. And a flock of chickens.

Some crops, especially perennial ones for which seed set is not the be-all and end-all, will keep right on going if I neglect them. But they still may not be as productive if ignored. I've noticed this with raspberries. Rainy weather can make the fruits moldy, but if I keep up with the picking, the mold on a berry is less likely to spread to the berries touching it. This makes a good case for checking them every day and stuffing any ripe ones into your mouth whenever you walk by the row. There's a lot of responsibility attached to that job. But I'm on it.

Hot

Summertime, and the beanpoles are leaning. Fish are jumping, and the squash vines are creeping out into the lawn.

I love my summer garden but as July turns to August it has lost some of its freshness and so have I. Wade into the scratchy squash bed? Not right now. Pull out the dead peavines? Maybe tomorrow. It's not easy to summon the energy for garden chores when it's hot, but here are a few strategies that work for me.

- Work as early in the day as possible. Daybreak is way cooler than sunset, and the garden is breathing easier too. A cloudy day is always worth catching, or one with a nice breeze.

- Straw hats might be standard equipment for sunny days, but I find them itchy and irritating. A cloth hat is more comfortable, especially when soaked with water as needed; the evaporation cools me off. A large wet bandana might not be flattering headgear, but it works too.

- Try wearing a skirt. Skirts are cooler than pants. We girls have been envying all you shirtless guys for years. Here's our chance to one-up you. Not the long gardening skirts that ladies of the Gertrude Jekyll era dragged through the mud. How about knee length and loose-fitting, with a stretchy waist?

- Pour a tall glass or pitcher with something cold, keep it in the fridge, and chug on it when you come in for frequent breaks. You can get very dehydrated out there without realizing it's happening. Everybody has a favorite quencher. I love iced coffee for the energy spike, but caffeine is dehydrating, so I often substitute a lean milkshake with milk, club soda, and a little maple syrup. Or an icy herbal mix of lemon verbena and mint, with a squirt of honey. Some favor beer, but I would need a nap after that.

This kitchen garden in Argentina keeps cool with a canopy of shade cloth.

- Take a nap. The midday siesta was developed in warm countries and has saved many lives—and gardens.

- Take the summer off. Some places are so hot in summer that not much food grows. There are some crops, such as squash and beans, that can adapt fine. But can you? Celebrate the gardening seasons of winter, spring, and fall.

Humid

A hygrometer is a tool that measures humidity's highs and lows but most folks rely on simpler data. At summer's muggy height towels do not dry. Saltshakers are shaken in vain. Beach novels you lent out are returned with their covers curled like scrolls. Even pages I write myself emerge from the printer cupped and on the wing, like paper airplanes.

In humid weather, my body slows and my spirit sinks. The only thing it improves is my hair, rendering it bouncy, full of body, and thick with curl. This lifts my mood almost as much as the humidity dampens it. If I were a scientist, I would call this the humidity-hair inversion.

The impact of humidity on the garden is harder to assess. Most plants like humidity—up to a point. The way they grow in the wild, grouped together, creates a little moisture cloud around them that helps keep their leaves from drying out. The power of the sun enables them to draw water out of the ground and circulate it through stem, leaf, flower, and fruit, carrying nutrients as it goes. Finally, this water evaporates into the air, which cools the leaf surfaces. If it is too hot, especially with a drying wind, the stomata (tiny openings in the leaves) remain shut to keep excess water from escaping. As a result, the movement of water from soil to plant to air slows or stops. Plants that are widely spaced, as they are in many gardens, are especially vulnerable and must be watered when it's hot and dry. This is especially true of leafy crops.

Too much humidity can make garden plants suffer if it goes on for weeks. If the air is saturated with moisture, it can't absorb the water the plants need to release. The leaves can then overheat, and the flow of nutrients can stop. Fruiting crops are especially susceptible. Calcium deficiencies such as blossom end rot on tomatoes (watery, sunken areas on the blossom end) show up in humid weather. There is not enough flow of water to move this important element up the stem and into the fruit. (This can also be caused by uneven watering, or by starting tomatoes in too-cold weather, followed by high heat.)

Nutritional deficiencies such as this are often mistaken for disease, but fungal diseases like leaf spot, mildews, and molds show up too, as lack of evaporation creates a perfect climate for their growth. What can you do? If fungal diseases are the problem with certain plants, spacing them farther apart may help. You can also drag yourself out from under that shade tree and clean up garden debris like dead plants, which can harbor disease organisms, and generally lighten the garden's load.

I like to remind myself at such moments that with crisp fall weather in sight I will have renewed energy for many garden projects long deferred. But I'll miss the curly hair.

Dry

As everybody knows, the best way to make it rain is to wash your car. As extra insurance, a superstitious gardener might provoke a shower by ordering a complicated drip irrigation system.

Or maybe there are better ways to prepare for a drought.

At the top of my list is: Make sure there is plenty of organic matter in the soil. This is a must in my garden because I have sandy soil that drains too quickly without the spongelike absorption that compost provides. Without it, I would have to water the garden much more often. I also try to restrict the amount of lawn at our place, because the lawn is the first place to suffer when there's no rain. Water is a scarce resource, and we all need to prioritize its use. For me, the kitchen garden is the top priority. Flower gardens come second, and then there's the lawn.

Gardeners in naturally arid climates work around dry weather the way I work around the long winter freeze-up. They grow vegetables during the coolest, wettest part of the year and stock up on what they can. They concentrate the thirstiest plants in one area so that they can be watered economically. Mulching the soil between plants, with straw or other materials, decreases evaporation as long as it is applied when the soil is wet. It's important to focus on when the plants need water the most—when they are newly sown, newly transplanted, and during fruit-set for the fruiting vegetables. Sometimes shade cloth on frames is put up over crops when they are vulnerable, or the crops are even put in greenhouses, where temperature, water supply, and humidity can be closely controlled.

What crops you grow makes a difference, of course. Some crops need less water than others, but it seems to me that people will try to grow just about anything they like to eat by relying on planting strategies and by looking out for drought-resistant varieties, heat-resistant varieties, and food plants that put down permanent roots, such as asparagus and grapes. In some cases, less water can improve the crop. You wouldn't want to grow dry-farmed celery, but dry-farmed tomatoes can have an excellent concentrated flavor.

When you do water, it's important to do it deeply, rather than just sprinkling the surface, which might settle the dust but then quickly disappear. I always look to make sure I haven't left a dry layer between the water I've applied and the moisture deeper in the soil. This is called "making the moisture meet."

It's also important to have watering equipment that you can live with, and that does the job right. We try to have our system in place at the beginning of the season, starting with big, black, sturdy, nonkinky rubber hoses and high-quality brass fittings. We prefer a type of brass coupling called Quick Disconnect (presently available at dramm.com), which locks securely in place with minimal leakage. Any nozzle or sprinkler we use is supposed to have a Quick Disconnect on it so that we can easily shift things around.

Drip, trickle, and soaker systems are often installed at soil level at great expense because most conventional sprinkler systems have one serious flaw. Because they atomize the water to a fine spray, they lose some of it to evaporation and waste even more when the wind blows the droplets away from their target. You can avoid that by using a relatively new type of low-pressure sprinkler head called a Wobbler. It spins, emitting uniform drops too heavy for the wind to blow around. The Senninger Xcel model we use is mounted on a tripod sprinkler stand.

I also like an oscillating rod-shaped sprinkler that sits on the ground and can be easily adjusted to fling water back and forth with great exactitude over a specific area. Both Gardena and Hozelock make one.

For container plants, I leave one solitary hose on the terrace with a wand called the Wonder Waterer, which delivers a soft, gentle spray. But I also keep handy an old-fashioned, hard-stream, suds-busting pistol-grip nozzle I can put on the hose if the rain never comes and I must resort to the old strategy of washing the car.

The heavy drops from these Wobbler sprinkler heads aren't blown away by the wind.

Freshness Is All

A garden may inspire any number of grand culinary adventures, but it also yields a steady supply of fast food. Much nibbling and grazing goes on right in our garden's rows, and every bite reminds us of why we do all this soil-building, and the care that we give our crops.

The outdoor snack bar is always open, starting in spring with little red-tipped French Breakfast radishes. Crisp spring carrots and peas are not far behind, then summer cherry tomatoes, strawberries, blueberries, raspberries, and, finally, apples and little white Hakurei turnips in fall.

You will never eat any morsel fresher than one just picked from the garden. Here's Harold McGee in his book *On Food and Cooking: The Science and Lore of the Kitchen*: "Most vegetables contain only moderate amounts of sugar and acid, and these are quickly used up by the plant cells after harvest. This is why vegetables picked just before cooking are more fulfilling than store bought produce." When you fresh pick a fruit or vegetable, it is still a living, breathing thing, taking oxygen from the air and releasing carbon dioxide. But it can't live indefinitely. The food you put in the fridge is literally eating itself—consuming its stored reserves. It no longer draws water from the soil, although its pores continue to release water vapor, costing it firmness and fullness. Mighty oxidants such as carotene and lycopene, proud guardians of our own personal shelf lives, start to lose their clout.

Some types of produce keep better than others. The decline and fall of a butternut squash might take eight months, stored in a cool, dark place. An uncovered bowl of spinach on a hot day might not last fifteen minutes.

There is much you can do to keep produce lively. The proper mindset is essential. I'm not the touchy-feely sort, but I do think it helps to imagine a fruit or vegetable as a sentient being that will scream "ouch" if handled roughly. Dings, nicks, or bruises provide entry points for bacteria and fungi, the handmaidens of rot. Greens should be cut with a sharp knife, not ripped from the plant. Squash need to be placed gently in a harvest basket, not dropped, lobbed, or flung. Tomatoes piled eight deep in a bucket, or rolling about in the back of a car, will suffer internal injuries that are routes to decay.

Timing is also important. Often I must pick something right away in order to keep my plants producing more of it, despite the fact that there's more than we can use right away. Even if I had meal planning and gift giving down to an art, some things would always need to be stored. When this happens, it's important to prevent as much moisture loss as possible. Food picked in the heat of day, when it looks a bit limp, will have trouble bouncing back. Early morning is the best.

What I do with it next depends on whether the crop is a cool weather or a hot weather one. Those that thrive in hot places, such as tomatoes, melons, peppers, eggplants, and bananas, are best stored above 50 degrees Fahrenheit. They actually decline in flavor, color, and food values when refrigerated.

The crops that thrive in cool areas, or during cool seasons, need chilling if not eaten promptly. These include all the leafy greens, cole crops such as broccoli and Brussels sprouts, and some northern fruits, especially berries. Cooling keeps these fresh and alive in three important ways. It reduces moisture loss by slowing down transpiration. It preserves oxygen levels by slowing respiration. And it reduces the effect of ethylene, a colorless and usually odorless gas naturally present in fruiting bodies that makes them ripen.

Leafy crops, with their large, porous surfaces, are the most at risk. Plunging them into a sink full of cold water will rehydrate them, get rid of "field heat," and flush out insects that otherwise would stay around to dine.

When storing produce we walk a fine line between giving them too much air and water and too little. A bag that is too tightly sealed will accumulate excess carbon dioxide from respiration, which affects quality, and excess moisture, which encourages decay. A crisper drawer works better, or a lettuce spinner put in the fridge to let greens drain gently while cooling.

Whether to wash produce before storing depends on the crop. Root cellar ones such as carrots and potatoes keep best if stored grimy, although

Greens, such as lettuce, should be refrigerated as soon as they are picked.

I do wash carrots being stored for same-day consumption, because scrubbing them is easiest if done right away. All squash store better unwashed, but I remove any rotting flowers that cling to them. Leeks and scallions can be washed, but onions and garlic should never get wet.

Good fridge management pays off. If there are two bags of something, it's often best to cook the one most recently picked and compost the other. Backlogged food soon becomes a sordid mess.

The wonderful thing about being a home gardener is that you can choose varieties of vegetables and fruits for their flavor, not their ease of shipment or storage. There is rarely a need to pick them green and then ripen them. There is a day on which each one has reached its full potential and is perfect for eating.

Seize it if you can.

A Soup Happens

In summer, so many vegetables beckon from the garden that it's sometimes hard to choose which ones to feature in a meal. That's when I turn to a tried-and-true theme. It's not the same thing as a recipe that would tell me which ingredients to choose, their weights or measures, what method of cooking to use for each, in what order, and for how long. It's more like an ideal and a flavor profile. Take the French vegetable soup pistou. What makes it a treat is the last-minute addition of basil, garlic, and olive oil, pounded and ground into a paste in a mortar. The pounding implement, the pestle, is what gave pistou its name.

If the ingredients in pistou sound familiar it's because they're much like the ones in the Italian sauce called pesto, which includes pine nuts and Parmesan cheese. Both are fine enhancements, and, if you like, you can substitute another cheese, such as Gruyère. It's hard to enforce authenticity in a dish that began in Genoa, then crept along the French Mediterranean coast to Provence. By the time it gets to your own kitchen it is your recipe. Your soup.

To construct the recipe, go out into the garden and make sure there is plenty of basil. Ideally there is also fresh garlic to harvest and either snap beans or shell beans, or both. Summer squash and tomatoes are frequent players, but rarely brassicas, such as broccoli. To me brassicas are part of the fall flavor profile and tell a different story. Some cooks add pasta, such as macaroni, and the inclusion of meat makes this a robust one-pot meal. A meat broth is also a good base. But for me, vegetables sautéed or simmered with a light touch to highlight their freshness are the soul of this dish.

My slow, rainy-day version of this soup starts by making a long-simmered vegetable broth that is then strained. More chopped sautéed vegetables are then added to that, and the pesto might even be mortar-and-pestled by hand. The quick, sunny-day version starts with broth that was made on a rainy day and frozen. The pesto is made by stuffing as many basil leaves as I can in a food processor with garlic and chunks of Parmigiano-Reggiano. This whirls very briefly while I drizzle in enough olive oil to make a sauce that is thick, not runny. With either version I peel the tomatoes by pouring boiling water over them to loosen the skin, cut them into biggish pieces, and add them at the last minute. After mounding the vegetables in each person's bowl, along with the cooking liquid, I spoon a big dollop of pesto into the center so everyone can admire the bright green color, inhale its heady fragrance, then stir it in themselves. It feels like the outdoors is contained in each bowl.

If It's August, This Must Be Italy

My favorite summer medley is an Italian-style antipasto, for which all the vegetables are gently cooked in extra virgin olive oil and then served at room temperature. It might take two hours to prepare, but it makes for an extra festive treat. I've found I can speed up the process by sautéing some of them on top of the stove while the others bake in the oven. With some planning and constant attention ("Out of the kitchen, people, unless

An antipasto celebrates late summer vegetables.

you're helping!") this can work fine. The vegetables I most like to use are summer squash, eggplants, sweet pepper, bulb fennel, onions, artichokes, and paste tomatoes. Gathering them all together at the beginning, washing them, and prepping them so that they're all ready to go will make the operation smooth.

For the tomatoes, this means slicing them in half lengthwise and setting them, cut-sides up, on a rimmed cookie sheet slicked with olive oil, then drizzling more olive over the top and sprinkling them with salt, pepper, and a few herbs. For the onions, I use ones of a uniformly medium size, peel them, and trim the root ends so that they can sit flat, but with enough of the base intact to hold their shape. I slice about ¼ inch off the tops, then drizzle them with olive oil and sprinkle with salt, pepper, and herbs just the way I did with the tomatoes. I crowd them into a baking dish so that they can hold each other upright, with ½ inch of water in the bottom.

I slice the peppers into rings, removing the seeds. For the fennel bulbs, I trim off the stems (and any brown parts), leaving the base at the bottom intact. Then I hold them upright and slice them down lengthwise into ¼-inch-thick fans.

For summer squash, I use any size (except for the monsters), slicing large ones in rounds about ¼ inch thick, and small ones in half lengthwise. I slice the eggplants the same way, then salt them generously and lay them on paper towels. After the salt has forced out some of the liquid, I wash the slices under a running tap, squeezing them gently to compress and moisten them without letting them get too soggy. This keeps the slices from absorbing too much oil in cooking.

I bake the tomatoes and onions at 350 degrees Fahrenheit for forty-five minutes to an hour, until they're soft, sweet, and caramelized. The tomatoes are reduced in size but still feel pillowy on the bottom. Both can share the same oven if you like, but keep checking them to make sure they don't burn.

While they're cooking, I get my biggest iron skillet, pour in a generous amount of olive oil, and sauté all the other vegetables, slice by slice, adding a little garlic from time to time. I find I can keep two skillets going at once if I really hover over both, flipping the slices to give them a uniform golden color. I might splash a little water on them as needed to hasten softening and prevent burning. As they finish cooking, I transfer them directly to serving platters.

Everybody has their own way of putting together an antipasto. All the vegetables might be roasted, grilled, or even pickled. Often cured meats and cheeses are included and may even dominate, in the style of an Italian salumi or French charcuterie plate. I'm particularly fond of the all-veggie version.

What has always astonished me is the role that any Italian antipasto is designed to play. The word translates as "before the meal," and even after the most lavish display of antipasti a great deal of food is expected to follow. I happily stop at the antipasto table that greets the diner in old-fashioned Italian restaurants. Traditionally, I am supposed to move on to pasta, rice, or soup from the *primi* course, then to meat or fish from the *secondi* course, more vegetables from the *contorni* course, salad from the *insalata* course, fruit and more cheese from the *formaggi e frutta* course, and finally *dolce*—dessert. It would take me from sunrise to sunset to eat a meal like that. But then I can sure think of worse ways to spend a day.

Houseguest Season

Planting season may be winding down, so we can catch a breath, but only a quick one. After school is out, houseguest season is just around the corner.

Now don't get me wrong. I like having company. It's much easier to set a few extra seats at the table for good friends and family than it is to get on a plane and visit their distant homes. And guests are less underfoot in summer, when life spills outdoors. But if your work is farming or gardening, there's no getting around the fact that visitors are on vacation, and you are not. Perhaps the solution lies in the old Swahili proverb: "Treat your guest as a guest for two days, but on the third day give him a hoe."

This approach has left me with so many good memories. Gardening with my sisters, Eloise and Anne. Gardening with my friend Joyce at her Australian farm—and mine, in Maine. Gardening with nearby vegetable-worshipping chef friends like Odessa and Devin. Some of the best conversations happen when you are working down the row with someone.

Guests who recognize weeds and can extract them, roots and all, are especially welcome, but I'm happy to instruct anyone in the fascinating art of garden maintenance. Men like big jobs with dramatic results, like planting a tree. Children can be surprisingly useful. They like picking off and drowning potato beetles. They will stand there with a hose as long as they can fool around with it a little. Small ones are endlessly absorbed with watering cans.

The best use for guests comes at dinnertime. With many to feed, there is less time for harvesting, and hands of any age can be put to work. Kids are always up for picking berries or cherry tomatoes, stealing some along the way. Even the most useless guest can help: "Henry, would you mind taking that cigarette outside, and while you're out there, cut me a few zucchini? It's the plant with the great big leaves and yellow flowers."

Cocktail hour brings a small army of potential prep cooks, so I pass out peas to shell, beans to snap, and tomatoes to slice, instead of canapés and Brie.

If your garden is near the house and its play areas, it allows you to socialize while you work. If not, that's fine too. When the hive is just a bit too abuzz, it's also the perfect place to hide.

Planting for Fall

Well before July, Eliot and I start thinking about fall crops. We make sure we've ordered seeds of what we'd like to grow and start pulling out spent crops so that we'll have some empty beds where we can sow rows of turnips and beets around July 15. We might sow some crops indoors, such as broccoli, cauliflower, Savoy cabbage, and bok choy so we'll have transplants of those to go in about that time as well. If you're in the habit of buying vegetable transplants at a local nursery, it might be hard to find one that stocks any for late planting, but encourage one to do so.

If you are really organized, you can keep your seed packets in a shallow, narrow box, with labels sticking up that divide it into sowing dates, week by week, both for direct sowing and transplanting. Another way is to just let the garden be your calendar. Basil that has gone to seed is the signal to plan for parsley and chervil, once the weather starts to cool. Having too many tomatoes is nature's way of telling you that you're not growing enough kale.

Timing your plantings is so much easier in spring because seed catalogs and seed packets offer time-tested data on when to sow and how many days until maturity. Later on, you have to turn the whole thing upside down. Instead of going from cold to hot, you're going from hot to cold. Instead of taking into account the last expected frost, you're looking for the first one. Instead of lengthening days, you have shortening ones. Sowing dates will vary, of course, from one climate to another, so instead of following the rules, you are forging your own personal journey and getting there will take some trial and error. You'll find that the more local

These beets, sown in midsummer, will make an excellent fall crop.

information you can find, the better, so you might start by asking the Cooperative Extension Service in your area if they have any lists of planting dates for fall and winter gardens. Keeping a journal that records what you planted, and with what outcome, will give you guidelines you can use next year.

The main thing to keep in mind is the difference between warm weather vegetables and cool weather ones. In case you're not sure, the first frost will tell you.

CHAPTER 11

Fall

I once knew a woman named Dot Gray who lived in a seaside town and planted gardens for people. By the time she got around to her own it was July 1, which some would call "too late." Dot, who also dug clams, knew the truth of the old proverb "Time and tide wait for no man," but, having no choice, she did in July what she'd hoped to do in April. Somehow, she always had a productive garden.

As gardeners we all rely on planning, but the guidelines we learn so carefully can seem more a belief system than a science. "The last expected frost date" after which the planting of most food crops is safe is no more a signpost than a blaze on a tree that has fallen across a trail.

Good guesswork has always been one of a good gardener's skills and will remain so. Although forecasting temperature, rainfall, and the like has gotten more sophisticated and perhaps more accurate, the weather itself has gotten more extreme and at times "unseasonable."

As a response to a life of weather uncertainty, I've become less attached to the idea of a gardening year with well-defined seasons. Scolding yourself about the nonsowing of spring peas is less helpful than ordering seeds for fall ones, and planning for a garden that will perform from early September, into November, December, and beyond.

Harvest, Dried and True

Opposite: Our garden in early October

When I was in third grade, our teacher taught us how to make an Indigenous survival food called pemmican. We combined dried beef, raisins, and Crisco, mushing them into a paste with a hand grinder and forming them into gummy balls, wrapped in aluminum foil. We then embarked on a field trip to the forested hills of Inwood Park, the only place on Manhattan Island where you could still look around and see absolutely no sign of modern life. We could imagine the scene as centuries old, with only our presence giving it away. Wearing flannel "Indian costumes" we had dyed brown with walnut shells or red with pokeberries, we spent the day exploring caves, identifying birds, and trying to eat our pemmican.

It may not have been the tastiest food lesson I'd ever learned—swapping bacon fat for the Crisco would have helped—but I'm still intrigued by this ancient trail mix, a high-calorie package of protein, fat, and carbohydrate that once fueled many travelers on their journeys through the boreal forests and arctic tundra. It needed no oven and lasted indefinitely. The meat would have been venison, caribou, bison, elk, or bear, dried over fire on a willow lattice and mixed with the animal's fat. The fruit could be cranberries, blueberries, serviceberries, or whatever berry was at hand. Nuts were sometimes added.

Pemmican has not yet become part of my repertoire, although other dried foods have. Nothing, of course, quite compares with food eaten fresh from the garden, and most foods stored or preserved by other methods still partake of that primal, integral moisture, the "water of life." Most dried foods aren't pretty, but a long, gentle drying process does leave most nutrients intact, not to mention their original fiber. Flavors are concentrated and, in the case of fruits, the texture is pleasantly chewy. Of the "vegetables" that can be dried, only certain fruiting bodies such as tomatoes can be left with a leatherlike consistency. Once past the sticky stage, their sugars and acids help prevent spoilage. But most edibles must be dried until more brittle, to prevent mold. I've dried red peppers by spreading them on a cookie sheet set above a woodstove. A heat register,

Tomatoes in a dehydrator

warm attic, or even the space near the ceiling atop a kitchen cabinet works too. One friend used to make "leather britches"—an old-time name for green beans strung on a stout string like a necklace. After a while they would get dusty, and she had to resist the urge to leave them above the stove for their homey look. Properly stored, they were tasty enough when reconstituted in water and cooked with bacon or ham.

Folks in cactus country can dry all sorts of things just by spreading them out in the sun, while I must deal with humid summers, dewy nights, and rain. An oven set to "warm" with the door ajar will dry many foods, but I find that electric dehydrators, with their numerous shelves and low temperature settings, waste less fuel. A thermostat keeps the heat constant, and a fan blows the moisture away. Setting the temperature at 115 degrees Fahrenheit is best for sweet items like peaches and tomatoes that can so easily scorch. It's important to slice items thin—¼ inch at most—and to turn the dryer off when it's not under your watchful eye. I've had good results with eggplant and apples. I've even dried kernels of blanched sweet corn for later use in fish chowder or shepherd's pie. After rehydrating they are pleasantly chewy.

One of the best things about drying food is the convenience of always having certain flavors on hand. Sometimes you want a hint of celery in the soup, or onion, or fennel. It's comforting to always have some dried lemon or orange rind, a few dried mushrooms for an omelet, a handful of blueberries for pancakes, and plenty of herbs. Dried produce, because of its reduced volume, also takes up little space in storage. (Tightly capped jars are best for excluding moisture.) Dried fruits pack well for long car trips.

But for me it's all about not getting into the car, not going to the store, not paying for the thing, not having to throw its packaging away. Odd, isn't it? As life out there gets more complicated, the old trail foods could help us to stay home.

Frost

Frost on Tuscan kale

At first, there's devastation. Whatever structures were supporting the tomatoes, cucumbers, and beans are now, overnight, festooned with limp stems and soggy, formless fruits. Whatever plans I might have had for them are cancelled. Sometimes that's a relief. I can now redirect my attention from those somewhat demanding summer crops to what remains in the garden. Just look at the way the multicolored stems of Bright Lights chard are glowing when backlit by the morning sun. The last Savoy cabbages and fennel bulbs need to be picked and eaten soon, but all the perennial herbs are in great shape, the hardiest lettuces are still pickable, and the Brussels sprouts have miles to go before we eat.

Besides, frost is beautiful. A few earlier "grass frosts" have touched the tips of the lawn grass in shady spots so lightly that I have to go and feel them to find out whether I'm seeing sparkly dew or crunchy crystals. The next one might just blacken the basil—always the first soldier to fall—and the uppermost tips of the squash leaves. Some mornings frost has covered the kitchen window or the car's windshield with fernlike fractal patterns, self-replicating smaller and smaller versions of themselves as they branch out and spread across the glass, just like real ferns when they unfurl in spring.

Some of the many crops that keep on going in cold weather are sweetened by frost. For me, one of the most dramatic ones is kale, which loses its slightly mustardy bite and can become almost sugary—especially the smooth kales, and especially the smaller leaves at the center of the plant. Carrots are another. Frost in the soil turns them into what we call "candy carrots," so sweet you could eat them for dessert. Kids love to pull them up, wash them off, and eat them as a snack. In winter, when there are fewer insect pests around, plants must cut back on the harsher chemicals they would otherwise produce as a defense, making them milder and sweeter for us to eat. That's one explanation, but a Japanese study published in 1996 showed that when cabbage plants were gradually acclimated to cold, they turned their stored starches into sugar as a sort of antifreeze. This revelation occurred in a lab, but you can replicate the experiment quite simply in your garden by planting fall cabbage and enjoying the tasty result. With carrots for dessert.

So frost has its sunny side, but it is still helpful to know when it is about to happen. One theory says that the first frost always comes during the week preceding a full moon, so you might watch the moon along with the weather report. Even if the "F" word is not mentioned, check the sky, because a clear night with no blanket of clouds to block Earth's radiational cooling is a frost omen. Find the Pleiades and if you can see more than five little stars in the cluster, the night is clear. Also beware the calm night with no wind to mix up the layers of warm and cold air. Or a dry one, with no moisture particles to trap heat. We check the outdoor thermometer at 8:00 p.m. and if it is above 42 degrees Fahrenheit there will be no frost. Maybe.

Ready or not, frost comes. Say goodbye to the tomatoes, make a great mixed salad from all that remains, put on Édith Piaf singing "*Non, je ne regrette rien,*" and check the glass on your cold frame for fractals.

Muster the Gear

Somewhere between Halloween and Thanksgiving is a good time to gather up anything that is lying around the place and might be soon covered with snow, blown away, run over, or just lost in the sands of time. A lost tool is, as my mother used to say, "right where you left it." Unless, of course, someone who is usually attuned to your needs has taken it for his or her use. We all do this. "I'll bring it right back," you vow—and indeed you would, if you could find it.

Your county extension agent doesn't have a diagram of it, but both farms and home gardens can fall victim to the Tool in the Grass Cycle. It begins with people leaving rakes, forks, hoses, and such in the grass next to the beds where they've been working. The grass grows up and hides them. Somebody brings the mower around to cut the grass, sees the tools, and puts them in the driveway so they won't get mowed, and there they stay. Drivers get used to steering a slalom course around them until they can't stand it any longer and toss them back into the grass until it's time to mow again.

Life is not perfect, but it can be improved by having a place where all the implements belong. It could be an actual toolshed, a barn, or a designated part of the garage. Indoor storage space keeps equipment free of rust, though in a pinch you can hang all of it on an outdoor wall if there is an overhang to keep it dry. Our house has a furnace room and a wood room, both of which have shared space with garden tools.

This year, aflame with the spirit of clearing out, cleaning up, and simplifying, we attacked some areas that had the feng shui of a blocked artery. Tools and supplies, like plants, can multiply. So the first step was to purge the space of anything obsolete, redundant, or broken beyond repair. Out went the leaky buckets, torn row covers, left-hand gloves with no mates, and stinky mosquito sprays that repelled nothing but people. What remained was suddenly manageable, and you could even walk across the floor.

Plant supports,
tamed

Still, certain trouble areas stood out. The worst was my collection of metal plant supports for the flower garden, in various shapes and sizes. Even after throwing out the bent and poorly designed ones, I needed a plan for the corner where they were kept or, that is to say, sprawled. I sorted the vertical supports by height and corralled them in three upright containers. The circular ones were falling off their shared wall hook, so I put up more hooks and sorted the supports by size and style. Did I really need circular wire grids to hold up bushy perennials? I kept a few because they hold firework tubes safely upright.

If space is limited, all the long-handled tools can be stuck into one or two garbage cans with the working ends up, but if you have a wall where you can hang them on hooks, that's great. These can be as simple as single screw-in hooks, like giant cup hooks, which are especially good for medium-sized tools like loppers, hedge shears, and hundred-foot-long tape measures. Another wall-mounted type is a bar that extends outward, perpendicular to the wall, and can support any D-handled tool, long or short. The farther out it projects, the more forks and spades it can hold. Even a long-handle tool without a D-shaped opening can be hung if you turn it upside down and rest the blade between two projecting supports placed just enough distance apart.

The worst way to arrange tools is to lean them against the wall, where they will always fall down.

However well designed a tool wall is, it's only as good as the empty space in front of it. You will never put away a tool if you first have to get past a lawn mower, bicycle, bagged fertilizers, and the stuff on its way to the dump. Place bags of soil amendments in tubs or buckets where they can harmlessly rip and spill. Stack pots and pot saucers on shelves, in tidy towers.

Any kind of netting—bird net, deer net, plant support net, volleyball net—will catch on your feet and get tangled up with the tools. Store it somewhere off the floor and out of the way. Hoses are almost as bad and are best suspended from hose hangers. I favor those with a wide, downward-facing metal arc that you can loop the hose over, with an upright piece at the end to keep the hose from falling off. Those are also good for extension cords and ropes.

In the end, though, it's the countless little odds and ends that do you in. A metal utility shelf unit allows you to sort them and caddy them. A plastic seedling tray could hold trowels, another could hold hand pruners and scissors, still another hose connectors, timers, and nozzles. A small wooden box that tangerines came in could take care of small tape measures and thermometers. One shoebox with gloves, another with balls of twine.

For even smaller items, such as plant labels and tomato clips, use the best storage receptacle ever invented, the one-quart plastic yogurt container. Eat enough yogurt, and soon you'll have a collection of them, each marked with a black Sharpie, another tool without which a gardener would be lost, especially when marking wooden plant labels. In fact, I just labeled a yogurt container "Black Sharpies."

A perfect step for the next gardening year.

CHAPTER 12

Winter

One of the most limiting factors of our country's garden culture is that it's a popular summer pastime, not a life support system. We are not used to thinking of food growing as the necessity it once was. Anywhere you lived, adaptations had to be made, by means of crop choices, storage, and protective devices, to make sure the supply was year-round.

Think of how desperate the Pilgrims must have felt after landing in what is now Plymouth, Massachusetts, and trying to live off the land. Not only was the soil sandy, rocky, and poor (just like the soil at our coastal farm before it was amended with organic matter), but the climate was much colder than that of England, and most of the other countries in Europe, warmed as they are by the Gulf Stream. It's easy to understand the pioneers' drift westward in search of fertile soils, and on to the balmy, sunny West Coast. It's even easy to understand our current dependence on what is grown there and shipped eastward.

There's another side to the story though. The entire United States occupies a position on the globe that puts us closer to the equator than most of the places from which our immigrant ancestors came. Our farm in midcoast Maine is on the same line of latitude as Genoa, Italy—a city

on the Mediterranean where basil, the most frost-sensitive of herbs, is a roadside weed. That means that on any given day of our frigid winter, we have the same length of day—and amount of sunlight—as Genoa does. The whole rest of the country south of us has even more. As long as we make adjustments to the climate, with regard to crop choices, storage, and protective devices, Eliot and I and other Maine growers can harness the benefit that this sun-washed land confers upon us.

So why aren't Americans growing more year-round food? Some of them are, of course, and doing it well. My mother grew up eating that way in Louisiana. But she didn't talk about turnips and collard greens the same way she talked about tomatoes and watermelons. The fact that winter fare isn't always juicy and luscious might have helped destroy the old growing techniques and traditions. But personally, I'd rather eat the orange flesh of a richly flavored roasted butternut squash than a tomato picked green in Mexico, gassed with ethylene to ripen it, and served up after a thousand-mile road trip in a fuel-burning eighteen-wheeler.

A 24-foot hoop house in our yard, cold frames, and snow-covered Tuscan kale

Eliot, who has spent decades developing and teaching a year-round approach to growing food, has covered this ground in much greater detail than I will here. (His book *Four-Season Harvest* is specifically aimed at home gardeners.) But I can give you a good idea of what it's like to live it.

Unexpectedly, it has meant less work, or maybe it just seems that way. One objection I've sometimes heard to the gardening "season" is that it's exhausting, and the gardener needs a well-earned winter rest. My experience is that spreading the effort over twelve months makes it more doable. There is no pressure to grow everything within a short, frantic time span, often producing too much and having it go to waste. I also do less canning and freezing of vegetables than I used to do—just a few favorites like sweet corn, tomatoes, and peas—because there is always plenty of fresh food at our place for the picking. I shop less, because the only produce items I buy regularly in winter are lemons, mandarin oranges, grapes, and pears. I don't have to check the labels on much of our food, because I know exactly how it was grown. If a blizzard or ice storm is coming, I don't have to rush to town and "stock up."

There are trade-offs where weather is concerned. Brushing snow off a cold frame might be a challenge if the wind-chill factor in a given day is brutal, but at least it's outdoor exercise, and no mosquitoes are biting. During the coldest months, with evaporation at a minimum, less watering is needed. Just as there are warm weather weeds like purslane, there are cool weather weeds like chickweed, but since growth slows down as days shorten and temperatures drop, it's easier to keep ahead of them. This is also true for the crops. During the coldest stretch (depending on climate zone), garden vegetables reach a point of suspended animation—alive and there for the picking but making little or no growth. It's like having money in the bank, except that the "green stuff" is delicious, gut-cleansing, pesticide-free food.

Crop Coverings

Say what you will about Louis XIV, he ate his fruits and vegetables. His great kitchen garden at Versailles, masterminded by the brilliant Jean-Baptiste de La Quintinie, was a monument to horticultural ingenuity. Prodded by the Sun King's prodigious appetite and taste for delicacies, La Quintinie used every trick then known to give his master out-of-season fare. The Potager du Roi, as the garden is still called, is now tended by students. You can visit the antique greenhouses, the ranks of cold frames, and the hundred-year-old grapevines.

Few of us garden on such a regal scale, but the cold frames at Versailles show how universal and timeless the best garden devices can be. "Frame" is a good word for this simple structure. Like a picture frame, it's just a shallow, bottomless box, covered with some transparent material. Placed on the ground, it admits the sun's light and captures its heat within. Chilling and drying winds, pounding rain, snow, ice, and other winter vicissitudes are excluded. Though glass wasn't invented until the fifteenth century, the ancient Romans protected winter crops with sheets of mica, and the basic concept remains to this day. It's like a greenhouse, but much smaller.

A cold frame is useful at any time of the year. You can start seedlings in it, sown either in flats or directly into well-prepared soil in the frame itself. Later, they can be hardened off right there, to adjust them gradually to outdoor life. You might get an earlier harvest on most any crop by planting it in the cold frame, but especially ones that don't mind cold soil, such as spinach, lettuce, and radishes. Remove the protective lid when it's no longer needed. Then, in September, fill the frame with winter fare. Root

Winter crops growing in a cold frame

crops such as carrots and turnips can go in, but the biggest payoff lies in the huge choice of winter greens, such as spinach, lettuce, arugula, mâche, tatsoi, and parsley, just to name a few. All will love the chilly but protected conditions you've given them, and most will regrow when cut. Any empty spaces can be instantly planted with new crops for early spring.

Managing plants in a cold frame is easy, as long as you follow a few basic rules. We water the ground well before planting, and thereafter as needed, since it isn't getting rained on. With crops like spinach and mâche, which will take night freezes—up to a point—we need to wait until they have thawed later in the day before we pick them. Most important of all, we make sure that we vent the cold frames so that they don't overheat. This can be done using a notched stick that props the lid in a range of positions, but even just a single stick that lets hot air escape is better than nothing. Sometimes we just slide the lid over a bit. Even on a cold, cloudy day, if there is any chance at all that the sun will come out, it's best to vent just in case. Excess heat will kill the plants quicker than the cold will.

There is a number of ways to build a cold frame. Ideally, it is highest in back, with sides that slope gradually toward the front in the direction of the strongest sunlight. It's best to have the front wall either very low, or transparent, so that the sun's rays reach all the area within. You'll find numerous cold frames available online, most of them quite small, in varying degrees of sturdiness. Lids made of polycarbonate are popular these days because they weigh less than glass and are less breakable. Typically, they are hinged at the back for easy opening and closing.

You could try one of these, but there is a long-standing tradition of homemade cold frames among home gardeners. The classic model has a wooden frame you bang together and cover with a row of old detachable storm windows. A more makeshift version can be made by using straw bales for the back and sides and letting the top of the windows rest on the back bales, slanting toward the ground. Avoid this technique, though, if voles are a frequent pest, or they will take up residence in the bales. Another caution: Storm windows may seem heavy and sturdy, but they become improbably light when a big gust of wind gets under a corner. As George H. Copley warned in the book *Growing Under Glass* (1945), wind that gets under glass tops "will lift them like pieces of matchwood, and when at last they reach terra-firma their condition can be better imagined than described." Because this did happen to one of ours, I will describe it: The glass exploded into thousands of little pieces where the frame landed. Nevertheless, apart from that moment, we have never been sorry that we had cold frames. Thanks to them, we have enjoyed many fresh-picked salads on our winter table.

Lettuce protected by a row cover clipped to wickets

There are even simpler solutions, such as row covers made of white spun-bonded polyester. Invented by DuPont in the 1930s as a filtering material, these sheets let in moisture and sunlight but exclude pests and provide some measure of frost protection. Sometimes they're called floating row covers, because, even though they're usually supported on wire hoops or wickets, they can also just float loosely over the plants, which lift the lightweight fabric as they grow. This concept has evolved to give even better protection, with stronger, slightly taller hoops made of ten-foot lengths of bendable, ½-inch plastic electrical conduit. We use whole fields of these at the farm, and they are useful in our home garden as well. We cut off the bulbous part at the end of each section of conduit, then poke both ends into the ground to form a hoop. Each length will span two 30-inch beds, including a foot-wide path in between. That's how simply and inexpensively a winter garden area can be covered. Hoops can be spaced up to five feet apart in the row, but in colder areas two feet will better support a load of snow. For further reinforcement, build them of metal conduit, sold as EMT (electrical metallic tubing) pipe. This requires buying a simple arched form around which you bend the pipe.

You can also upgrade the row cover to greenhouse-grade plastic. We install the floating stuff first, then add a second layer, of clear plastic, for the colder, snowier months. We run our rows east to west, burying the covers in the earth on the north side and using sandbags or bricks to hold them down on the sunny south side, removable for venting and harvesting.

The old glass solution had one advantage in that glass reflects the radiating heat back to the growing beds in a way that plastic does not. However, when the air cools, moisture from the earth collects on the plastic's underside and this water reflects heat back to the crops.

Here's another trick: Round up some sawhorses and have them straddle a few rows of plants. Drape them with plastic film and weigh its edges down. You can even make your own sawhorses with two-by-fours inserted into ready-made brackets. Look in the hardware department for a three-way bracket that fits over two legs and clamps onto a third two-by-four to make a ridgepole. If you're covering crops that are best dug standing up, such as leeks and carrots, make the legs long enough to make a tent you can step inside, or use plastic or metal plumbing pipes and their corresponding connectors. Cover with plastic film and either weigh it down or bury the edges on the ground. Rig a door flap at the ends, held shut with rope ties.

Bell jars, glass greenhouses, and tidy wooden frames may seem like more elegant solutions, and they look nice in the yard. But there's something to be said for these inexpensive plastic tents and tunnels that are so easy to create. And what is more elegant than a plate of just-picked dark green spinach on a winter day? Just remember to vent any device as needed, lest your spinach cook before it's time for dinner.

A Home Greenhouse

It doesn't take much imagination to move on from these modest tents to a simple greenhouse. Gardeners often do, with mixed results. I once saw a plastic tunnel-shaped one built over rebar hoops stuck in the ground, but with little other means of support. It seemed to have been built by the least practical of the Three Little Pigs and, sure enough, the first windstorm huffed, puffed, and crumpled it. I've seen examples of careless joinery that might have been built by the second hapless pig. So, what would the admirable third pig's greenhouse look like? It would be firmly

anchored to the ground and able to support the covering of choice—plastic film being the lightest and glass the heaviest.

Film, rigid plastic, and glass all provide roughly the same degree of insulation, but while the best film might last three years at most, the other materials are more permanent. Glass tends to last a lifetime, and is the most attractive, but costs the most. The real challenge is to develop the perfect do-it-yourself greenhouse—simple, durable, functional, economical, and gorgeous. For that, we'll need someone with a good appetite and a great sense of style. Paging Miss Piggy.

There are home greenhouse kits for sale, which are very popular. Some are covered with plastic film, others with rigid, double-walled polycarbonate, others with tempered glass. Some are framed with aluminum or galvanized steel, others with rot-resistant woods such as cedar. Some come with roof vents, fans, heaters, watering systems, humidity controls, shade devices, flooring, and lights. Many are pleasant and useful spaces equipped with waist-high benches, perfect for bringing houseplants into bloom and starting seeds in potting mix, but rarely are they shown

Above left: This small, simple greenhouse in our garden is easy to make with plastic sheeting clamped to metal pipe.

Above: Eliot thins spinach protected by a floating row cover inside a small home glasshouse.

with plants growing in the ground. You could grow salad crops on those benches, but I wonder how many people do.

Compare these with one Eliot and I saw in the hills of Tuscany in 1994. It belonged to an elderly couple, living off the land. After a glass of their homemade wine, they proudly showed us a greenhouse about fourteen feet long and eight feet wide, home built, and framed mostly with saplings sunk in the ground and lengths of rebar. The clear plastic sheeting that covered it was a bit worn but anchored firmly, with a flap for the door. Even in the low light of February it glowed with edible greenery—endive, arugula, and Tuscan kale. It had a narrow path down the center, flanked by beds of fertile soil. It looked the way any garden might look except that it was covered.

Having grown food in plastic-covered greenhouses for years, I can vouch for the simplicity of the idea. In the lower light level of winter, plants need little or no watering. Condensation alone provides a handy "drip" system. Just getting the plants out of the wind puts them in a warmer climate zone, while the soil collects the sun's warmth and gives it back at night. The bigger the greenhouse, the more heat it retains. You can also double that effect by spreading sheets of floating row cover over the crops, just as you do in the garden. In fact, this is even easier inside a greenhouse where there is no wind to lift them. A few clothesline clips holding them to the hoops is all you need.

When siting a greenhouse (or any protection device), it's best to find a spot protected from heavy winds, for greater warmth. But good drainage is even more essential, especially in a climate where water can back up and freeze, depriving the soil of air. Ample sunshine is always welcome too. Yes, the winter sun is lower in the sky, and less intense. Its working days are shorter. But all those sun-blocking leaves have fallen from the trees. Take that, summer.

Winter Storage

Storing root crops isn't the necessity it once was, when they stood between you and starvation from late winter to spring, but it's great to have a stash of them on hand for the winter table.

I'm going to assume that most of you don't have a root cellar. You are more likely to have a wine cellar, or maybe a bomb shelter, or just a crisper drawer in your fridge. But there are other storage solutions less ambitious than the traditional cavern, filled with potatoes, carrots, beets, turnips, celery root, kohlrabi, and more.

Let's start with the garden. For fall storage, I like to leave as many crops in the garden as long as I can, before the soil freezes up. Parsnips are the champion when it comes to in-ground storage. I have also seen carrots winter over in a garden row as far north as Vermont. Leafy brassicas, such as cabbages and kale, may be harvestable for much of the winter. Spinach,

At the farm, our winter greenhouses are filled with food.

too. Even potatoes may keep if you pile straw or evergreen boughs on top of them, keeping the soil diggable—unless you have an active vole or mouse population. They may take this nice mulch as an invitation to move in, and feast.

If you have a cold part of your house, or an outbuilding, that stays cool in winter but offers some protection against freezing, that's a good bet. The garage? A shed? An enclosed porch? (The best way to test a spot is to put a cup of water there on a cold night and see if it's frozen hard in the morning.) A spare fridge also makes a good minicellar if you have room for one. Gardeners have come up with ingenious personal solutions. My friend Debby stores root vegetables in her car.

You can also use metal garbage cans as outdoor minicellars if you sink them into the ground vertically. Use one can per crop, or divide one vertically with a piece of plywood, so that two crops can use the same space. Insulate each lid with a disk of foam insulation, or stuff a plastic bag full of dry leaves beneath it. Plastic or metal picnic coolers will work too.

But let's say you get very serious about this and decide to dig a real, old-fashioned root cellar. What would it look like? In the old days, a family had a root cellar under the house, barn, or shed, accessed by a staircase or ladder. Sometimes it was a cave-like room dug sideways into a steep hillside. Building materials included wood, stone, brick, sod, or just earth. It was common to give the cellar a dirt floor, as certain crops, especially the hearty greens, can actually be stored there in the dark with their roots in the ground. One year we tried digging some full-grown cabbages—stem, roots, and all—and planted them in soil in our root cellar. They kept just fine.

A cellar's purpose is to use the earth's warmth to keep food from freezing but cool enough to keep it in suspended animation so that it can last until new crops start to bear aboveground. The ideal temperature for most food is just above freezing. Crops vary as to the ideal humidity. Most prefer moist air (90 to 95 percent), and it helps to spritz water around the space with a hose from time to time to keep it that way. But a few—notably onions, garlic, pumpkins, peppers, tomatoes, and squash—store best if the humidity is 75 percent or less. Winter squash are well-behaved, odorless keepers, and are just fine stored under the bed in a cool guest room, with the door closed except for occasional use.

We have two root cellars at our farm. One is built of concrete and is partly cut into a steep hill behind our barn. Large rock formations stopped us from digging farther, but soil heaped on top to extend the hill made up for that. To speed up cooling of the cellar in fall we use a low-energy CoolBot system, powered by an ordinary air conditioner. But soon the temperature settles into the ideal 33 degrees Fahrenheit or so and all the vegetables stored there keep beautifully.

Our other cellar is underneath a concrete slab. It has two rooms, one for potatoes and one for apples. It is important to store apples and other fruits in a separate place. The ethylene gas they give off will cause vegetables to ripen and prematurely spoil and, in the case of carrots, lend them a bitter flavor. Even vegetables alone will give off some ethylene, so it's best to build a vent into your root cellar to let the gas escape, and to circulate some cold air in. Even with two root cellars, I find it handy to keep a few small buckets of root crops in the house, closer at hand.

Gardeners often wonder if they can just store their root vegetables in an ordinary basement. In my experience, yes, but not as long, especially if they share space with a heat-emitting furnace, woodstove, freezer, fridge, washer, dryer, or some combination thereof. The best solution is to close off a cool corner of the basement, preferably on the north side, with a window, using two insulated walls and a door. Ventilate the space by replacing a windowpane with a piece of insulated plywood through which two 6-inch pipes are fitted. One pipe is short and removes the warm air from the top. The other is angled down to within a foot of the floor. This pipe draws air from outside and keeps the little room cool. Use a cap or a built-in valve to stop the flow of air if it is too cold or too warm outside. Keep the room dark.

In our bounteous land we often take our food for granted, but I like having some of mine socked away for a snowy day. Security isn't knowing that the credit limit on my platinum card has been extended. It's the thought of all those lovely carrots, potatoes, and beets, just a few steps down.

Top: Our above-ground root cellar

Bottom: Our underground root cellar

Here Comes the Sun

"As the days begin to lengthen, the cold begins to strengthen." The old saying sounds puzzling, but it's true. After the long night of winter solstice, December 21, there are a few more minutes of sunlight each day, and each day the sun sails higher in the sky, clear and bright, instead of hugging the horizon, filtered through the murk of Earth's atmosphere. It should warm us, but it does not.

A logician will call this a veridical paradox, an apparent contradiction that is resolved once an explanation has been found—in this case, the fact that Earth holds onto the warmth of summer well past that season, just as the chill of winter lingers into spring, so sunlight and temperature are not aligned. Emotionally, we are stuck in a paradox living and true, because the more light there is, the more all of us—animal, human, or plant— yearn to take part in the rebirth of the growing year.

Agrarian societies in the temperate zone all have festivals linked to the yearly cycle of light and dark, warmth and cold. In the Celtic tradition there were eight: the opposing pair of summer and winter solstices, when the year's longest and shortest days are noted; the spring and autumn equinoxes when night and day are equally long; and in between the four festivals that celebrate the quarter holidays: Imbolc on February 1, Beltane on May 1, Lughnasadh on August 1 (a harvest rite), and Samhain on November 1.

Imbolc, originally a celebration of the Irish goddess Brigid, was later Christianized as Saint Bridget's Day. It celebrated the birth of lambs and the flow of milk from the ewes, spring cleaning, and the emergence of wild animals from the forest (as with its successor, Groundhog Day). Such lore only accentuates the climate difference between Ireland and midcoast Maine. Here, at Imbolc, you know it's going to be downright frigid for at least two more months. The view out the window is one of snow and ice, witch hazel flower buds not yet open, crab apples and chokeberries long stripped of their fruits by scavenging birds. The odd deer, emboldened by hunger, might emerge from the woods in search of expensive nursery-grown shrubs to browse. But still there is, day by day, that little increase in light, and the potted plants next to our south-facing windows are feeling its effect. The Meyer lemon is blooming; the foliage on the sage is newly lush and tipped with tiny round buds; the passion vine has scaled the Venetian blinds. The magical ten-hour day has returned, and the plants know it. The cluster flies know it, buzzing between the ice-cold windows and the screens left in place after summer. And we know it.

The momentum of this sunny but chilly time can trigger mad acts in humans, such as starting tomato plants too soon or applying a spade to wet clods of soil. But almost anything that gets us outside is good, as long as we have warm clothes on, since we are not out of the woods yet.

SHARING THE GARDEN

PART FOUR

CHAPTER 13

Sharing with Friends

Our gardens don't exist in isolation. They are always interacting with the natural world around them, which includes weeds and critters, neighbors, and friends.

Farm Lunch

It was late spring, ten years ago, and the day had started with a chicken. Even before I'd finished my coffee the bird was simmering in the pot. In those days it was my custom to make a big noon meal for our crew. The numbers, counting us, fluctuated between five and eight, depending on the season. That day we were seven, plus two visitors—Jen, who was writing something about farming and Evan who would take photos to go with her piece. Evan used to work here, so he knew to arrive in time for farm lunch.

Meanwhile, I was steaming potatoes from the root cellar, as well as some of our early vegetables—baby carrots, spring onions, tender young fennel—to combine with the chicken once I'd removed the bones. At this point the dish could go in several directions, perhaps to Greece as an egg-lemon soup, or to India as a curry. Since there were still a few apples left from the fall harvest, I went with the latter, chopping the apples and tossing them in, along with the chicken and vegetables, coconut milk, cumin, nutmeg, and cardamom. I picked some mixed lettuces and herbs for a big salad. Then I was out the door by 9:00, because I had a little garden work to do before lunch.

At 11:40 Eliot informed me that two more people, aspiring farmers, had appeared. Would I feed them? Sure. I thawed two pints of homemade chicken stock from the freezer as I heated up the curry and stirred them in for extra volume, along with cream and leftover rice. I quickly grilled some extra cheese sandwiches on a cookie sheet, in addition to the ones I was making for Jasmine, our vegetarian worker. At noon Evan burst into the kitchen with his camera, shouting "Paparazzi!" and I hollered out the back door, calling the crew to come in and eat. They trooped in, grimy and ravenous. Eliot handed out beers and an uproarious meal began. Halfway through it, Travis, another former employee, rocketed through the door. "Am I too late?" he asked, pulling up a chair. Thank God for the grilled cheese. After lunch the crew did dishes or settled down with mugs of coffee and tea.

My friends, knowing that I hate housework, thought I was crazy to feed a dozen people on a busy day. But to me the ritual of farm lunch had little in common with tasks such as cleaning or laundry. Our noon meal was the center of our day, a socializing ritual during which we'd let off steam, kid around, and discuss plans for future work. Most of all it was the time we celebrated what we grow, comparing and evaluating new varieties while all our appetites were sharp. Everything we do on the farm is aimed at making food as tasty as possible, and our biggest perk is eating it fresh from the fields and greenhouses each day.

A hundred years ago a big farm meal (often called "dinner") was commonplace, a generous interval in which you could escape the heat of the midday sun or stoke your inner furnace against the cold. People working hard need plenty of fuel. I've seen other American farms that did what we did, often hiring a cook if the crew was a large one, and in many countries it is still the usual thing. A French farm we once visited fed us

a three-course lunch and then offered us a place to take a nap. In many countries it is common to close the stores for a couple of hours so that everyone can go home for a family meal—so much better than a hasty sandwich at your desk. But long commutes and the pressures of the modern workplace are eroding this tradition. And the fact is, other demands on my time have since caused me to break with the farm lunch tradition, although improved kitchen facilities at the farm itself have helped to compensate.

Fortunately, there are ways of putting farm lunch back into everyone's life, in spirit if not in precise timing. Even when everybody works it is possible for families to reunite at the end of the day for a cooked-from-scratch meal. Beans, soups, and stews can be simmered all day in a slow cooker. Quick meals of pasta and stir-fries from fresh garden produce can

A neighborhood potluck to celebrate spring

take forty-five minutes or less. When these are made with love it is only natural to include others at the table—friends, schoolmates, neighbors.

It is often said that nobody has time to entertain anymore, but I find that planning, not time, is the big deterrent. Feeding people is more fun when it happens spontaneously. And this works best if you have a garden. I like to call someone up when a crop comes into season. "Hey, our tomatoes are ripe and I'm making gazpacho," I'll say, or "There's enough strawberries for a pie," or "Come over and help us eat up all this corn." Back when I actually planned dinner parties, juggling the schedules of us and two or three other couples was like a bad day at air-traffic control. We all finally landed, but it was a bit exhausting.

A last-minute feast inspired by the garden, on the other hand, has its own permissive code. I can ask guests to bring something from their garden or just cheese from the store. Nobody has to dress up, and I don't have to vacuum. Now that's a ritual a busy person can live with.

A Potluck Life

Food at our place is shaped by the season. Even the oddities of weather can determine what we actually pick and eat on any given day. I can harvest spinach in the snow, but sometimes I'd just rather not do that. Dinner is the luck of the pot.

In our neighborhood most people have gardens, and we get together often for a potluck feast. We take turns hosting, providing only one dish and the table. Each person brings their own plate, cup, fork, and a dish to share. Nothing is planned, or assigned, so half the fun is seeing what turns up. In spring it might be the first asparagus and foraged fiddleheads or nettles. In summer, blueberry pies and the overflow of everything. In fall, kale salad and Asian cabbage slaws. In winter, garlicky medleys of roasted root vegetables, scalloped potatoes, and apple desserts.

We've come to recognize people's individual styles, so that we know they've arrived before we see them or their cars. One couple often brings a beautiful Greece-inspired plate with strong-flavored olives, vegetables, and hummus drizzled with olive oil. One regular's well-remembered trademark was pine nuts and edible flowers. Another's is her homemade pickles. One is known for his roasted red peppers with kasha, another for her Japanese spring rolls stuffed with tender greens from her winter greenhouse. He Who Does Not Cook always supplies homemade wine. If it's early June and succotash appears, it means that a certain woods-woman is clearing last year's corn and beans out of her freezer.

There are occasional times when everyone, hilariously, walks in with the same dish. We have had strawberry nights, spinach nights, and acorn squash nights, but since everyone's recipe is different, we all learn new ways to handle a surplus.

We've mastered the art of the quick, last-minute contribution. A bowl of fresh shell-your-own peas delights everyone, as does a big plate of sliced tomatoes with basil and balsamic dressing. Some of my favorite quickies are cucumbers with dill and sour cream, raw veggies with feta cheese dip, and ripe melons cut in wedges, on a platter.

Room temperature is fine for almost any kind of food. And if someone is coming straight from work and all they can do is stop and buy a special cheese, a pizza, or a couple pints of ice cream, that is okay. More than okay, actually.

CHAPTER 14

All Creatures

Even before summer, a picnic is being prepared in the backyard. From the swelling of the first pea to the fall of the last apple, children, grandchildren, and other visitors will come to graze. The garden will be a giant tablecloth, spread for random snacking, outdoor feasts with friends, and ultimately the household's year-long produce supply. This program requires that the whole yard be pesticide-free. The grandkids are too young and I am too old to keep track of the "safe days to harvest" one must observe every time a poison is applied to food—safe, perhaps, for family and friends, but not for the bees, birds, butterflies, and other essential nonhuman neighbors. More important, I have found in my years of gardening that such applications are unnecessary.

Numerous animal species can make growing plants difficult at times. They range in size from creatures larger than us, such as deer, to ones too small for us to see, such as mites. Don't let their numbers discourage you. Don't imagine that they are lined up out there waiting for you to plant something. Generally, they're not, and there are solutions to problems that arise if they do. My approach to unwelcome visitors consists of a few steps that have stood me in good stead.

Flower flies gather-
ing nectar in doron-
icum blossoms, and
doing no harm

Step 1. Understand that the natural world is a complex web and
includes many predators that help you keep pest populations in check.
You have probably heard about some of them, such as birds, predatory
wasps, and lady beetles. It's essential that you maintain a nontoxic
environment that keeps all of them safe, and able to continue their work.
But it's important to understand that these are not "good creatures" as
opposed to "bad" ones. They are all part of the web, and just as with a spider's web, a few tears in it can imperil the whole structure. So, when one
creature is not busy eating your plants, it might be busy eating another
one that could be. Eliminating too many pests by spraying can backfire
by robbing helpful predators of their food, and thereby decreasing their
numbers. And many of them that survive your spraying may breed
pesticide-resistant traits into their offspring, so that the whole species
becomes immune.

Step 2. Grow healthy plants. Plants that are under stress are more
vulnerable to insects and diseases, so give them adequate light, water, and
air circulation. Make sure they are growing in a living, fertile soil, rich in
organic matter and with an aerated, crumbly structure. This helps them to

manufacture their own defensive substances, thereby strengthening their immune systems.

Step 3. If a pest shows up in large numbers, it's okay to kill it to save your food, but this is best done by simple mechanical means. Picking off beetles or caterpillars may be tedious but doing it every day can be very effective. Even if you don't get them all, you can minimize the damage enough to still get a good yield. A shop vacuum cleaner can suck up bugs very well if you use a slot attachment, which is relatively easy on the plants. (Afterward, remove the machine's bag and put it in the trash, in a well-sealed container.) This trick is often the only way to catch insects that are easily startled into motion, such as leafhoppers and cucumber beetles. Webs of tent caterpillars can be burned out with a propane torch or drowned in a bucket. Aphids and mites can be blasted off plants with the force of a hose. Simple traps such as boards or half-filled bottles of beer lying on their sides will attract slugs and snails so they can be disposed of.

Step 4. Erect barriers. Netting in varying degrees of fineness, to exclude any insect, is available to spread over a crop if a surge from a frequent pest is expected. (It's important that the same crop did not grow on that spot the previous year, in which case the same pest might have overwintered in the soil.) The netting can be removed briefly for weeding and harvesting. Floating row covers will also exclude most insects, but one advantage of the netting is that it doesn't raise the temperature beneath it in hot weather.

Step 5. Get to know your pests. Insects can have as many as four different phases: egg, larva, pupa, and adult. Recognizing them will help you to find and outwit them at any stage of their life cycle. Learning the various habits of furred and feathered creatures is helpful too.

Step 6. As a last resort, apply only the most harmless, targeted treatment, such as a squirt of vegetable oil to the young silks of corn ears to foil corn earworms. Even supposedly benign products such as Bt (*Bacillus thuringiensis*, a disease used to kill the soil-dwelling larvae of Japanese beetles and others), rotenone, and agricultural soap sprays carry a price tag in terms of money, time, and environmental side effects.

Eliot folds a little screen tent over each squash plant to keep out the squash bugs.

Step 7. Evaluate the damage level. Often, it's minimal enough to ignore. Corn earworms don't crawl very far in, and the oil is a nuisance to apply, so we just chop off any messed-up tip before cooking, and heartily enjoy the rest of the ear.

Potato Beetles

Nicky and I are both working in the garden, but she's having a better time. Clad in a skirt and a peasant blouse, she gathers armloads of larkspur, baby's breath, and sunflowers. I'm in the potato patch nearby, picking Colorado potato beetles off the plants and dropping them into a quart-sized yogurt container half-filled with dish detergent and water.

The beetles are bad in this section, but another planting, at a distance, has none at all. Eliot and I do rotate crops to avoid pests that overwinter in the soil, but potato beetles can emerge and then walk or fly a short way in search of potatoes (and eggplants, which they like as well). So far so good on that far patch.

"This is so wonderful!" Nicky exults, as she moves into a row of annual butterfly weed (*Asclepias curassavica*). "These plants are full of caterpillars." I know which ones she means. Striped with yellow, black, and white, they will eventually turn into monarch butterflies. In fact, numerous adult monarchs now hover above the plants and feed on nectar from the yellow and red flower clusters, as well as pollinating them. They'll lay eggs on the leaves, so that when the larvae hatch, they'll find ready nourishment. Like all milkweed relatives, this *Asclepias* is a chosen larval food for monarchs. We like hosting a plant species that benefits a pollinator at risk, so Nicky is careful to spare the caterpillars as she picks.

Meanwhile, I'm "harvesting" both the adult potato beetles (hard-shelled, with ten brown stripes on a yellow background) and the larvae (fat, humpbacked grubs that vary from pinkish-tan to salmon-red, with prominent black spots), and since both are devouring leaves and stems, both are sent to a sudsy death. They perch on the upper sides of the

leaves, usually near the top of the plant, which makes my job easier. I try not to shake the plants, lest my prey fall to the ground.

At the tips of the branches are clusters of many tiny young larvae, newly hatched from patches of yellow-orange eggs. Over the next few weeks, they'll go through several molts, enlarging each time, then they'll fall to the ground and turn into yellow oval pupae, and finally into the striped adults. I rarely see the pupae, but I do find the eggs, especially on the undersides of the leaves, and I squish them. The sooner that is done the better.

While I work, I keep an eye out for lady beetles (also called ladybugs), which are hard-shelled, round, and bright red with black spots. While their favorite food is aphids, they munch on potato beetle eggs and larvae as

Monarch butterflies, feeding here at their winter home in Big Sur, California, find nectar at our farm in summertime.

well, so I'm glad for their help and try not to disturb them. They may also be attracted by all the nectar and pollen in Nicky's flower world nearby.

The much-studied potato beetle was first noticed not in Colorado, but in Iowa. "This insect," wrote entomologist R. A. Casagrande in 1985, "resulted in the first large-scale use of insecticides on an agricultural crop … influencing generations of agriculturists to depend on this unilateral approach for managing this pest and others." And to little avail. From Paris green to DDT, to the highly toxic neonicotinoids of the present day, the beetle has developed resistance to every chemical employed to destroy it, even the less toxic spinosad formulations, which were created by fermenting a natural soil bacterium, and are approved for organic growers.

Scientists theorize that the beetle acquired this power through its evolution in Mexico with potato-related host plants that were full of natural toxins. In addition, our overeager blanketing of crops with poisons has actually encouraged resistance, because only resistant individuals survive to breed. We'd do well to heed Casagrande's thought that "the solution may require a reevaluation of many practices throughout agriculture."

Moving down the row with my cup of suds, I ponder, as I so often do, how lucky I am as a home gardener to have a simpler solution than a farmer would have to a common problem. Without too much effort I can keep the beetle population down by picking them until the spuds form underground. I will still have a decent crop, and can then get rid of all the above-grown parts of the plant. Groping in the loose, dark soil and turning up the delicious pale tubers will be as gratifying as gardening gets, and even more fun than picking flowers.

Conquering Cutworms

One spring the cutworms were so bad that my neighbors stopped complaining about the deer. Newly planted cabbage seedlings lay toppled. Freshly sown rows of spinach and beets sprouted merrily—then vanished. Even flats of transplants left carelessly on the ground overnight were empty in the morning. The creature became such an emblem of the season that one friend named his new little sailboat *Cutworm*, but there was nothing cute about the situation.

Not every year is like that, but cutworms are always something of a problem, as they are everywhere in North America. They attack tomatoes, pepper, corn, all the brassicas, eggplants, lettuce … well, you get the idea. As adults they are small, usually gray or brown moths called "millers" or "owlets" that fly around at night. As larvae, they are fat, hairless caterpillars an inch or so long in shades of gray, brown, or black, with paler tummies. They're nocturnal in this phase too, working their mischief under cover of darkness.

Some cutworms tunnel in the ground and devour root systems, while others climb plants as tall as fruit trees. But the most typical ones work very close to the ground, severing a small plant at the base, eating a bit of it, then leaving it for dead or dragging it into a burrow. Desperate people will go out with a flashlight at night in hopes of catching them in the act.

If you have better ways to spend your evenings, an easier solution is to find the larvae while they are sleeping just beneath the soil surface, too full to crawl far, but positioned for the next raid. If I probe with my forefinger in the soil all around the damaged plants, I will usually turn them up, especially first thing in the morning. I'll know they are cutworms if they curl up when touched. If I keep this up, I can make a dent in the population and, once the plants grow stronger stems, most cutworms will leave them alone. It helps to have some extra seeds or seedlings on hand to quickly replace a crop.

I also find that it's worth putting collars around the stems of seedlings as I'm setting them out. I make these out of bottomless plastic cups—or just 3-by-5-inch cards—settling them into the soil a bit and having them project several inches above. One gardener I know puts a toothpick right next to each stem; he claims that the cutworm thinks the plant has a woody stalk and turns away. It's also reassuring to know that grub-eating birds, toads, skunks, spiders, ground beetles, and the parasitic trichogramma wasps all prey on cutworms. If I keep the yard free of poisons that can harm them, they'll have my back.

Deer-proofing

In February 2006, sixty-four years after frisking across the screen in his original star turn, Bambi the orphaned fawn reappeared in *Bambi II* and the franchise marched on. I'm guessing future Bambis will have less to fear from hunters than from gardeners, maddened by the sight of chewed broccoli.

In 1942, everybody loved deer—graceful, big-eyed symbols of wild nature. Their numbers, once in serious decline, were on the increase as abandoned eastern farmland grew up in forest. Forest, in turn, was yielding to suburban development, and deer predators such as mountain lions, wolves, coyotes, bears, and bobcats had long since been driven out. Deer, by contrast, adapt wonderfully to residential areas. The typical home landscape offers the classic "edge habitat" between fields and woods that these hoofed browsers love—a shrubby smorgasbord of tender-tipped azaleas and yews, made all the more toothsome by doses of fertilizer.

The results have been bad for everybody. Large deer herds face hunger during harsh winters and dry summers and collide with motorists on roads. They wipe out native forest plants such as trillium and lady slipper while allowing barberry and other less tasty invaders to dominate. They carry deer ticks, which spread Lyme disease. And no solution is without problems, from hunting (dangerous in populated areas) to birth control (promising but expensive). Gardeners who find deer beautiful struggle for a workable détente.

Repellents can have some effect. There are countless recipes involving hot pepper, garlic, rotten eggs, curry powder, or ground chicken feathers—and many commercial formulations. But most need to be reapplied often and involve so much time and money that one's thoughts turn to venison instead. Bunches of human hair and dangling bars of deodorant soap work only for a short while. You could spend more time making your garden noisy, flashy, bad-tasting, and smelly than you do tending it. Still, a bag of dried blood from the local garden center is worth keeping around. A dusting, reapplied after each rain, does protect irresistible hors d'oeuvres such as emerging tulips, daylily shoots, and young broccoli.

A good fence works best, especially for a manageable area like a vegetable garden. I've even seen small food gardens caged completely, with mesh ceilings. Electric fences are effective but expensive. An ordinary six-foot wire-mesh fence will often do the trick, though in areas with high "deer pressure" even eight feet is too low. Two fences spaced four or five feet apart are said to deter deer, and fences with baffles that slant outward in the direction of approaching deer have the same effect. As long as you make sure the deer can't wriggle through or under a fence, anything you can do to make them nervous about jumping will help. A solid fence or one with a dense hedge along it will keep them from seeing where they will land.

Fences needn't be ugly. I once deer-proofed the whole front yard by running an attractive wooden lattice fence out from one end of the house, to support vining squash and beans, then running a stockade fence along the road with lilacs and other shrubs on both sides. I took the next stretch of fence through a patch of woods, nailing black polypropylene mesh from tree to tree, then rejoined the house at the other end, with a decorative iron gate and more lattice, festooned with clematis. In time, rabbits chewed up the polypropylene in the wooded section but the people who bought our house replaced it with mesh made of steel.

In the end, the system worked—certainly much better than the "deer-resistant plantings" we often read about. I have a big file of plants to avoid because they are deer favorites, and another file of those that deer dislike. Many plants are on both lists. Sadly for gardeners, deer are often so hungry they will eat anything. Sad, too, for the deer.

A fence, with a gate, is the best way to keep out deer.

Life as a Predator

The tiny, furry body hurtles across the gravel walkway, from the shelter of one garden bed to that of another. It is a meadow vole (*Microtus pennsylvanicus*), a mouselike rodent that nests and hides among grasses and other herbaceous plants, munching as it goes. When in full view it's always on the run, to escape the eyes of its many predators: hawks, crows, owls, foxes, raccoons, possums, skunks, weasels, snakes, snapping turtles, and even bullfrogs. The lifespan of a vole is brief—a year or so at best—and 80 percent die before maturity. But as I watch the one in question disappear into the leaves, neither these grim statistics nor the creature's cuteness inspires much pathos. It is headed straight for our beets.

A vole has a sweet tooth, nibbling strawberries, Swiss chard, parsnips, baby turnips, and the roots of endives. When fall frosts arrive, extra sweet carrots may become orange-tinted hollows in the ground. And don't forget the salad course. Cold frames and greenhouses full of tender winter greens can become vole playpens.

As generally happens in nature, this vole's vulnerability is balanced by strategies that have ensured its survival. It's had a long time—since the Pleistocene era in fact—to develop not only speed and cunning, but also a reproductive strategy that puts most rodents to shame. A female vole can get pregnant when less than a month old, deliver three weeks later, and get pregnant again that same day. Breeding year-round, she might have as many as ten litters in one year, with five or six babies in each. They prefer moist, grassy areas, but are highly adaptable and are common in most of the United States.

Voles are easily confused with mice (which are smaller, with longer tails), shrews (also smaller, with more pointed noses), and moles (which have outward-facing digger's hands). True meadow voles, also called field mice, are five to seven inches long—counting the short tail—and plump, with dark, beady eyes and brownish fur.

If you're a gardener, you've probably seen places where voles have been. Some spring bulbs you planted never came up. You went out to divide a clump of hostas or Siberian iris and found that something had done this for you and half the roots had vanished. The lower bark of your precious young fruit trees was girdled by tiny teeth, and the trees died. The fall lettuce you hoped might overwinter was devoured in patches and hid a complete subway system of tunnels under its leaves. If narrow surface runways have appeared anywhere—as if miniature dirt bikers had held a rally—then you'll know that voles are in residence. If you find a ball of woven grass in a slight hollow in the soil, that's where a mother has reared her young. No matter how reverent we all feel about the web of life, there are times when the list of predators must include you.

The first line of defense is to keep the areas around beds closely mowed, exposing the scurrying creatures to their enemies. To protect young trees, wrap them in mesh cylinders made of metal window screening, buried an inch or two at the base and stapled at the sides, leaving plenty of space for the trunk to grow. A circle of crushed stone around the base will deter voles that strip the bark and sometimes tunnel in the soil and destroy roots. The same collars protect against borers and, if about two feet tall, against rabbits as well.

When vole populations soar, Eliot and I start trapping. Plain old mousetraps work—up to a point—if placed perpendicular to a well-used runway, with the trigger right in the path of their oncoming feet and baited with apples or peanut butter. But these sometimes attract and kill birds. Besides, the voles in our garden have learned to associate those flavors with death, so Eliot found a better method. Unbaited mousetraps are placed inside a simple wooden box equipped with little entrance holes in opposite sides of the box walls. The traps are set just inside the entrances. If a box is put in a runway, voles will scurry into it to hide, and land on a trap. The top can be lifted off to place the traps and remove the prey.

One of Eliot's home-made vole traps

For a ready-made version, a plastic fishing tackle box with holes cut into it works fine. We have tried commercial ones such as the German *Wühlmausfänger* but that one was clearly designed to catch an Arnold Schwarzenvole of more strapping proportions—the Eurasian water vole perhaps. Our tiny American ones just skittered past its inner mechanism.

Attacking little furry beasts is not pleasant work, but they can eat half the garden if not kept in check. If you haven't the stomach for trapping, you could sabotage their burrows by stamping, spading, or flooding them with a hose, though some survivors will return. Be consoled by the fact that a vole population explosion is often met by an increase in predators. If you hear owls calling at night, take heart.

The Easter Bunny

Without much growing in my northern garden, come spring, a glimpse of brightly colored, half-hidden eggs is a cheerful one, especially if they are real eggs, home-dyed, rather than candy ones wrapped in foil (though my inner four-year-old would disagree).

In any case, I've always found this a charming but puzzling tradition. I suppose it's quite logical that the rabbit, associated as it is with the ancient fertility goddess Eostre (whose name gave us Easter), should be a spring totem. After all, a rabbit can produce eighteen bunnies a year. As for eggs, they're a fertility symbol too. One legend about Eostre had her turn a freezing bird into a rabbit in order to give it warm fur—hence the rabbit that delivers eggs. Of course. As for the future, let's hope that some biotech lab doesn't engineer some sort of furry Frankenfowl that lays rainbow eggs. Sometimes science is stranger than myth.

Meanwhile, thoughts of bunnies at Easter time occupy the minds of many a gardener: bunnies eating lettuce, bunnies eating spinach, bunnies gnawing the trunks of young apple trees. Shooting rabbit trespassers is hard to do. If you are close enough to get a good shot you can probably see how their little noses quiver, and admire their soft, floppy ears.

Trapping isn't any easier. Eliot once showed me a baby one he'd caught in his cap, and the best we could bear to do was relocate it well down the road. As with deer, a sprinkling of dried blood works as a repellent, if you have the patience to resprinkle it after every rain.

The permanent solution is a rabbit-proof fence, which means one with openings no bigger than one inch. (Tiny rabbits, because of their numbers, can be just as destructive as big ones.) It needn't be tall: two or three feet will do. In fact, you can buy rolls of "rabbit guard" fence, with wide mesh above and finer mesh at the bottom. Chicken wire works as well, but it's best to bury it at least six inches down, in hopes that nothing

tunnels under it. You can also try bending it and laying some of it flat on the ground, weighted with bricks or stones.

Fencing only works if you keep the gate closed. Remember Mr. McGregor? You don't want furry creatures trapped *inside* the garden. Check to make sure no crops are getting nibbled. Hopefully there are only rabbit tracks outside the fence. And no eggs.

Sunflowers offer bounteous pollen and nectar to bees.

Chapter 15

Making Alliances

Many good deeds go unseen and unrewarded in your garden. You may not love the lumpy tunnels the moles are making in the lawn but think twice about stomping them flat with your feet. Underground they might be gorging on Japanese beetle grubs that are getting ready to hatch and go to work on your grapes. As you spray that yellowjacket nest with Raid, remind yourself that yellowjackets eat the earwigs that feast on your zinnias, your apricots, your lettuce. And those earwigs? They eat the larvae of many pest insects—and their eggs. Acknowledging these hidden allies, even if you must sometimes restrain them, will help you develop a humble, democratic view of your garden's complex environment. Resist the urge toward total control.

One popular "solution" to pest problems is to buy and release insects called "beneficials," such as lacewings, lady beetles, and parasitic wasps. But unless these hired mercenaries are released in an enclosed space, there is no guarantee that they will stick around, and there's no way you can tell them what to do. Better to maintain a nontoxic yard, full of diverse native trees, shrubs, and flowers, including lots of nectar-bearing ones that attract pollinators. Be curious about what goes on there. The

A bird called the killdeer loves to lay her eggs on farmland, where the ground often makes good camouflage for the nests. She and her family eat pest insects in return.

more you learn about the flora and fauna around you, the more you will enjoy your partnership with them.

Bird Diplomacy

If you were a lad in nineteenth-century rural England, chances are your first job would be bird-minding. To protect newly planted grain seeds, farmers stationed children as young as eight or ten in the fields from sunup to sunset, armed with little wooden clappers hinged with thongs to frighten hungry birds away.

In the view of H. J. Massingham, who chronicled bygone practices in his 1939 book *Country Relics*, such an outdoor childhood was preferable to uninspired schooling, or the cruel environment of the factories. But it was child labor nonetheless, with a daily wage as low as "one penny and a swede" (a rutabaga). The birds themselves provided protein to supplement the children's diet: "blackbirds and thrushes which they killed with catapults [slingshots] and cooked over a wood fire under the hedge."

Needless to say, bird-minding is no longer a part of agrarian life. Farmers use automatic devices that range from the simple—a popgun that goes off every minute or two—to the complex, such as sonic devices that mimic the distress signals of specific birds.

Red chokeberry (*Aronia arbutifolia*) provides late berries for the birds.

Attitudes toward birds have changed too. Enlightened growers view them as allies that devour pest insects. People love to watch birds feeding and nesting in their yards, and increasingly avoid poisons that could harm them. Garden centers stock up on birdhouses, birdseed, bird feeders, and—even better—trees and shrubs with berries that birds love. I once spent the winter watching from my window, aglow, as grosbeaks, finches, and grouse munched the golden fruits of a Snowdrift crab apple.

Still, though, birds are sometimes pests. When spring came, all the hungry grouse returned to the crab apple and began tearing off and eating the tree's lovely emerging flowers. I admit I rushed outside and drove them off. Similar stories can be told about the red, red robin, bobbing along and eating the just-ripe strawberries. The seed-stealing finches. The crows that always know when you've just planted corn. Herons, in all their majesty, would wear out their welcome fast if they snapped up the expensive koi fish in your ornamental pool.

I doubt if any amount of money could turn modern America's youth into conscientious bird-minders, but another old-time technique—the scarecrow—is still with us. It's fun for a family to build one, dress it in everyone's old duds, then watch the birds perch on it and nest in its hat or its pockets. It doesn't matter if the scarecrow doesn't work, because it's part of the great American tradition of backyard folk art. Being able to create something fun and useless in your garden is what this country is all about.

So, what about those nuisance birds? First of all, they aren't a nuisance very much of the time, and some devices actually divert them, such as owl scares. Not the ones that just perch on a fencepost, which are no better than scarecrows, but ones like the great horned owl from Bird-X, which has a convincing hovering motion. To foil blackbirds, Eliot has used kites shaped like hawks that can be dangled from a tree or pole or lofted up on a tethered helium balloon. Those orange Terror Eyes balloons are some-what effective. Bird-X even sells a plastic floating alligator head to foil her-ons. All of these devices work best if you move them from place to place.

We've had success with the long, shiny ribbon you string above or around a vulnerable seedbed, vineyard, or berry patch, twisting it so that it not only moves but also glints in a way that both birds and mammals find spooky. Other devices use motion sensors to trigger a startling action. One, called the Scarecrow, shoots a strong jet of water at anything that comes near—hopefully not you.

You can also cover seedbeds with mulch, chicken wire, or floating row covers until they've sprouted. You can drape plastic bird netting over berry bushes. In England I once admired raspberry beds growing under a net ceiling, supported by wooden posts. Each post was capped with an overturned flowerpot to keep it from poking through the mesh.

Our crab apple tree was too tall to protect with netting, though the shiny ribbon might have done the trick. But it would have been ugly.

It takes a bit of trial and error to work out a solution, often one that combines several techniques, used only when the plantings are vulnerable. What we need is a device that's as picturesque as a scarecrow, but with all the modern bells and whistles of sonar, holography, and electronics. An action figure for the old-fashioned gardener. Easily programmed by anyone young enough to be good with computers.

Know any ten-year-olds?

Understanding Bees

For champions of wildlife, the insect world can be a tough sell. Gardeners might eagerly plant flowers to lure butterflies, even embracing the caterpillar stage through which these winged visitors pass. But many buzzing, crawling creatures give people the creeps.

Bees have a mixed reputation. They can sting, but they're also models of industriousness and communal effort. Honeybees manufacture a healthy, high-nutrient sugar substitute. We know their economic importance—most of our food plants could cease to exist if bees did not pollinate them. We feel concerned about threats to their well-being, such as agricultural pesticides, habitat loss, diseases, and predatory mites. But about bee populations in general we're usually quite ignorant.

To most people the representative bee is the honeybee, an imported species that now dominates because of its use in agriculture. Most recognize bumblebees as well but are unaware that there are some four thousand native bee species that are of great importance in our lives. These are highly efficient pollinators that can move so quickly from one flower to another that they're sometimes gone before you see them. Some are active earlier in the season or earlier in the day than honeybees are, and some have a niche pollinating specific crops such as squash, blueberries, or potatoes, emerging just as their favored crop has begun to bloom. Even those with broad tastes tend to work one crop at a time, to their benefit: Pollen from a squash blossom would be wasted on a geranium.

Many native bees don't sting, and even those that do are nonaggressive, stinging only when they or their colony are threatened, and with a mild bite at that. These types include bumblebees and sweat bees—small insects often colored a brilliant metallic green that may alight on your skin, attracted by the salt in your perspiration. Ignore it and it will ignore you. With any bee it's best not to swat it or pick it up with your fingers.

Native bee colonies are tiny compared with those of honeybee hives, and most don't form colonies at all. These "solitary bees" are born in little homes the females build. Here the eggs are laid and sealed into individual chambers along with a nourishing supply of "bee bread"—a mixture of nectar and rich pollen that nourishes the hatchlings as they grow.

The names of these lesser-known bees sound like the listings in the "Services" section of the Yellow Pages, each denoting a different skill in nest construction. The carpenter bee drills a little tunnel in boards or logs. The mason bee uses an existing hole, filling it with a kind of plaster she makes from mud. The leafcutter bee, with supreme artistry, moves into a hollow stem, then forms larval chambers from pieces of leaf, each cut to size. Even more numerous are the digger or mining bees who make tunnels in the ground. One digger, the polyester bee, makes a polymer with which to waterproof and separate her brood cells. When the time is right, bees emerge from all these specialized cells and begin to forage.

Many of the foods we eat, from fruits and berries to tomatoes and melons, are pollinated either entirely or in part by native bees, and we will count on them even more as honeybee populations continue to decline. Natives are resistant to prevalent honeybee mites, and do not interbreed with the aggressive African species misleadingly called "killer" bees.

But they face dangers too, and do not have the visibility and economic support given to honeybees. Gardeners can help. As physicians are told, "First do no harm." Avoid toxic sprays, dusts, and soil drenches. Next, make sure there are plenty of nectar and pollen sources by planting a wide diversity of the native flowering plants with which our bees have co-evolved. Our season begins with spring-flowering trees like shadblow, willow, and wild cherry. For summer I have flower beds filled with salvias, coneflowers, bee balm, catmint, anise hyssop, sunflowers, and numerous others. I planted fragrant summersweet bushes (*Clethra alnifolia*) for late summer bloom. The season finishes with asters and goldenrod. Bumblebees especially appreciate these late flowers. Though first to arrive, they are the last to call it quits in late fall.

Providing nesting sites is a bigger challenge. It means leaving patches of ground where tillers don't till and mowers don't mow. It includes bare soil uncovered by asphalt or mulch where digger bees can dig. Bees like messy places—railbeds, roadside ditches, embankments, pondside thickets, hedgerows between fields. Why not turn portions of schoolyards, cemeteries, and golf courses into the sunny meadows that bees need? Plant roadsides with flowering shrubs and trees.

Bees in Lavender

Gardening can be a solitary activity, and pleasantly so. But on a recent sunny day, harvesting lavender for our farm stand, I found myself in the middle of a busy marketplace. Butterflies were visiting the blossoms,

Bees feeding in lavender blossoms

especially the painted ladies with gaudy, multicolored spots on the underside of their upper wings. Small grasshoppers perched here and there, as did tiny green inchworms. A few lady beetles came by, foraging for aphids. Most conspicuous were the wild bees, mostly bumblebees—hundreds of them, zipping from one open floret to the next to gather nectar. It was a joy to see them in such large numbers. There were a few large bumblebees but most were smaller, with horizontal russet stripes on their backs. The whole lavender bed quivered with their activity and resonated with their sound—like the entire string section of an orchestra drawing their bows.

I felt very comfortable, moving my hands through the bee-laden flowers. When I pick sunflowers, their center disks usually have bees in them, and I gently flick them off with my finger before bringing them into the house or the car. They don't want to be in there, buzzing up and down a window.

I knew that the bees in the lavender posed no threat. They were gathering a crop, just as I was, not protecting their home, and there was plenty of lavender to go around. So I just went about my business, looking for sprigs whose pale florets had started to open among the purple-blue buds, selecting those with the longest stems, counting as I went to make bunches of a hundred. Dodging the bees was instinctive and I soon relaxed into the dance, my hands moving among them, knowing that the bees had more important things to bother with than me.

The truth be told, I do get stung while picking things in the garden if a bee is accidentally obstructed by my hand. But it's very rare. And on a sunny day, working in a companionable group, when the air smells of lavender, it seems a small price to pay.

Spiders and Snakes

It's the last day of the year and there are still spiders in the house. While some manage to survive the winter outdoors, or lay eggs that do, our home's warm corners are inviting, and many have moved in. With no shrews, frogs, or birds afoot (or so I hope), the only predator lying in wait for them is the feather duster. Presently, one spider is eyeing a bit of down pillow fluff caught in her web, as if to say, "What am I supposed to do with *you*?" I wonder what there is for her to eat here. Dust mites?

Since they are more fun than mosquitoes and flies, I tolerate a few spiders in the house, up to a point. But in the garden, they are among the most welcome of beings. Their diet consists of any insects small enough for them to eat, and since they are active early in the season, there they are, waiting in huge numbers for the first biting flies of spring. Among helpful predators, only the dung beetle, which breaks down manure and makes its nutrients available to plants, is more underrated. Spiders feast on almost every insect pest, from tiny aphids and mites to grasshoppers and cucumber beetles.

If you make your yard comfortable for spiders, they will come. The spinning types, especially, prefer grassy, weedy areas, with lots of tall stems on which to hang their beautiful webs. Some are artists, such as the spectacular yellow-and-black argiope spider, with her large, complex orb web. Others are hunting spiders that actively pursue their prey rather than simply lay traps.

Some wolf spiders are known for carrying their newly hatched babies, known as spiderlings, on their backs. Emerging from burrows in loose leaf litter, they come forth at night, and I've been told that you can see their eyes as tiny glittering specks if you hold a flashlight next to your own eyes

Spider web in wild carrot plant (Queen Anne's lace)

Our garter snake

and aim it at the ground. I haven't tried that yet. Nor have I yet seen a hummingbird hovering before an orb web, stealing insects from it. Or a spider's web laid across a carnivorous pitcher plant, using the plant's fragrant lure to trap insects before they can disappear into the deadly funnel. Such scenes reward the sharp-sighted. If you look closely at enough open flowers, you may find crab spiders, which change colors to match the petals, and thereby hide from their prey.

Another creature whose reputation is sadly in need of rehabilitation is the snake. Never mind that unfortunate incident in the Garden of Eden. We were meant to live with snakes. They're here, we're here, and mostly we stay out of each other's way.

I've never understood why these reptiles strike so much fear, loathing, or, at the very least, wariness, into the human heart. A few are poisonous, but those are the ones most likely to avoid us. Far more common are the ones such as garter snakes that can be seen slithering about the yard. They are domestic snakes.

You can recognize a garter snake by its yellowish stripes, running lengthwise against a dark background. Most often you'll find it quietly sunning itself on stones or in warm grass. Unlike birds or mammals, snakes don't make their own heat, and must pick it up from sunshine. I once had a garter snake in residence all summer long in a crevice between the stone steps of the house, winding away when people came in and out the door. I defended it against those who felt like stomping it with their feet.

I'll admit that the sudden sight of a snake can be startling. Even the sinuous motion of a windblown, snakelike stem can make you jump. Just tell yourself that a resident snake is not after you. It wants grasshoppers, toads, and frogs. It might be on the prowl for rodents. If one is patrolling your compost pile for rats, give it a salute.

One summer when the vole population had peaked, to the great detriment of our garden, I watched as a snake devoured one of these furry plant destroyers on our terrace. It held the creature aloft in its fangs, weaving back and forth, then enjoyed its meal.

Snake haters will point out that if you keep brush piles, woodpiles, stone piles, or other such accumulations, snakes may take up residence. Grassy verges, especially around ponds and other wet places, also attract them. I like to encourage them by leaving some areas natural and wild.

Snakes are indiscriminate carnivores that will consume earthworms and other garden helpers, but they won't nibble your salads or gnaw the bark of your young trees. They'll gobble up slugs and Japanese beetle grubs.

You may not see your snakes, even if you have them, although you might come upon the silvery skins that they shed as they grow, a fascinating find, especially for kids. Teach yours to look around for snakes, admire their beautiful silent motion, and let them be.

Gardening with Bufo

People with gardens like the chance to spend time with the wild creatures that live and work there, or are passing through, and will excitedly report a visit from a hummingbird or a rose-breasted grosbeak. But few ever mention a toad. Bulgy eyed, warty, and rather sleepy looking as it squats among the bean rows, it's what conservationists call an uncharismatic species in need of a champion. Toad-dom has no Kermit. There are no Teenage Mutant Ninja Toads.

If you've gardened with a toad you know what good company they can be. Those that we find belong to the species *Bufo americanus*, the American toad. As babies they are smaller than my thumbnail. Full-grown they are plump (especially the females) and nearly as wide as my hand. A toad will often sit and sun itself next to where I am weeding, within easy reach if I choose to touch it. When I move a foot down the row, the toad moves the same distance, keeping just ahead of me.

One summer a particularly large toad was a frequent visitor. We named it Leroy, before we figured that she was probably a girl. Because toads are not plant eaters, she never interfered with my work. Her job was simply to bear witness, nabbing any insect, worm, or grub that happened by.

Although she ate some garden helpers such as earthworms and spiders, a large part of her diet was slugs, mosquitoes, tent caterpillars, sowbugs, and snails. Like a frog, a toad has a long, sticky tongue that it flicks out to catch its meal. Interestingly, it will only eat prey that is moving. I can relate to a creature that insists its food be fresh.

Though slow and easy to catch, I left Leroy alone. Her parotid glands secrete a substance that would irritate my eyes and mouth if I got it on my hands. (Just watch a dog with a toad in its jaws.) But I liked her company.

Toads, like their close relatives the frogs, begin their lives in ponds. Unlike frogs, they stay there only a month or two, and even a springtime pool—no more than a large puddle—is enough to start them out in life. This is where the adults mate. You can hear the males' high-pitched courting trill and see the females' long strands of eggs. These hatch quickly to produce thousands of tadpoles. As soon as they are land worthy, those that have escaped predators make their way into fields, woodlands, and gardens. The adults follow later.

When choosing a home, toads like to be near some form of water, which they must absorb periodically through their skin. This could be just a shallow garden pool, but it needs to have gently sloping sides, or at least a log they can use as a ramp. Even a ground level birdbath is helpful if it is kept full. Uncovered swimming pools, on the other hand, are death traps, and ponds with hungry fish also pose a danger.

Toads need a place to burrow during the heat of the day (most of their hunting is done at night) and hide from snakes, skunks, and large birds. They'll live under a brush pile or a log, or in a hole under a rock or a board.

Sadly, toads are diminishing worldwide, as are amphibians and reptiles in general. Possible causes include loss of habitat, stronger UV rays resulting from the thinning of the ozone layer, and countless air, water, and soil contaminants, to which these animals are especially sensitive. So the most important thing you can do for them is to avoid poisons. Providing water is helpful, but don't try to import them into your yard—just let them come. They're the best judges of where they can survive.

One winter a toad took up residence in our plastic-covered greenhouse. Instead of burrowing into the soil to hibernate, she just hung around and let us feed her the cutworms that were nibbling our winter salad crops. Come spring she went off to lay her eggs, but we hope that someday she'll return. Toads have been known to live as long as thirty or forty years, so it could be the start of a long partnership.

Ants in Your Plants

One March, at a lodge in coastal Mexico, I stood in a courtyard smelling the jasmine and I happened to look down. All along the edges of the terrace, thousands of ants were marching in tidy, ordered lines. The scene looked like the subway map of a major city. My host explained that the ants had free run of the place. "They clean the houses," he said. "They eat all the dropped crumbs, spiders, and scorpions."

I admired his view, one I try to cultivate at home. Sometimes, in spring, small black ants journey through the kitchen and, realizing that they do no harm, I have stopped squishing them. Once I found a honey pot full of them, but I now put the honey pot in a saucer of water and they don't cross the moat. Problem solved.

My anthill, covered with sedum

Outdoors, the buds on my peonies swarm with ants attracted to the nectar the buds secrete, but they open and bloom, unharmed. In my flower garden, ants sometimes make nests among the plants lining the gravel path. It looks a little messy, but as I have learned how useful ants can be—aerating the soil with their tunnels, pollinating flowers, eating aphids, removing and composting debris—I've stopped pouring boiling water on their homes to drive them away. For years now, I've had a small, dome-shaped ant mound, covered by the sedum variety Weihenstephaner Gold, right at a corner of a formal perennial border. Normally that plant creeps along the ground, but now it covers a tiny mountain, always as healthy as can be, where ants come and go, carrying things.

Even if I wanted to, I would find ants hard to manage. The real control is in the hands of a powerful queen ruling her empire from a bunker deep in the earth, far from boiling water, dried molasses, and organic pesticides. She will immediately replace any ants you destroy, and the best you can hope for is that she'll move the operation to a less bothersome place, leaving the earthworms to do all your soil aerating for you.

It's hard to like ants that sting, as many native species do. Nonnative ones can do even more harm, because, like so many imports, they have not brought along the natural predators that keep their numbers in balance at home. Fire ants are the most notorious example, both the South American ones that have caused havoc in our southern states, and the northern ones recently arrived from Europe, which injured the eyes of a friend of mine when she mowed an infested lawn.

In time we will adapt to the existence of fire ants, just as we've come to terms with bedbugs. Maybe we'll find a use for them—perhaps a crop that just loves the way they rototill the soil.

Does that sound crazy? Not long ago I read about a creature whose deadly venom can be used to treat brain cancer. You'll never guess which one. It was the scorpion.

Domestic Partners

I once spent some time with a Peruvian family that had a townhouse in the heart of Lima. The roof was a minifarm, crowded with rabbits, guinea pigs, and assorted poultry, all of which supplied protein for the household below. This arrangement is uncommon in the United States, where municipal rules for urban livestock range from strict forbiddance to a grudging "Don't ask, don't tell."

The association between domesticated livestock and gardens is a natural one, quite apart from any food the critters provide. Their manure lends fertility and organic matter to the soil, and any excess greenery from the vegetable patch in turn goes to supplement and improve upon their grain diet. Poultry also offers the extra benefit of pest control. A flock of chickens turned loose in the garden in fall will scratch up the ground and neatly dispatch any insect pests that might otherwise spend the winter there.

Our baby chicks start out in a little moveable house with a fenced yard.

Chickens are great, but if I were to suggest only one type of backyard livestock, it would be the duck. Its eggs are like chicken eggs but larger and can be used in all the same ways, and ducks are much less destructive, because they don't scratch the soil and pull up everything that's green. They're content to poke around among the plants with their bills (an activity we call "snarffling"), looking for beetles, cutworms, and other tasty morsels. Slugs are like gummy bears to ducks, and wherever they are raised, plants are largely slug-free.

Tasty salad crops, especially while young, must be fenced so that the ducks won't nibble them. The best plan is to enclose the vegetables but let the ducks roam around the perimeter of the garden to keep slugs from crawling in. In the fall you can let them in to do a cleanup. They won't bother big crops such as well-established fall kale. You will be astonished at how much the calcium in the greens you feed them improves the quality of their eggs. After you've seen the brilliant orange yolks of fresh eggs from grass-fed ducks or chickens, you'll never want the pallid supermarket kind again.

Although ducks are waterfowl, a pond is not a necessity. They need ample water to drink, and prefer to mate in water, but even a big rubber dish about two feet wide, available from a feed store or pet store, is adequate for a few ducks, and easy to clean out. A pond can even be a drawback. If too small, the ducks can muddy and foul it. If too large, it's hard to get them off it at bedtime. (We shut poultry up at night to protect them from raccoons and foxes.) Foxes will get them during the day, as will neighborhood dogs, so it is wise to fence your birds in and predators out. A coop will also keep them warmer in winter, especially when insulated with straw bales.

For duck housing, Eliot and his son, Ian, once devised an elegant little roofed box about two by three feet with a hardware cloth bottom to let droppings fall through. It was built with two wheels from a garden cart attached to the sides and two cart handles in front. We could wheel it three feet each morning to the next patch of grass, eventually fertilizing the whole lawn. They named it Duckingham Palace.

We have tried several duck breeds, but our favorite is the Indian Runner, a bird that is no more able to fly than you are. It looks like a tall bowling pin on webbed feet, and the only thing funnier than the sight of one jogging across the yard is a flock of them doing it together, moving as a synchronized team. They are superb layers and foragers and like to stay close to home.

Both baby ducklings and baby chicks can be ordered by mail. I love getting that call from the postmaster: "Barbara, you have a package. It's quacking." Or peeping, as the case may be.

Good citizen that you are, you'll wonder whether duck raising will compromise the sanitary condition of your surroundings or disturb the peace. No worries. Duck droppings, unlike those of chickens or geese, are nearly invisible, and sink rapidly into the earth. As for sound effects, you'll get some low-decibel quacking, far softer than a goose's blaring honk or a rooster's salutation to the dawn. Unlike a hen, a female duck does not loudly and triumphantly proclaim that she has just laid an egg.

Indian Runner
ducks at La Ferme
Biologique du Bec
Hellouin

It is likely that you could keep a few ducks in your backyard without anyone being the wiser. But you didn't hear that from me.

As far as rodent control goes, you are lucky if you have a talented and
dedicated dog or cat that can help you with that. Outdoor cats are problem-
atic, since in addition to voles and mice they also eat songbirds. At times
we have considered recruiting a dog bred to pursue rodents, such as a Jack
Russell, a fierce and overactive little ball of fury, happy to "go to ground"
and pull out its prey. I even contacted a farming couple that had tried that
solution. "They definitely solved our vole problem," they said, "but they
dug up the plants in the process. We now grow things only in pots."

One day, upon discovering a large garden area completely destroyed by
voles, Eliot could stand it no longer. "We're getting a Jack Russell," he said.

"We. Are. Not. Getting. A. Jack. Russell." I replied.

"Okay, how about a Jack Daniel's?"

"Fine."

CHAPTER 16

Weeds

Weeds may often seem like a gardener's worst enemy, but when you get to know them better you may find them more interesting and even more valuable than you might have thought.

What's a Weed?

My mother always said a weed was just "the right plant in the wrong place." Our young French friend Mélodie seemed to agree. She explained that the traditional French word for weed, *mauvais herbe*—which translates as "bad plant"—is now obsolete. All plants are good, and to deny that would be politically incorrect, or at least a faux pas. The preferred term is now *advantice*: a plant that has wandered into your garden and availed itself of your hospitable soil.

Weeds have long had their defenders. In 1950 the biologist Joseph A. Cocannouer wrote the book *Weeds: Guardians of the Soil*, which championed weeds as free and abundant sources of organic matter. They enrich and aerate the soil, especially "deep driving" ones such as ragweed, pigweed, and lamb's quarters that mine the subsoil layers for nutrients

and thus "enlarge the feeding zone for a cultivated crop." Weeds stabilize soil, improve its structure by "fiberizing" it and keeping it moist. Edible weeds are often more healthful to eat than the crops we grow. A book published a year later by F. C. King called *The Weed Problem: A New Approach* also pleaded for coexistence, and even advised raising weeds for the compost pile.

Comfrey is beautiful in bloom, and purportedly medicinal, but also quite weedy in the garden.

These books are good touchstones. They remind us of the importance of plant diversity and are antidotes to the reigning practice of monocultural farming. Neither of them argues for letting weeds ruin our gardens. But even as we exclude weeds, the yard can be a place where foraging and gardening meet. A cultural bond exists between the crops we grow on purpose and certain adventitious weeds that deserve our respect.

Driving through Europe, even in wintertime, you will sometimes see people poking about in the meadows and stuffing green plants into

Mats of purslane are easy to pull out.

baskets or plastic bags. They are foraging, a practice as old as the human race. Many of our most common weeds were originally brought over either deliberately or accidentally from early immigrants, and our more developed greens, such as spinach, lettuce, and kale, were originally wild. Researchers are finding that the closer a plant is to its primitive form, the more nutrients it contains, and a number of common weeds are being described as "superfoods." Yet even for those of us who value weeds' virtues, it's often a love/hate thing.

Take purslane, for example. I once tried out a horticultural version of that plant and it did quite poorly in my garden, unlike the weed version, *Portulaca oleracea*, known in Mexico as *verdolagas* ("green lakes"). As sure as the sun will rise to its zenith in late June, purslane will appear in my garden and spread its verdant mats from shore to shore. Another word for it, fatweed, well describes its leaves—little paddles that ooze a milky juice. Equally succulent are the red stems, which fan out from the center of the clump. Its role in nature is not to torture you but to cover disturbed ground and prevent the soil from blowing away. Years ago, as a farm-worker, I would munch it in the field to tide myself over until lunchtime. Now I'll add it to a salad for a crunchy texture, as well as iron, vitamin C, vitamin E, beta-carotene, and omega-3 fatty acids.

Still, its ambitions must be contained. Purslane is easiest to weed out when mats have formed: You just grasp the center and pull out the whole thing with a satisfying swoosh. But leave it there in the path, and it will

not die, but bask in the sun, put down new roots, and, as soon as it rains, form seeds.

No plant announces spring with more fanfare than the dandelion, with its happy yellow dots everywhere you look. It needs no pollinating insect to set its fuzzy balls of seed, scattered by the slightest wind. Many a weed killer displays a deep-rooted dandelion plant on its container like a mugshot, a symbol of Mother Nature out to get us. But clearly, dandelions were given to us to keep us from getting too serious about our lawns. Dandelions were once universally praised as one of the most beneficial plants known to humankind. The purpose their mighty taproot serves is to bring up minerals from various soil layers, along with a wide range of vitamins. The Chinese call it the "earth nail." Devotees rush to cut and savor the first tender leaves for salads. More mature leaves are best boiled, sautéed, or fried as fritters, to take the edge off their bitterness. The roots are edible too, but it's that first "mess of greens" that perks up the system.

It's good to know that something in my lawn might someday save me from scurvy, or starvation, but it is not welcome in the garden. I find the best way to remove a dandelion is to loosen the soil around it with a garden fork. Removing the whole root intact is like batting a home run, sinking a basket, or bowling a strike. Any piece of the root left in the ground can regrow, and you won't know that it has until you see yellow.

Chickweed (*Stellaria media*) is a cool weather weed with dainty little rounded leaves. Like purslane, it makes great annoying mats. But this mineral-laden plant is so mild and tasty that it is sometimes included in gourmet salad mixes and is among the wild greens sought after by adventurous cooks. I once supplied a notable chef with some, through his professional forager. Honestly, it seemed a little tacky to take money for something we normally fed to our chickens, so the next time the forager appeared I pointed to a greenhouse where chickweed was taking over. "Remove it, and it's yours," I said. Not since Tom Sawyer and his fence has a job been pawned off with more glee.

I could go on endlessly about edible weeds I have known. Lamb's quarters, a summer weed and nutritional powerhouse best cooked like creamed spinach. Burdock, which makes fistfuls of round burrs that attach themselves to your dog, your socks, your sweater. Take revenge by sautéing its taproots in lots of butter. Wild sorrel—infuriating because it loves bark mulch, scurrying across the surface on long, threadlike runners. It's easy to pull up, though, and a tasty little devil. Its tiny, spade-shaped leaves lend a tart, lemony zing to salads. Even the despised stinging nettle, which causes such pain to a careless gardener's hands, turns up in our neighborhood potlucks in soups and rice dishes.

One day I found one of our workers, Mee-Young, yanking up the ubiquitous red-root pigweed after quitting time. It turned out she was picking it for supper. "With sesame oil, garlic, chopped scallions, and miso paste,"

she said. When shepherd's purse (*Capsella bursa-pastoris*) dotted our farm with its pesky little rosettes, Mee-Young gave it a similar treatment, but added rice vinegar, sugar, and chili powder. Plantain leaves, too tough for salads, she tamed with blanching. They are a seasonal treat in Korea, her home country, where they suddenly appear in all the markets, sold by "old grandmothers with baskets."

Not all wild foods are fabulous. I am not impressed with dandelion root as a coffee substitute. (Where's the caffeine?) I honor the skinny white root of Queen Anne's lace as the mother of the modern carrot, but it's her orange descendants that make it to our table. I love the honesty of famous forager Euell Gibbons in his classic *Stalking the Wild Asparagus*: "In research for this book, I tried several hundred different kinds of plants and disliked most of them."

One must also be careful when foraging of the property rights of others, and also the appalling toxicity of our roadside soils and the water in our streams. Even when you know a plant is safe, make very sure you have identified it correctly and washed it thoroughly. Taste just a bit of it, at first, in case you have an unknown allergy.

Start by getting to know the weeds in your own poison-free organic garden. They can teach you a lot. My mother maintained that weeds are very crafty and will grow next to garden plants they resemble, to escape notice. Perhaps this is because plants with similar structural properties like the same spot.

Actually, they're even smarter than that. They're sneaking in through the kitchen door.

Galinsoga

It came in with the millennium, invading every garden in our neighborhood, and has irked all of us to madness ever since. Growing only two feet tall at most, it might seem overshadowed by other weeds but none match its persistence. Not only can one plant produce as many as 400,000 seeds in a season, but there can also be multiple generations of it before frost gives it a winter recess. I have even seen it flowering and producing seed at two inches tall in my newly mowed lawn.

The local galinsoga obsession included, at first, its purported edibility. "A common staple in China," the rumor went, though no one could come up with an Asian recipe. But a quick online search turned up a classic Colombian dish called *ajiaco*, associated with the city of Bogotá. Some friends had even eaten it on a recent trip, recalling it as a hearty soup or stew with potatoes and chicken in broth. My kind of meal, I thought.

Recipes I uncovered insisted that galinsoga (botanically *Galinsoga parviflora* and called *guasca* in the land from which its now-global march began) is essential to *ajiaco*. Without the distinctive flavor of this "native mountain herb," it is not *ajiaco* at all. Hilariously, homesick Colombians plead for advice on Web forums, asking where they can find the plant. "Everywhere," the world replies.

I picked and nibbled a few leaves from the galinsoga forest taking root in some recently emptied beds. It wasn't strong, bitter, or hot. Strangely, it had almost no flavor at all. Still, I'd resolved to prepare a reasonably authentic *ajiaco*, so I set about simmering some chicken, potatoes, corn, onions, garlic, and galinsoga in rich homemade stock.

Because the dish is ordinarily served with an array of garnishes—avocado, diced hot peppers, capers, cilantro, and sour cream—I set those out too, in little bowls, and summoned the farm crew to the table. We loved this one-pot meal. We devoured it. But the importance of including the bland galinsoga remained a mystery. Perhaps if you grew up in Bogotá it is a subtle taste memory that speaks of home. Or maybe the plant is terribly rich in vitamins and antioxidants, so invigorating to those who eat it that they can rip the plants from their gardens for hours on end without tiring. I also wondered whether it was originally a famine food, something indestructible that was always there to eat, even if your garden's crops were not.

The ajiaco I made was so good that it will always be a permanent part of my life. So will galinsoga, I fear, like a medical condition you can manage but not cure. Meanwhile, there will be other garden ills to gripe about—new bugs, new weeds—but famine will not be one of them.

WHAT TO GROW

PART FIVE

CHAPTER 17

Tomatoes

It's a spring day in our greenhouse and the Pointer Sisters are belting out "I'm So Excited" as the young potted tomato plants raise their branches up toward the sun. Eliot and I dance around them, lifting our arms to the beat. It's a joyous ritual, our ridiculous salute to exuberant new growth. Anyone will tell you that the sisters' song is a double entendre. We agree. It's about tomatoes.

There is something very seductive about tomatoes, often gardeners' favorite crop, a gateway drug that lures them into the garden, and then on to melons and corn. They are luscious, of course, but, better yet, their flavor, more than any other, defines the difference between store-bought and fresh-picked. Most commercial ones are harvested green, then gassed with ethylene to make them "ripen." Your own are picked red, and taste of sunshine.

What Makes a Tomato Taste Good?

Given half a chance, a tomato vine is mighty and fruitful. A perennial in the South American tropics from whence it came, its natural inclination is to creep over the sun-warmed ground and it will grow indefinitely if not killed by frost. At our farm we once had a greenhouse so full of the vines' rank growth that I feared it would burst in a great explosion of red sauce.

As you'd expect from their tropical origin, tomatoes are warm weather creatures when grown in temperate zones. It's best not to set them in the ground before the soil temperature is at least 60 degrees Fahrenheit. Those set out too early will just sit there and sulk, and any planted later will soon overtake them. There is also a flavor arc over the course of their season. The first one to ripen will seem delicious, a small miracle, but you'll find the flavor intensifies as the fruits bask in the warm midsummer sun. If any of them soldier on into October you will be grateful, but the cold will render their flavor bland by comparison. This is why one never stores tomatoes in the fridge.

Certainly, the care you give tomatoes will pay off too. A fertile soil with plenty of organic matter and all the right macro- and micronutrients is needed to produce all those leafy vines. Giving them consistent water will help avoid a lot of tomato ills. But that doesn't mean excessive water-ing. If anything, it's best to keep them just a bit on the dry side, so as not to dilute those rich juices. Whenever possible, let them ripen on the vine, not off it. Nature is adding ingredients to the recipe right up until the moment of pick-and-eat.

Taste is also a matter of what kind of tomato you grow. There are two broad, general types. The indeterminate tomato is the original, function-ally immortal "vining" tomato. The determinate tomato, on the other hand, created via a genetic mutation in 1914, terminates both its growth and its fruit production by midsummer, having given you a large harvest in a relatively short time. This makes the plants smaller and easier to take care of, and it is handy if your major goal is to put up a lot of tomatoes in jars for year-round eating. The oval-shaped plum or paste tomatoes are often chosen for this purpose because their dense, concentrated flesh can be boiled down more quickly for puree or sauce. But indeterminate toma-toes are what you want for a long season of fresh eating, and they have a flavor advantage as well. Their greater ratio of leaf to fruit concentrates both the sugars in the fruit and its flavor. "Think of foliage as solar panels for the sugar factory" my tomato farmer friend Andrew Mefferd once said. Fruits from a rambling, leafy tomato vine will pack ten times the taste of a petite pixie patio tomato in a little pot. Because they ripen later, they also have had more time for their flavor to develop.

Tomatoes vary greatly as to size, from beefsteak monsters down to pea-sized "currant" tomatoes and the popular cherry tomatoes. I find cherry tomatoes—so sweet when ripe—the ultimate snack food for setting out on the table in a bowl or, better yet, as a right-off-the-vine treat while you're out weeding the garden. The fact that the tastiest ones split easily forces you to eat them at their brief moment of absolute perfection. One called Matt's Wild Cherry, a primitive strain from the mountains of eastern Mexico, is probably the closest you will get to the flavor of the original, primordial tomato. But even our most modern "cherries" have some of its qualities: sprawling, vigorous, and disease resistant, the fruits full of character, and wild at heart.

It's not surprising that the best-tasting tomatoes are often the oldest varieties, known as heirlooms. Naturally those that have withstood the test of time are likely to be the tastiest. But it's more than that. The definition of heirloom is limited to varieties bred before the end of World War II, when the commercial seed trade switched over to patented F[1] hybrids. Before that, all varieties were open-pollinated, which means that you can save seeds from a favorite one and pass it down, like any family heirloom, from one generation to another. But seeds saved from F[1] hybrids cannot produce fruits similar to the ones from which they came, which means you have to go back to the seller for more seed. Flavor has changed as well. In keeping with the industrialization of agriculture, tomato varieties began to be bred more for storability and ease of shipping than for taste.

Heirloom tomatoes, as a group, win the flavor prize, but they do have drawbacks. They are often less productive than modern ones—all vine, and few fruits. This is sometimes due to poor disease resistance. But the best modern breeders, in my view, improve the originals just enough to increase productivity but keep the yumminess. Take the case of Brandywine (Sudduth Strain), a very old and popular heirloom with

Squeezing paste tomatoes

Top: Brandy Boy tomatoes are lumpy—and luscious.

Bottom: Paste tomatoes are wonderful roasted with olive oil and herbs, cut-side up, with the bottoms still a bit pillowy.

pink skin and richly flavored bright red flesh. Its shape is lumpy and indented, so that you cut it into chunks rather than tidy rounds. Burpee Seeds sells a hybrid called Brandy Boy (Brandywine crossed with a more disease-resistant French tomato) that retains enough of the original's goodness and character to satisfy me, and it yields a much bigger harvest. Because it's not open-pollinated I can't save the seeds, but it makes better use of my garden's space.

In the end, it comes down to personal taste. The ideal tomato flavor is thought to be an ideal balance of acidic and sweet. As with any fruit or vegetable, sweetness must be combined with whatever gives it a unique character. For instance, some people go nuts over the muddy-colored heirlooms such as Cherokee Purple or Black Krim. Their flavor is complex, but to me they're a bit tart. Some of the yellow ones such as Garden Peach are sweet but lack zip. Striped German, which looks like a red-yellow-orange sunset, is so gorgeous and delicious cut up in a salad that I almost excuse its poor yields. Some people are gaga over the green ones such as Green Zebra.

Most gardens aren't big enough to grow and serve the whole tomato rainbow on a platter, drizzled with good olive oil, freshly ground pepper, and coarse salt. But if each gardener in the neighborhood grew one kind, we could hold a tasting, with a serious discussion of what makes a tomato good, bad, or ugly. We'd also have a mighty fine meal.

Taming Tomatoes

They must call it "spring" because that's when plants spring forth and rocket skyward. In summer, if fruiting crops have put on more weight than they can bear, they will then sag their way into equally well-named "fall." Tomatoes, especially the indeterminate ones, do best when lifted up into the sun to ripen, away from soilborne diseases. This also makes them easy to pick. Wise gardeners install supports for them ahead of time, before their heavy vines and fruit bring them to their knees in a tangled mess.

There are a number of ways to do this. Tomato cages—wire cylinders or boxlike structures that surround a single plant—work well only if they are strong. Eliot and I have made them out of concrete reinforcing wire, purchased in five-foot-wide sheets from a building supply store. This rigid mesh has six-inch-square openings through which you can easily reach for the tomatoes. Using a bolt cutter, we cut pieces long enough to form into cylinders about sixteen inches in diameter and set them over the young plants, which are placed thirty inches apart in the row, to guide their ascent. If necessary, you can anchor a cage by driving in one or two

pointed wooden grade stakes or metal T-posts and tying them to the mesh, lest it blow over, but so far this has not been necessary.

A tomato plant will grow happily in a cage, making side branches that grow outward, resting its elbows on the wire, so to speak, and bear fruit. But pruning is required to keep the plant growing vertically and bearing fruit in a controlled way. Look closely at the first leaf branches that form and you will see a tiny shoot called a "sucker" emerging in the angle between those branches and the main stem. Pinch them out. As the plant grows, keep pinching out excess suckers in the leaf branches to keep the plant from producing a jungle of fruiting branches, which are unlikely to bear ripe fruit before the season's end. You want just one main stem. The fruiting branches that bear your tomatoes will emerge straight from that main stem with yellow blossoms visible. Guide their growing tips to stay within the cage as they travel up. If a plant is indeterminate a five-foot cage is fine, though it's best to snip it off when it reaches six feet. If it is determinate, the cage could be as short as three feet tall since growth will cease on its own. This is a great way to grow determinate paste tomatoes.

Another support technique is called "stake and weave," a simple matter of running two strings down a tomato row, supported by a single row of wooden stakes, so that the plants are captured and held upright between the strings. To do this, remove the lowest suckers and set the plants out

The stake and weave method

two feet apart. Hammer in pointed four-foot wooden grade stakes at three-plant intervals. (Begin and end with metal T-posts or use those throughout for exceptionally vigorous varieties.) Then tie untreated, non-stretching, compostable sisal twine to the first stake, eight inches above the ground, and loop the twine around every stake and along alternate sides of each plant, keeping it taut. (This works best as a two-person job, one holding up a plant and the other weaving the twine.) At the end of the row, come back down the other side, doing the same thing. Once a week add a new level of twine, six or eight inches higher each time, as the plants grow. Remove suckers here and there if your Great Wall of Tomato threatens to be visible from outer space.

The most elegant method, with vining tomatoes, is to train the plants vertically, supported by sturdy twine. If you have a greenhouse, even a small one like Helen Nearing's lean-to, you can suspend these from a metal or wood purlin (horizontal bar). This will give you extra-early tomatoes by keeping frost at bay and provide late ones in fall. However, you can also train outdoor tomatoes on vertical strings. Construct a wooden frame consisting of a post at each end of a planting row, the posts no more than six feet apart in between and a two-by-two bar across the top. The posts should be sunk at least a foot in the ground for anchorage, and you might even want to string guy wires at right angles to the top

Tomatoes trained vertically on strings in a home greenhouse

bar for additional support. (Thick vines in late summer can act like sails in a gale.)

Plant the tomatoes sixteen to eighteen inches apart and tie a soft string loosely to the base of each stem. Tie the other end to the bar, with enough slack to let you twist the string gently around the vine as it grows. Prune each plant to one stem by pinching out all the suckers that appear, to keep them from making the plant unmanageable. Pinch the growing tip when it reaches the bar. If you are vigilant, you will develop a case of "tomato pruner's thumb," which dyes your thumb a brownish green, easily removed with lemon juice. Or flaunted with pride.

I like to plant some lemon basil plants in the same row. Do they repel pest insects, as some sages promise? I doubt it. But they go handily into the harvest basket along with the tomatoes for a hearty tomato and basil salad, flavored with a mix of balsamic vinegar, olive oil, a bit of honey, coarse salt, cracked pepper, and sunshine.

Hornworms in Full Sight

Sometimes a pest insect is so intriguing you almost hope to encounter it. Almost. Take the tomato hornworm, which feasts on tomato plants and their relatives, such as peppers and eggplants. In its larval form it is a huge caterpillar, up to four inches long. Sometimes the damage it does is slight, if there are few larvae and many plants, but because of its size it can be voracious. If you notice foliage missing from the tops of the plants, and even nibbles on the green fruits, hornworms may be the culprits. If so, you'll also see their dark-colored droppings on leaves below their picnic area, helping you to locate them.

Finding them is harder than you'd think. A tiny aphid is more visible. Tomato worms are well camouflaged, having spent millennia learning how to resemble tomato stems and leaves, and with their pale green color they look exactly like part of the tomato plant itself. One way to beat that defense is to go out at night with a black light—that gizmo we used to view psychedelic art with back in the '60s. Medical pathologists use it to

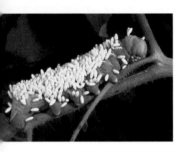

A tomato hornworm
parasitized by a
braconid wasp

illuminate certain viruses and bacteria. Policemen use it to detect bodily fluids and counterfeit bills. And you can use it to light up the bioluminescence in a tomato worm.

When you do come upon one, you'll recognize it by the upright black horn that it carries on its hind segment and the white V-shaped markings on its sides. The tobacco hornworm, which has a similar look and appetite, has a red horn and the markings are diagonal stripes.

When hornworms have grown to maturity, they pupate in the soil, turning into sphinx moths and hawk moths with five-inch wingspans. These are also called hummingbird moths and are often mistaken for those birds as they hover before an open flower, buzzing their wings energetically during pollination. Don't harm them. You may have the moths without the larvae ever being a problem.

If they do become a problem, take comfort in the fact that you have helpers, and encourage their presence by keeping the yard poison-free. Green lacewings, lady beetles, and other insects eat the larvae when they are small. Mature ones are often parasitized by braconid wasps. If you find a hornworm covered with what looks like grains of rice, leave it be! A braconid wasp has laid tiny eggs on its body and these have hatched into larvae that consume the caterpillar from within. These then pupate inside the white, rice-shaped cocoons that you see. In time, adult wasps emerge from those cocoons, finish off their host, and go off to parasitize more hornworms, thus carrying out a life cycle of great value to the gardener.

For hornworms without the cocoons, the job is up to you, and hand-picking is the best defense. Many people find this extremely distasteful, even those not normally repelled by creepy-crawlies. When poked, a tomato hornworm will start to emit a bright green goo. I have also heard that a hornworm, when disturbed, will often make a noise, a sort of clicking sound, so that shaking the plant a bit may help you find its hiding place. I have not heard that with my own ears, but someday I would like to. In someone else's garden.

CHAPTER 18

Salad Greens

Willi
illiam Shakespeare's plays abound with images of gardens and the natural world. Take the moment in *Antony and Cleopatra* where Cleopatra refers to her youth as her "salad days," when she was "green in judgment." What better emblem of youth than fresh, tender greens emerging from the soil? And in one's lifetime, one can only hope for many days when these greens can be picked from the garden and rushed to the plate.

A bounty of salad days favors gardens in moderate climates where it is neither freezing cold nor scorching hot. Most gardeners in Canada and the American tier of northern states must arm their tender greens against winter cold. An even more daunting task is faced by those in sunbaked lands, such as that of the great Egyptian queen.

In either case, there are ways and means. One of them is to simply expand the idea of what a salad ought to be.

Serendipity Salads

There is nothing like a happy by-product of error. Let's say I've sown a row of lettuce, but too thickly, leaving each plant too little space in which

Gorgeous lettuces in tidy rows

to grow. So I pull out enough seedlings to adjust the spacing and what do I have? A basket of small leaves, tender and delicious. Pulled at two or three inches, they're an instant baby-leaf salad harvest. Pulled even smaller and they're microgreens: little bits of greenery for which chefs pay great sums to garnish plates. At any size, all I need to do is toss them into a sink filled with water, swish them, drain them, then spin or blot them dry.

Spring is the best time for a thinnings salad, when many crops have been direct sown. A row of lettuce here, a row of arugula there, and I have a tasty dish. Spinach seedlings need to be thinned to a hand's width apart, with plenty of small treasures in between.

Some of the best thinnings are ones that aren't even being grown for salads. Both Swiss chard and beets are the ones most likely to need thinning because they grow from small capsules with several seeds inside them, separable only after they have sprouted. Radish leaves, though fine for cooking later on, are tender and mild enough to eat raw when small. The same goes for brassicas such as cabbage, collards, and kale. Fennel thinnings, which are wispy, flavorful fronds, are also great in salads. Were the peavines planted extra close in the row as insurance against poor germination? At two inches tall their tips have none of the toughness or stringiness they will later develop, so out the thinnings come, soon to glisten with vinaigrette.

Since a salad is even better with fresh herbs, I head for the dill patch next, the one composed of self-sown volunteers from last year. I give them a spotty haircut with a pair of scissors, allowing the strongest to remain. And if any brassica plants such as kale have made it through the winter and now are going to seed, with masses of edible yellow flowers waving above the plants like out-of-season goldenrod, I might pick a few of those to scatter over my salad, as just another accidental harvest.

Thinnings of assorted vegetables make delicious additions to a salad.

Is Iceberg Still Cool?

Back in the 1950s Iceberg lettuce was about the only salad green you could buy. Round, hard, and pale green, it is cabbage-like in its density and keeps for weeks. It went to war with the troops, preserved the structural integrity of lunch-bag BLTs, and was always there for you in the back of the fridge, no matter how seldom you went shopping. No wonder it was called bachelor lettuce.

Iceberg lettuce is not gourmet. The fanciest it ever got was when the local steakhouse cut a wedge of it and topped it with a dollop of creamy blue cheese dressing. It's a head lettuce, as distinguished from a leaf lettuce, in other words, one whose leaves are compressed into a dense ball, as opposed to ones that flare out like a cancan dancer's ruffles.

The original Iceberg is an heirloom variety that was introduced by W. Atlee Burpee & Company in 1894, and the general type known as crisphead is older still. The claim that the name derived from its being shipped by rail in containers filled with ice has been disproved, but "Iceberg" certainly has become a symbol of industrial agriculture and its focus on bulletproof, long-keeping varieties that can withstand nationwide transport—as opposed to ones chosen for nutrients and flavor. And yet, that sturdiness and shelf life have always sat well with home cooks, as they sliced and wedged it into the culture of American cookery.

Our farm's salad mix

With the 1960s, along came greener, softer, more nutritious lettuces, from the Boston, butterhead, and oakleaf types to the crunchy but nutritious romaines. Next were Euro-style market treats that took the idea of salad greens well beyond lettuce, with arugula, mâche, radicchio, and spring mixes, inspired by the wild-foraging traditions of the Mediterranean countries—mesclun in the Provence region of France, *misticanza* in parts of Italy, and *horta* in Greece. Asian greens such as mizuna, tatsoi, and spicy red mustard jumped into the rapidly expanding bowl of flavorful, multicolored salads. At one point our farm was growing and selling a winter salad mix consisting of red and green lettuces, baby spinach, arugula, golden-colored frisée endive, tatsoi, mizuna, claytonia, baby Red Ace beet greens, and a grasslike leaf called *minutina* or, in English, buck's horn plantain. Because its contents represented so many different botanical families, it was like a multivitamin in a bowl.

During this long and exciting period, Iceberg lettuce still maintained much of its market share, but style-wise, its sun had set.

For home gardeners, one way to jump into the wide world of exotic salads is to purchase, and plant, a carefully curated mix of seeds, chosen not only for their diversity but also for their uniform rate of growth and harvest times. Often, they will regrow nicely after cutting, for a second crop. John Scheepers Kitchen Garden Seeds has always had a number of these blends, some all lettuce and some mixed with chicories, Asian greens, and other nonlettuce favorites. One summer I grew one of their lettuce mixes and found it especially pleasing because one of its components was especially crunchy and gave a nice loft to the mix. It added some air to the salad bowl and kept the softer leaves from matting down at the bottom in an oily pool. So I started growing a crunchy lettuce all by itself—a heat-tolerant variety called Summertime.

Work has been done to cross the Iceberg type with leaf lettuces and romaines, but it's a tough sell to customers who celebrate the end of the Iceberg age and have no use for a lettuce with no more nutrients than a volleyball (as Iceberg is generally perceived). But Iceberg is still here.

Sometimes it's just sold as a crisphead; other times the "I" word is brazenly used. After all, there has been a bit of a retro steakhouse craze.

Eliot once approached a very young restaurateur with this suggestion: "Take one of these crispheads, cut it into wedges, and spoon blue cheese dressing on top of each one. It'll save you lots of time." "Wow," she replied, in all sincerity, "What an amazing idea."

Revelations of Romaine

Finding the ancient origin of a popular food is always intriguing, especially if it leads to a new adventure in the kitchen. Take ordinary lettuce. The oldest lettuce type is the upright, long-leaved romaine, its ancestor on full display in Egyptian bas-reliefs from the third millennium BC. The French name *romaine*, a reference to its presence in papal (Roman) gardens, merely points to a step along the journey to modern times. Its other common name, cos lettuce, links it to the Greek Island of Kos. But that too was a way station. According to William Woys Weaver in his book *100 Vegetables and Where They Came From*, "Those large, long, stiff-leaved sorts were consciously selected by Syrian gardeners so that the leaves would develop strong ribs and spoon-shaped foliage. The reason for this was simple: the lettuces were used as an edible scoop or spoon when eating tabbouleh-like foods." That's still an excellent reason to grow romaine.

Red Rosie, a glamorous romaine variety

Seed catalogs list many tried and true romaine varieties. Parris Island Cos, bred in South Carolina in 1952, is large, crisp, and mild tasting. I also like the ruddy-tipped, chill-tolerant Rouge d'Hiver, and the red, carnival-like speckles of Flashy Trout Back. Speckled lettuces aren't for everyone, though. The first time Eliot saw Flashy Trout Back, he said, "It looks diseased." I tried to sway him with Gerard Manley Hopkins's poem "Pied Beauty," which begins "Glory be to God for dappled things," and celebrates "whatever is fickle, freckled." Hopkins would have loved Flashy Trout Back. One of his favorite "dappled things" was that very fish, with "rose-moles all in stipple upon trout that swim." Then again, a customer at our farm stand once pointed to a speckled variety and asked, "Has this lettuce been spattered with mud?" To each his own.

Managing Lettuce

Gardeners love to compare notes, but it's always a little weird with my friend Joyce Wilkie. For many years she—along with her late husband, Michael Plane—has grown vegetables at her farm in Gundaroo, Australia, near Canberra, so our conversations have an upside-down quality to them. In February, when I'm deep in winter, Gundaroo is beastly hot. When my garden is in its spring kickoff phase, Joyce is getting her winter greenhouse into fighting trim. Once I decided to pick her brain about lettuce. "Do any survive your summers?" I asked.

Of course, it's not really about survival. A lettuce plant thinks it's doing just fine when the combination of long daylight hours, dry weather, and temperatures about 80 degrees Fahrenheit causes it to bolt. This simply means that it's time to make seed in order to perpetuate itself. The center of the leafy rosette begins liftoff, rising several feet in height, if you let it, and will eventually make flowers. (Lettuce flowers are beautiful, by the way.) The ancient Egyptians found this a powerful image, equating the plant's upward thrust and milky sap with virility. More to the point, they grew lettuce mainly for its seed, from which they extracted cooking oil, so bolting was part of the game plan. But modern gardeners are less impressed. I have actually tried braising the stems of lettuce and found that they remain tender and tasty even after the plants "start to move," as Joyce puts it. But by then the foliage has grown too bitter for salads.

"We never grow the frilly, fancy ones in summer," Joyce says. "We grow mesclun instead, sowing it in the shade and cutting and recutting while it is small. For heads I grow the big, hard crisp types, which are so crunchy and sweet my boys pick them and eat them like apples. But you can never allow lettuce to get stressed. Transplant stress, wind stress, water stress—avoid all these and Bob's your uncle."

Just for fun, let old lettuce bolt sometime and admire the flowers.

The Wilkie-Plane solution involves shade cloth, stretched across a framework made from rebar and black poly pipe. The reduction in light, coupled with vigilant watering, holds the plants' procreative urge at bay. This is excellent, clear advice in any hemisphere, except for the phrase "Bob's your uncle," which turns out to be an expression meaning, roughly, "It's as simple as that." Less clear: who Bob is, and why I should want to be his niece.

In California it is quite common to grow summer lettuce in a shady spot with rich, friable soil. And shade cloth is easy to put over a lettuce row if you use the same wire wickets and metal or plastic hoops that hold up floating row covers for protection against pests or winter cold. Joyce uses quite a dense weave of this dark material, one that excludes 70 percent of ultraviolet rays. Roll it up at the sides to permit good air circulation because in climates more humid than Australia's lettuce is prone to summer rot. I would also avoid mulching lettuce with hay or straw, which will, without fail, attract slugs. If possible, use pine needles or leaf mold instead.

If you grow summer lettuce, make small sowings every few weeks, so there is always a fresh young row coming along. By the time mid-August arrives, it's time to start lettuce for fall. Either start seeds indoors where it's cool, or cover an outdoor row with moistened burlap, checking daily for germination and removing the cover once that occurs. If you keep the crop irrigated, it should hang in there until the days are 70 to 75 degrees

Fahrenheit, with cooler nights and more rain—just the weather lettuce like best. And then—Bob's your uncle!

Like all lettuces, romaine is a cool weather crop. In climates where summer heat arrives in April, it's wise to sow lettuce seeds indoors by early February in order to have seedlings to transplant outdoors at least by early March. For a later spring planting, the Israel-bred, heat-tolerant Jericho is a good choice. Lettuce plants should be set out twelve inches apart, in a fertile, moisture-retentive soil, rich in organic matter.

Romaine's robust texture makes it a versatile salad lettuce. It has nearly the firmness of the Iceberg type, but usually with more vivid color and more nutrients. Cooks love the way it holds up well against heavy dressings such as warm anchovy and garlic, or the classic Caesar with egg and Parmesan cheese. To use it as a dipping scoop, choose the smaller inner leaves.

For the tabbouleh test, you must wait for the first tomatoes. This wonderful dish of bulgur wheat dressed with olive oil, parsley, and garlic requires the presence of chopped tomatoes picked vine ripe, and would be excellent scooped up with the first romaine of fall. While waiting, try a lettuce-scooped Provençal tapenade made with black olives, capers, and anchovies, or the Greek *htipiti* (I pronounce it "ti-PITTY" but I'm probably wrong), a puree of feta cheese, olive oil, lemon, and roasted red pepper. Or an ultra-garlicky Middle Eastern hummus, with tahini, chickpeas, and olive oil, which is fit for a banquet in ancient Mesopotamia.

The Green Leaves of Winter

It was nothing as dramatic as the fall of the Berlin Wall or the race to the moon, but by the start of the new millennium America had opened her doors to peppy international salads. Those who were jarred by this intrusion blamed a growing wave of effete foodies, too cool to eat a hot dog. Yes, there will always be those of us who love to try something new. But, ironically, all of these new delicacies were very, very old. They were not foods for the elite, but peasant foods. Many could be described as weeds.

The gateway green was arugula, a soft, bright green plant you pick when it's no more than three inches tall. It has a distinctive mustardy bite and, while you can eat it all by itself, its greatest use is to toss a handful of it into a salad of milder greens, to liven it up. Arugula doesn't keep well, so this is best done just before dressing, tossing, and serving. There are ways to cook it, but its flavor is more prominent in the raw leaf.

Arugula, whose botanical name is *Eruca sativa*, is native to the Mediterranean region. Though the name we use for it is Italian, you'll also see it in Italy as *rucola* or *ruchetta*. The Flemish call it *krapkool*. In France it's *roquette*. It's strange that we've latched onto a European name for it when there was already an English one: rocket. As rocket, it was brought here by early British colonists and then more or less ignored. But overall, it has been known as a mighty health-bestowing plant, a good luck charm, even an aphrodisiac.

The most important thing for a gardener to know about arugula is that it is best grown in cool weather. If you've tried arugula and found it too strong, you may only have tasted summer-grown plants. In heat, they struggle, losing their bright green color. They fall prey to flea beetles—little hopping insects that stipple the leaves with tiny holes. It truly shines as a fall and winter crop, when neither pests nor heat trouble it. Sow it every few weeks as the summer heat starts to ebb, in moist, fertile soil, thinning to a one-inch spacing to prevent bolting. You may often get a second harvest after cutting. In Maine, we grow it in fall and winter, with protection against freezing, for a tonic that tastes like spring.

Another tasty introduction was mâche, pronounced "mosh." There is nothing in its flavor to offend, which is why the French call it *doucette*: the little sweet one. Mâche heads are soft and fluffy, with a loft that lends volume to a salad. Its slightly cupped leaves, joined at the base, hold a dressing well. You might know it by an old English name, corn salad, a reference to its habit of growing wild in grainfields, the word "corn" denoting small grains in general, not the maize of the New World.

You'll rarely see this cool weather green for sale because it is too tender and perishable for easy transport—a good reason to grow it at home. In

Arugula is best cut in cool weather at baby-leaf size.

Mâche grows in small, soft, mild-tasting heads.

Europe, especially in the Alps, it's a crop for winter because of its cold tolerance, and I have never grown a green so winterproof. My friend Verena Stoll, who grew up in the Swiss city of Basel in the 1950s, recalls the arrival of mâche in the October markets, trundled through the streets in barrows by farm women from nearby Alsace. She loves it dressed with vinaigrette, a finely diced hard-boiled egg, croutons, and crumbled bacon. "This is a crop that gets us through the winter," she says. Nowadays mâche is greenhouse grown in France's Nantes basin, near the mouth of the Loire. There are California growers as well, but I think mâche shines the most as a home gardener's crop.

A lush bed of mâche has fed our household all winter in an unheated greenhouse or cold frame. We harvest the little heads by running a small, serrated knife just under the soil surface, severing them from their roots. After a thorough washing, I toss them whole in a salad bowl. When the days lengthen past ten hours, and some of the heads enlarge to four inches or more, we can pinch them near the base of the plant and release individual leaves. Soon after that, the plants start to go to seed, and while bolted mâche is still tasty, I like to have a young spring crop coming along outdoors.

There is no such thing as summer mâche. It will not even germinate in warm weather. But a crop sown in early fall will reach maturity in time for the cold season, and a robust salad of mâche with baked beets is the best winter tonic I know.

In 1996, wandering through Italy and France in January and February, Eliot and I learned a lot about winter salad greens, and much of it had to do with chicories. These plants are in the same family as lettuce, but they tend to be less improved and more like their wild ancestors. Their flavors are strong, often to the point of bitterness. With these assertive tastes comes an impressive package of vitamins, minerals, fiber, inulin (a low-glycemic fiber), and other nutritional signposts. But you can tame their bite by growing them in cool weather, cooking them, or blanching them, that is, depriving them of light. The result makes the foliage lighter in color, but the original purpose is to make its flavor sweeter and milder. Chicory and endive are often confused. One of the two important chicory species, *Cichorium endivia*, contains the popular frisée endive, sometimes just called frisée because of the fine, frizzled texture of its slightly flattened heads. Planting them closely, as little as eight inches apart, will crowd them just enough to bunch up their centers and blanch them a bit.

The other true endive is escarole, which makes great big heads with large, wavy leaves. I love to eat it in the Italian way: simmered and drained, then sautéed with olive oil and garlic. Both frisée and escarole are popular in winter salads, especially in France. Every market we saw in the southwest of France had piles of both on display—huge, fresh heads of greenery with glowing, pale gold centers, and every place where we ate served a salad composed of them, in which the green parts and the blanched part made a nice balance of mild and strong, sprinkled with bacon lardons and vinaigrette. It was clearly the January salad.

Near Perpignan, in Catalan country, we saw those heads being blanched in the field by placing white plastic dome-shaped hats, slightly smaller than Frisbees, over them, and pinning them down with stiff wire pegs to keep them from blowing away. One section of the field would wear the hats for ten days or so until the centers were blanched, then be promptly picked and sold. I've copied this trick successfully by inverting clay pot saucers over heads of escarole. (Plastic saucers can be used too if you weight them down with bricks or rocks.) The result is a lovely pale, mild center.

Poking along from village to village we saw frisée and escarole in many home plots. At one spot we stopped to chat with an elderly gardener in a beret. "Do you ever grow mâche?" we asked. "No, they grow that up around Nantes," he said. "What about mesclun mix?" we ventured. "Why do Americans always ask about that?" he replied. "That's for early spring in Provence. We grow these." He pointed to his rows of escarole and endive. "That's the tradition."

Moving along to Italy, on our winter greens tour, we found more local traditions to celebrate, especially in the Veneto region of northeastern Italy, which is the center of radicchio production. Radicchio, *Cichorium intybus*, is a chicory species, but not an endive. Radicchio heads we had grown in summer, richly streaked and spangled with red tones, were gorgeous to look at but too bitter in salads for our tastes, and much better grilled with olive oil and garlic. We were interested in seeing how they were dug up in fall, forced (compelled to sprout new growth), and simultaneously blanched in the dark for winter use. Varieties we had ordered from seed companies, and grown, were often named for towns in the Veneto that specialize in a certain style: Treviso (long and narrow, striped with white and deep red), Chioggia (round and predominately deep crimson), and Castelfranco (blanched to pale yellow, speckled with red).

Essentially, they were doing the same thing we do when we force witloof chicory, otherwise known, erroneously, as Belgian endive. (It originated in Belgium, but an endive it is not.) Eliot and I plant a chicory variety called Totem in summer, dig it up in fall, cut off the foliage, leaving the growth point at the top of the root unharmed, and cut the long taproot to about nine inches long. We then place the roots standing up in buckets or tubs of water, cover them with enough thick black plastic to make it extra dark, and wait for delicious little creamy white heads to emerge. The French call these *chicons*. You don't need a root cellar to do this. We have forced chicons in the cupboard under our kitchen sink.

Does the U.S. have any comparable salad tradition? Was Iceberg the best we could do? Hidden away, is there some unheralded native son? The answer is yes.

Discover Claytonia

Claytonia in bloom

Claytonia is a weed found in northern California and other parts of the West Coast that are damp in wintertime. It's the kind of weed you like to have. It flourishes in winter or early spring, when greenery is scarce, and it fortified prospectors in the Gold Rush days with ample vitamin C, as a protection against scurvy—hence one of its common names, miner's lettuce. It also feeds wildlife, stabilizes disturbed soil, and is one of the first plants to sprout after fire, helping to heal the land.

From a firm base at soil level sprout dozens of thin stems, topped with little heart-shaped leaves. As these mature, each encircles its stem, clasping it, so that the leaf appears as a flat-topped parasol. In botany this is called a perfoliate leaf, the trait that gives the plant its Latin name *Claytonia perfoliata*. From the center of the parasol a tiny, fragrant white or pinkish flower appears, then a cluster, then a sprig that elongates as a continuation of the stem. The flowers are followed by brown capsules that scatter multitudes of tiny black seeds.

The leaves are nutritious and wonderfully fresh tasting, a great background for more assertive flavors in a mixed salad. Another of its common names is winter purslane, and though not as pillowy as the true purslane, the leaves contain so much air that when you wash them, they float on the water in your sink, like a raft of tiny lily pads. They rarely need washing, though, since they are held so erect by the stems that you can grasp them like a bouquet of violets. I cut them with just an inch or two of stem.

Sometimes I make a nest of them on which to set a fish fillet or an egg. Cooking them seems beside the point, although a few handfuls dropped into a soup will lend just a bit of thickness, the way sorrel does. This is one way to use the leaves if they have grown larger and firmer, as they may in milder climates. In my garden they are rarely more than an inch across.

Claytonia is a winter annual, which means that even though it drops its seeds in spring, they don't germinate and grow until fall. In a mild climate you can grow it all winter, cutting it repeatedly and having it regrow, for winter salads. It needs some winter protection in chilly Maine. It is not fussy about soil fertility or pH, but in the wild it chooses soil on the sandy side, often on the banks of a stream, in dappled shade, at the edge of the woods. If your soil is heavy, lighten it first with plenty of organic matter before planting.

As the days warm and lengthen in spring, and those brown capsules burst and scatter seeds in defiance of a garden's tidy rows, claytonia may become a permanent feature there. This is not a bad thing. It is easy to pull out—but you may not want to. It's not surprising that miners took claytonia with them when they went to seek gold in Australia, and why European travelers to the New World brought it back home with them. It is a weed that pays its way.

CHAPTER 19

Hearty Greens

Somewhere in the human organism, I am sure, is an ability to recognize food that is healthful and nourishing. Over the centuries we have been drawn to plants of power—those with dark green foliage bespeaking chlorophyll, carotene, folate, and other important nutrients. Noticing that some plants produced ill effects when eaten, we paid attention to certain strong flavors that signaled better outcomes: growth, good digestion, and general well-being. We must have learned to pair them with other foods, such as the fats that permit fat-soluble vitamins and phytonutrients to do their work. Otherwise, we would not still be here. We did not evolve on spinach alone. We also discovered butter.

These are the kind of foods I think about when I'm going into winter. When I say they are hearty, I mean that they are particularly nutritious and fortifying. They will keep you "hale and hearty" if you make them part of your diet. This is not the same thing as calling a plant "hardy," which botanically speaking means that it can withstand a certain level of cold and/or freezing. A lot of hearty plants are cold hardy as well, but I'm also talking about a certain kind of structural integrity. What happens when you turn on the stove and boil, steam, bake, roast, or sauté them in a pan or pot? Unlike the tender salads of spring, these plants, when cooked, are firm enough that they don't entirely wilt, melt, and almost disappear.

Spinach at Its Best

One of the most famous cartoons ever to run in *The New Yorker* magazine showed a small girl being told by her mother that the green thing on her plate was broccoli. "I say it's spinach and I say the hell with it," said the girl. Irving Berlin turned it into a song.

Ever the butt of jokes, it took the support of yet another cartoon figure, Popeye, to earn spinach even a small measure of respect. Why? It's full of folate and bursting with fiber. You can cream it, steam it, make a quiche with it—even a salad. What's the problem?

Here it is. There is good spinach, well-grown, and there is its evil twin—bitter, strong-tasting spinach, grown in soil with a poor nitrogen/calcium balance. Good spinach is both mellow and sprightly at the same time.

You can tell a lot about a spinach crop just by looking at it. In poor soil with too little fertility, it is pale in color, with poor growth, and quick to go to seed. Look at the shape of its leaves as well: they are often pointed rather than round when under stress. But don't be tempted to overdose it with the almighty N. You'll produce leaves with a blue-green cast and little flavor. Avoid high-nitrogen fertilizers and fresh manure, especially if you are growing it in winter in a cold frame or greenhouse. Dried alfalfa meal, or a good, mature homemade compost that will release nitrogen more slowly and contribute its natural abundance of trace elements, is a better way to go.

For a good crop of fall spinach, choose a spot in the garden where you have grown and harvested a summer crop and prepare the bed with compost. The key to having good germination is to wait until cool weather is just starting to settle in, but there are still enough frost-free days to bring the spinach to a respectable size. Many spinach varieties are hardy to 15 degrees Fahrenheit and can be harvested all winter long, especially if protected by something easy to remove, such as the lid of a cold frame or a floating row cover.

You can almost tell the time of year by the way spinach tastes. Spring-sown spinach has a tender freshness. In summer, spinach tastes all right only if you garden in a place with cool summers. Fall spinach is the best of all, sublimely sweet. At our place we leave it in the ground until spring, eating it all winter long. (At the farm we have a large unheated greenhouse full of spinach for winter harvest.) In spring it regrows rampantly when cut, but the sweetness is lost, and the flavor coarsens as it prepares to go to seed.

How you present spinach to a diner makes a difference too. If it is a dark, soggy wad, trailing long stems and looking like something that just washed up on the beach, only the polite will lift their forks. Removing big stems, then chopping the spinach, will produce a tidier mound. Boiling and draining it will remove some bitterness, but it will also send some of its nutrients down the drain, so it's better to start out with mild leaves in the first place. I prefer to sauté it just enough to barely wilt it in a large pan with a little olive oil, a bit of garlic, and just a flick of water from my fingertips. As I stir it gently with tongs, the moisture evaporates and doesn't collect in the pan. The leaves stay bright green.

A word about raw spinach. I like to eat it raw only when the leaves are small and tender. I admit that big-leaved spinach is excellent for holding a robust salad dressing such as honey-mustard or duck fat and cheese, and, conveniently, it doesn't wilt in the bowl. But I say big-leaved raw spinach leaves is tough, and I say the hell with it.

Spinach at tender, baby-leaf size

Brassicas in Bloom

Call it an odd blend of sex and religion, but some of the plants in our garden make the sign of the cross when they flower.

Botanical taxonomists often organize plant families according to the shape of their flowers, and the vegetables in the brassica family (Brassicaceae) are a good example. Their alternate name, crucifer (Cruciferae),

Above: This kale was allowed to go to flower in order to save some of its seed.

Above right: Flowers from a kale called Wintersweet; gentle cooking will let them retain their golden color.

which means "cross-bearing," comes from their cross-shaped blossoms, made up of four symmetrical petals. They include cabbage, kale, collards, broccoli, Brussels sprouts, cauliflower, kohlrabi, Chinese cabbage, mustard, rutabagas, turnips, radishes, arugula, and cress—all descended, amazingly, from a single wild species from the coasts of northwestern Europe. All share a great love of the rich, well-fed soil of home gardens.

Gardeners are not exactly reverent when these flowers appear, because it means that the plants are getting down to the serious job of reproduction. For us, the flowering usually signals a decline in the plants' usefulness. This doesn't happen very often, though, because most of the brassicas we grow are biennials and will therefore not bolt (make flowers) until their second year. So only if a cabbage or kale plant has made it through the winter would it flower, and by then it would normally have been picked and eaten.

An important exception to this pattern is broccoli, which triumphantly sends up masses of yellow flowers the first year unless you snip any stems that are about to form them. This means harvesting the large central head and the side shoots that follow it, even if you don't need that much broccoli for the table. If you don't, bolting will begin, and the production of new shoots will decline. So when flowers appear, they signal that the gardener is a sloven who can't keep up with her picking. At least that's the common perception. But the longer I grow brassicas, the more I seem to adjust my picture of them and expect the unusual from them.

For the bees in my garden (and other pollinators) the bolting of a brassica is a great moment. Those masses of flowers are gold to them. They are wedded to this flower form by millennia of co-evolution, so that by burrowing into the blossoms' reproductive centers they can nourish themselves and their hives with nectar and pollen, and while doing so, fertilize the flowers, and spread the plants' genetics around. That golden X marks the spot where they must land. Chances are that other plants are blooming in your yard at the same time, but crucifer blossoms are especially rich treasure, and the presence of bees will help ensure the pollination of many other crops besides these. If you have the space, leave some of them to keep on blooming. If there are wild mustards blooming in your yard, allow some of them to flourish as well.

An unexpected event early in the summer of 2011 turned my mind even further in this direction. For some time, our farm had been growing Asian greens. In the winter of 1997, we planted a whole 50-by-30-foot greenhouse in a wide range of them to see which would be worthwhile for us to grow. At that point in time, I knew more people who had gone to China than had grown Chinese cabbage. So we were delighted to discover something as beautiful as Tokyo Bekana, a Chinese cabbage of the open-headed or loose-leaf type, with bright yellow-green leaves. We fell in love with bok choy (also spelled pac choi), which looks a bit like Swiss chard but is bulbous at the base, with very large, tender white or green ribs. Favorite varieties proved to be Mei Qing Choi (whose name, I have been told, means "beautiful green vegetable"), the dramatic maroon-and-white Red Choi, and especially Joi Choi, whose snow-white ribs are wonderful in stir-fries at the mature stage. The most winter-hardy favorite of those we trialed was tatsoi, which starts growing upward, then spreads out to form a large flat rosette, with little spoon-shaped leaves

This Asian gem, Happy Rich, has sweet, tender stems and edible white flowers.

and a deep green color. We put together a winter salad mix of these Asian greens, but all its components could be stir-fried or dropped into soups as well.

But the brassica flower revelation of 2011 occurred in a section of our home garden where I often have trial beds for testing which unfamiliar plants might be worth growing and which ones (such as a prickly thing called saltwort) are not. I had been looking for an alternative to the newly popular broccoli rabe, a broccoli-like plant that doesn't form big heads but just handy, small shoots. I loved its "sprouting broccoli" growth habit, but no amount of good olive oil and garlic could make up for the flavor, which was simply too bitter for my taste. One could buy something called Broccolini, a trademarked green sold in produce markets that is a cross between broccoli and a leafier Asian version called gai lan, but seeds were not available.

So I grew a variety called Happy Rich, also a broccoli/gai lan cross, but one for which I could purchase seeds (from Johnny's Selected Seeds) and soon I had a bed of towering plants, like stately candelabras, somewhat blue-green and covered with small, tasty shoots. As with any broccoli,

I picked regularly to keep flowers from forming, but many did, and they were not yellow, but white. The whole plant was deliciously sweet and tender—stems, leaves, buds, flowers and all. We had long ago discovered that broccoli leaves were as tasty and edible (we learned this from our chickens, who spurned the heads). And the flowers of this new variety, unlike those of regular broccoli, didn't turn brown when cooked.

When I typed "Happy Rich" into my search engine, all I got was endless articles about how wealth will never bring us happiness. But this vegetable did. Eliot and I have been growing Happy Rich to the point where it has almost replaced broccoli in our home garden.

In my years of growing regular broccoli, I have always preferred the side-shoot stage that follows the cutting of the big central head, because, with their narrow, tender stems, the shoots are more uniform. They require less trimming, and they also cook more uniformly, so that by the time the stems are tender, the buds have not turned to mush.

If you still prefer to grow the classic broccoli, I suggest you try a variety we first encountered in 2006 called Piracicaba, from Fedco Seeds. "So good you can eat it raw," the catalog proclaimed. Bred to be unusually heat tolerant, it forms healthy vase-shaped plants with a small central head and numerous side shoots, whose buds are open arrangements of little round green balls. These sprigs cook quickly and evenly, and are delicious, but they are also, just as advertised, fine uncooked. In fact, one of the plant's best features is the way you can swipe a brushlike sprig of Piracicaba through a bowl of dip. It sure beats stabbing the dip with a hard stump of ordinary broc. A few flowers do appear if we are not paying attention, but on the whole our Piracicaba patch at the farm seems to be very well cut—grazed, even. I suppose it could be the deer. But at this point everyone is a suspect.

Nothing Boring about Cabbage

It's easy to take for granted, but cabbage is a remarkable plant. Just a hard round ball, more good for you than glamorous. More survival food than

From left to right, these are red cabbage, a pointed variety named Carex, and a Savoy.

epicurean treat. But what other green vegetable keeps all winter in a cold cellar? What crop is equally resistant to both heat and cold?

If you want to dress cabbage up a bit, steam it lightly and then drizzle it with butter, browned in a small pan with caraway seeds. If you grow the red kind, try cooking it in a little beef broth, with sour cream stirred in at the end. Or make it into borscht, with baked beets, onions, and small chunks of beef. Or bacon. Or both. And again, sour cream.

I often wonder why more Americans don't grow the Savoy type of cabbage. It doesn't keep as long, but the head is a green, loosely packed delight. Its chief feature is its crinkled texture, seemingly designed to hold butter more luxuriously. Its name comes from the popularity of crinkled cabbage in the French Alpine region of Savoie, from which it has spread far and wide—just not here. Its name has even been lent to a common vegetable characteristic. A crinkled spinach, kale, or lettuce leaf is "savoyed"—in case you've never figured out what that means.

If you want to vary your cabbage repertoire a bit more, grow some Chinese cabbage: the barrel-shaped Napa kind that slices so nicely crosswise with a bread knife for a sauté or a salad. After that, get ready for an even better cabbage adventure—in Portugal.

Everywhere in the world there is a local soup, one that begins with the region's particular soil and the crops that have adapted to it over the years. The soup may vary from province to province, village to village, and even from family to family, but within a single kitchen it stays the same. You make it the way your mother did. Don't ask for it without onions, just eat your soup.

Caldo verde translates as "green broth." A winter staple, it has been called the Portuguese national dish, even though it lacks the seafood so characteristic of that country's cuisine. The hot broth is thickened with potatoes, often mashed. Onions often figure in, as well as olive oil, drizzled on top. Coriander appears in some versions, as does linguiça—a delicious fat sausage inflamed by paprika and garlic. The fatter chouriço sausage, or slices of smoked pork loin called salpicão, may also be used. But the most important thing is a particularly Portuguese cabbage called couve tronchuda. Other names include sea-kale cabbage, Galician cabbage, Portuguese kale, and Braganza cabbage.

What traits lead a plant to become a local staple in a field as crowded as the brassicas? Among all the primitive landraces of cabbage-like, kale-like, collard-like greens, what caused this one to be singled out?

The couve tronchuda I have grown is sweeter and more tender than most cabbages and kales. It looks somewhat like collards, its large, rounded leaves sprouting in a bunch atop a short, thick stem. But the color is a fresher green, and it has thick, fleshy white ribs that are more tender than kale ribs, and can be used as a vegetable in their own right or chopped up and simmered in the soup.

It is easy to grow, and more easily adapted to warm climates than most other brassicas. Transplants can be set out after danger of frost has passed, two to three feet apart in the row, as it actually may form a rosette that large. Since it is a loose-leaf cabbage, you never have to worry about whether it will properly head up and form a ball. As with many leafy brassicas, the more the outside leaves are picked, the more the inside ones will sprout from the center. As you near the heart, those become paler and milder, with a frillier shape.

Transplants set out in late summer will carry you into fall, and even beyond if your winter is mild. The plant will not hold up under a hard freeze, but a sumptuous, soupy bowl of it will certainly be welcome as the weather turns crisp, and stirring a soup seems like just the right thing to do.

Kale Rising

There's nothing dainty about kale. As autumn's chill settles over the garden, crumpling the squash vines, kale marches on. The cold improves everything about it—its pest resistance, its color, the sweetness that counterbalances its cabbagey flavor.

Originally an ancient Mediterranean crop, grown by the Romans, kale spread throughout much of the world. The more rugged regions welcomed its vigor, ease of cultivation, and health virtues. Long before people began discussing fiber, minerals, beta-carotene, vitamin C, and cancer-fighting organosulfur compounds, they recognized a plant of substance that could keep them strong, even if all they had was kale, oats, and the family cow.

No folk are more associated with kale than the Scots. In their dialect a kailyard is synonymous with a kitchen garden. "Kail" might denote the vegetable itself, a soup, or even dinner. There was even a Kailyard school of Scottish authors in the late nineteenth century (including J. M. Barrie, the author of *Peter Pan*), who wrote nostalgically about the bucolic past.

Ach, what would they say if they could see the ornamental kales now displayed in garden centers, the green leaves encircling frilly white or rose centers? Technically these are edible, but even modern diners find them inferior as food.

Fortunately for the gardener-cook, there are excellent kale varieties from which to choose, many of which still bear the stamp of the Old World. (Kale is essentially a primitive cabbage, more typical of the brassicas grown before head cabbage was developed.) Many of their names signal their northern provenance, such as Dwarf Blue Curled Scotch, whose flattened rosettes hug the ground for easy overwintering, or the dauntless Dwarf Siberian. This one has flat, jagged-edged blue foliage with red ribs. It has a softer leaf, not quite as resistant to cold. For severe winters, choose a superhardy one such as Winterbor or its cousin Redbor, which turns a deep purple as cold weather advances. Kale will eventually succumb to ice and snow, but I find I can pick a lot of it before that happens, and stuff a big black trash bag full of it, put it in a cold room, and eat it for at least several more weeks.

Though not a southern crop, kale does fine in moderate climates as well. Many southerners grow collard greens instead, a close cousin to kale. We have found Blue Max the hardiest collard variety. But the kale varieties with "Vates" in their names, such as Dwarf Blue Curled Vates, were developed in Virginia. (The word Vates is an acronym for Virginia Truck Experiment Station.) And my absolute favorite kale is an Italian heirloom, variously called Tuscan kale, lacinato kale, dinosaur kale, and cavolo nero. It is a gorgeous plant with narrow, dark blue-green leaves that are pebble-textured and curl under at the sides. It has a particularly fine flavor and texture when cooked. Whenever a dish I've made looks a little pallid, like a bowl of buttered cabbage or an endive salad, I cut some Tuscan kale into very narrow ribbons, scatter them over the top, and immediately the dish seems healthier and more interesting.

Kale's recent fame as a superfood may not be enough to get your family to try it. But cooks have their ways. Most kale varieties have a large, firm central rib, which is best discarded by folding the leaf and ripping the stem and rib away. Fussy eaters may approach kale if it is sautéed with bacon, or with oil and garlic. Try baking it, generously topped with cheddar cheese. Add it to mashed potatoes, milk, and butter, and you've made colcannon, an Irish classic (rumbledethumps in Scotland). Or chop it and drop it into a soup: How better to add a hearty green to a meal than teaming it up with potatoes, dried beans, barley, carrots, turnips, and sausages? Or, if they're handy, oats and an ox head to cook up a fine Scots broth, seasoned with a bit of auld lang syne.

If your household still rejects kale, try steaming it along with sliced onions. This is my magic trick for any strong-flavored hearty green—using cooked onions as a sweetener.

Before the 1990s, kale was hardly a mainstay of the American diet. Then, suddenly, it was the new spinach, with a deserved reputation as a health food. Well into the new century, it is still a part of our vocabularies, our smoothies, and even our salads, but the spotlight has moved on. By 2015 a young friend, always up to date about food, said to me, "Kale is kind of over, though the name is still powerful." She paused. "Cauliflower is having a moment."

It's easy to chuckle about food trends but, even as one passes, it leaves us with knowledge and appreciation that will stay with us. Personally, I think kale mania took a big hit when people swore it should be massaged by hand with salt and oil, as if it were a Kobe steer, to tenderize it enough for salads. If you have ever performed this messy task, you might agree.

What has become the new kale? Cauliflower? Kohlrabi? Kelp? I don't know, but I am reminded of a strange tidbit from Florence Marian McNeill in her 1929 book *The Scots Kitchen*: "The vogue of kail … was originally confined to the Lowlands. The Highlander preferred the common nettle in his broth and appears to have regarded the use of kail as a symptom of effeminacy." Was kale a "vogue" of Lowland Scots in 1929? And nettle-eating a sign of virility?

Funny, but recently there has been a lot of talk about the common nettle (also called stinging nettle), once the scourge of every farmer. Abandoned, a farm will "go to nettles," since, once it appears, it is soon everywhere, inflicting a burning pain to every ungloved hand that tries to pull it out. Now, suddenly, it's the superfood of the hour, touted as a treatment for any number of ills, from allergies to arthritis. If you see a bit of it here at the farm you are welcome to come and take it away with you. Please.

Far from Brussels, Tiny Cabbages Sprout

Not every country has its own personal cabbage, but Belgium does. The Brussels sprout, named for Belgium's largest city, is essentially a cabbage with a unique growth habit. Like a regular cabbage, it grows one stout stalk, but instead of forming one large head, it forms miniheads in every leaf axil—that is, the V formed between a leaf's stem and that main stalk. These are bunched tightly along the stalk, and when they are dense, firm balls they are ready to eat.

   Brussels sprout plants are champions of wintertime, often the last vegetables left standing in gardens. In our climate we can pick them up until Thanksgiving, and sometimes even Christmas, before the cold finally gets them and threatens to turn the little heads to mush. It isn't a simple matter of the lowest temperature they can endure, but rather the action of freezing and thawing, and bombardments of icicles and snow. They are not glamorous winter specimens like white-bark birches or red-berried hollies. They have tall gawky stems, from which long, somber green leaves droop down. But note the clever way that form follows function. The thick stem has stored the nutrients that make those wonderful little globes appear, and the leaves hang down like that to shelter the sprouts from the cold as they grow.

The point of growing Brussels sprouts under such dubious conditions is that they taste so much better in the cold. Like many brassicas, they are sweetened by it, and I have learned never to pick them until after the first frost. The red varieties such as Red Rubine are comparable in color to red cabbage and red-leaved kales. You can watch the deep, rich hue of the sprouts developing as cold sets in.

Ironically, Brussels sprouts first entered this country via French settlers in Louisiana's Mississippi River Delta but it's not always easy to grow them in regions with long, hot summers. (Most commercial production in the U.S. is in California.) The trick is to time planting them so that the sprouts will be forming in cool weather. The Southern Exposure Seed Exchange recommends starting them indoors in early June, mid-May in the north. You might have to experiment for a few seasons before you find the perfect timing for your area. The good part is that you can direct sow the seeds outdoors in temperatures up to 86 degrees Fahrenheit and they will germinate. To do this, give them a compost-rich soil and sow in clusters up to eighteen inches apart in the row, then thin to one strong seedling per cluster.

Harvesting them is easy. You kneel next to the plant and twist off the little green balls with an upward, snapping motion, starting with the large ones at the bottom of the stalk. Those are the first to firm up and the first to open up in loose clusters if neglected. Since they mature progressively, the ones farther up will continue to grow.

Picking becomes less fun when frigid winds are blowing, and the sprouts are too frozen to pluck. At that point, we break off the big leaves of any stalks with sprouts still on them, and fell them like little trees, using loppers or a hatchet. Then we bring them inside and store them whole in the root cellar or the spare fridge, pulling sprouts off as needed, until we've eaten them all. We've even sold them in markets as whole stalks, and people love them that way. But to do that, we have to top the plants when the lowest sprouts reach about ¾ inch in diameter, so that they all reach full size at the same time. It's best to do that if your goal is to have lots of them for freezing.

If you think you dislike Brussels sprouts, you probably have been served ones that are old or ruined by overcooking—mushy little wads with a rank smell. To prepare them properly, first slice off the bottom of each sprout so that any outer, battered leaves fall away and only nice ones are left. My mother taught me to cut an X in the base so that the solider portion will cook faster and be done at the same time as the leaves. Simmer or steam them gently, then plunge them in cold water to preserve the bright green color. They can then be reheated briefly with butter in a pan, maybe with some chestnuts, caramelized onions, or little cubes of pork belly as well.

Roasting them has become popular, but few cooks have a light enough touch with that. The word "blackened" on a menu might entice me to eat a Cajun redfish, but not a Brussels sprout. But I will try the recipe for Cream of Brussels Sprouts Soup (*Spruitjesroomsoep*) in Ruth Van Waerebeek's *Everybody Eats Well in Belgium Cookbook*. It's a hearty dish thickened with egg yolks and would go splendidly with a tall glass of dark Belgian beer.

For Glamour, Add Chard to Your Yard

In gardens, as in comic operas, there are occasional cases of twins separated at birth. Beets and chard, for example, are intrinsically the same plant. It's because of differences in their breeding and environments that they occupy separate produce bins—or garden rows—as unlike in appearance as carrots and fennel.

Over the centuries, breeders have selected the plants with the largest roots to develop the beet we know today. Chard breeders developed plants with thick, juicy stalks that continued into the leaf as broad ribs. As a result, chard plants have no enlarged roots, and beet greens lack the enlarged ribs (although their greens, like those of turnips, make a good healthy dish). From one vegetable, two different ones were created.

The brilliant colors of chard mixtures light up both garden and table.

A common origin is reflected in the British names for chard and beets, which are leaf beet and beetroot respectively. The word "chard" comes from *carde*, the French word for cardoon, a type of edible thistle related to the artichoke but bred to have thick edible stems. *Carde* became a blanket term for tasty stalks. (The French have been known to eat chard stems alone and feed the greens to ducks.) Our common name of Swiss chard is a mystery, since the Swiss did not embrace the vegetable any more than did the rest of Europe.

Like most Americans, I never got very excited about chard until I discovered its versatility in the kitchen. It made a decent side dish as long as the ribs were separated from the green part and given a bit more time to cook. Then I figured out how fantastic both were in stir-fries. When mature, the leaves hold their shape better than most stir-fried greens. And they are so easy to cut into ribbons for a soup. After that came the idea of blanching large leaves briefly and using them as a wrapper for a stuffing of rice, pork, ground lamb, or vegetables. The little packets are great alone— or baked and topped, Greek style, with a lemony sauce. Chard harvested at baby size is mild and tender, perfect for salad mixes. At our farm we started selling young chard as "butter chard," for its tender, buttery texture, and suddenly the name was on local restaurant menus.

Meanwhile, chard has made a comeback all on its own. I think the trend started when Rosalind Creasy, as a pioneer of edible landscaping, popularized the red-ribbed types. The late-day sun makes the scarlet ribs glow, and they taste great too.

Next the multicolored chards such as Bright Lights entered the ring like a string of circus ponies, with ribs in shades of red, pink, yellow, orange, and gold. Bright Lights was not a modern novelty but a collection of old strains, reselected and strengthened for greater dependability by breeder John Eaton in New Zealand and Johnny's Selected Seeds in Maine. There are also varieties with only yellow ribs. Mixtures are often referred to as rainbow chard.

For a more delicate leaf, some gourmets favor the Euro-style narrow-stemmed types like Perpetual Spinach and Erbette, both available from

The Cook's Garden. Personally, if I were to grow only one, it would be good old Fordhook, developed in the 1930s by Burpee. It's a foolproof plant, good at any stage from salad-leaf-petite to palm-frond-huge.

Lazy gardeners consider chard their one true friend. Plant it now, and you will harvest it for many months, as it is less apt to bolt than summer spinach or lettuce. Cold tolerant as well, your planting might remain useful well into fall and even winter, though, ideally, you'd make a second sowing in July for more vigor.

How closely you plant chard depends on its use. For cut-and-come-again salads you can sow thickly, thinning to two to four inches apart, in rows as close as six inches. For champion-sized plants, space them ten to twelve inches apart each way, picking the outer leaves of all the plants in the row to encourage new ones to sprout from the centers. Leaf miners may make their wandering tunnels in the leaves of early sowings; later plantings are immune. In wet weather, slugs will occasionally turn the leaves into Swiss cheese—a mere cosmetic problem. (Perhaps *that's* the Swiss connection.)

One year an entire row of chard wilted and died suddenly in our garden. On close inspection all the meaty parts of the roots had been devoured. The culprits were voles—small, fruit-eating rodents that often nibble leaves but prefer treats like strawberries or sweetroots. To a vole, a beet is a beet.

Sorrel: Born to Be Soup

Before the first daffodil, long before the first spear of asparagus, the sorrel was up in all its green glory. Not much was happening in my herb garden except for a scattering of bright blue chionodoxa and scilla—tiny spring bulbs that had spread by seed. Not even the chives were big enough to snip.

Sorrel is a salad green, but is more common in herb gardens, partly because of its pleasantly sharp lemon flavor and partly because, unlike most edible greens, it's a hardy perennial, inconvenient in a vegetable plot that has a crop rotation scheme. Gardeners grow several kinds.

Top: Traditional garden sorrel surrounded by small-leaved French sorrel

Bottom: Profusion sorrel, a patented variety, comes up along with the earliest spring bulbs.

There's French sorrel, with its little shield-shaped leaves, and common garden sorrel, whose leaves point upward like a quiver of arrows. Both are tender and zesty in salads, especially if you divide and replant them every spring to renew them. I also grow a variety called Profusion, which is the one that caught my eye on that particular day when I longed for a fresh spring taste.

Profusion is a patented variety, from Richters Herbs, which you must buy as a plant, since it is sterile and does not produce seeds. This trait prevents it from bolting, so you can keep picking its outer leaves while tender new ones form in the center. Mine has sat in the same spot for years. Its foliage is a bit coarse and I treat it as a plant to eat cooked, not raw.

Sorrel, oddly enough, is not common in American gardens. In France it is as popular as spinach, and in the days when Paris was ringed with market gardens it was grown in cold frames to meet the demand for a year-round supply. Its lemony tart flavor figures prominently in classic French recipes such as the creamy, egg yolk–enriched soup called *potage germiny*. It was also used traditionally to curdle milk when making certain types of cheese. Rich in vitamin C, it was an important weapon against scurvy in times when cold weather sources of C could not be found.

Sorrel and I go way back, partly because I can't resist a plant that takes care of itself. It is one of the few perennial vegetables, overwintering even in very cold climates. In hot, dry ones you must provide it with ample water, but otherwise it's foolproof, requiring only a reasonably fertile, slightly acid soil. It prefers full sun, but will do fine in part shade, especially in summer's heat. A friend who grows sorrel might give you a clump to get you started. Otherwise, direct sow it in midspring, thinning plants to a foot apart. Harvest it by cutting the large outer leaves to encourage the small inner ones to grow, and remove flower stalks to keep the plant from going to seed.

There's only one problem with sorrel. As soon as moist heat is applied, the leaves turn army green, an unappetizing shade verging too closely on brown. This color has never stopped people from cooking sorrel, though. Added to the drippings of a roasted chicken, it makes a flavorful gravy, born to be brownish in this particular role. But on one particular day, the planets aligned just right for the best sorrel soup to ever come out of my kitchen. First, there were the last leeks of winter, dug the week before and stored in the fridge. There was good homemade chicken stock in the freezer, along with a bit of leftover mashed potato—better than flour for thickening a soup. Finally, there was parsley, bunches of it that had wintered over and not yet gone to seed. One of parsley's best traits is that it keeps its bright green color when cooked, so in it went, simmering in the broth along with the leeks. I pureed the soup in a blender for a velvety texture, then beat an egg yolk in a little cream and stirred that in at the end. A dash of salt, a grinding of pepper, and it was perfect. The sorrel flavor was there, but the color was pea green, not khaki, a green true enough to usher in spring.

There is also a wild plant called sheep sorrel (*Rumex acetosella*), one of the most infuriating weeds ever to enter a garden. It forms tiny rosettes, which, though tasty, spread maniacally on yellow, threadlike roots. Mulching does not deter it: in fact, it loves mulch. The noted food forager Euell Gibbons stalked it happily in the wild for his salads, as may you, but don't plant it. It is probably in your garden anyway, having crossed the Big Pond several hundred years ago. Now if we could just get it to return.

CHAPTER 20

Peas and Beans

There's always been a bit of mystery about the legumes, a large family of plants that includes peas and beans. To some degree that's true of all Earth's life forms—how they started, and how they grow. Nevertheless, new revelations about plant life do come to light as science marches forward.

In the ancient world, for example, farmers discovered that a crop of peas or beans improved the yields of other plants that followed in the same spot. But it wasn't until the eighteenth century that people found out why. Like all members of the legume family, peas and beans form lumps called nodules on their roots that allow them to assimilate free nitrogen in the air, which is abundant but otherwise unavailable, and turn it into a form that plants can use for growth. These nodules spring to life because of a symbiotic partnership that legumes have with soil bacteria called rhizobia. These rhizobia feed off sugars produced by the plant in return for the gift of nitrogen availability. When parts of the legume— leaves, stems, roots, and the nodules themselves—are left in the soil, that gift is passed along to whatever grows there next.

This trick of "nitrogen fixation" allows legumes to do well in relatively poor soil. This fact led to a misconception about one group of leguminous plants, the lupines. Since these often grew and flowered in waste places, they were given a name derived from *lupus*, Latin for wolf, with the assumption that lupines robbed the soil and made it infertile. The opposite was true: The lupines enriched the soil just enough so that they could thrive.

Legumes range in size from trees, such as locust and acacia, to meadow plants such as clover and vetch. Many, especially alfalfa, are important as forage crops for livestock and as improvers of the soil. Others, including peas, beans, peanuts, and lentils, are of great importance in the human diet because they are high in protein, B vitamins, and fiber. Each legume has a particular rhizobium species with which it has evolved—a fava bean has one, a lima bean another. Growers will introduce these into the soil as purchased inoculants, but you can also just borrow a few shovelfuls of soil from a plot where the same crop you are about to plant has been growing and sprinkle it onto your new pea or bean patch. Or just go ahead and sow; the crop will do fine.

Gardeners sometimes assume that because of legumes' special potency they don't need fertile soil but, in fact, nodulization is a delicate dance between the two partners. The stress of being undernourished may trigger the bacteria's assistance of the plant, but the plant must be vigorous enough, with enough green foliage, to feed the bacteria in return. Factors such as cold, drought, and infertile or acidic soil can inhibit the exchange. Very fertile soil, on the other hand, can make the exchange unnecessary—it's a coping mechanism the plant only uses when it's needed. So you still owe your peas and beans a decent soil, with plenty of organic matter.

Legumes have so earned my respect that I sometimes welcome weedy perennial ones when they turn up in the yard or garden. I'll let the odd vetch plant wave its wands of purple blossoms, and I'll welcome patches of white clover in the lawn. Knowing that legumes have proved to be the benefactors of grasses, wouldn't the use of weed killers on a clover-rich lawn be a step backward in human enlightenment? The eighteenth-century agronomist John Christian Schubert was knighted by the Holy Roman emperor Joseph II for promoting clover in Austria. At the very least, the extraordinary legumes deserve our admiration.

Splendor in the Ground

It was the third weekend in September and, as always, I could be found at the Common Ground Fair in Unity, Maine, a magnificent yearly celebration of rural life. I cruised through the craft booths and tasted local treasures at the cheese tent. Then on to the barns to see lop-eared bunnies and outlandish breeds of chickens with topknots and feathery feet. At the vegetable displays my step slowed to an amble as I admired heirloom tomatoes and corn, then came to a stop at the dry beans. There I went into the trance of a kid in a candy store, a guy at a car show, or a more normal woman at Tiffany's.

The beans at the fair are arranged in tidy little piles. There are creamy white ones, big black shiny ones, and wildly different colors, from purple to rich caramel. It's as if artists around the state had each turned a bean into their own personal canvas. There are speckles, splashes, blotches, and swirls. Sometimes their names are descriptive, as with the black-and-white Penguin, or Tiger's Eye with its golden background and dark brown streaks. One white bean with a large dark chocolate spot is simply called Aunt Jean's.

The infinite variety of bean seed patterns is a wonder of the horticultural world.

Beans in seed catalogs are just as seductive. How can you resist one called Paint Dry or Scarlet Beauty? I tend to buy from companies such as Seed Savers Exchange that are active in preserving the genetic diversity of heirloom beans. The amazing thing about these beans, other than that they seem too beautiful to bury, is that they all tell a human story. Each has evolved over the centuries in partnership with a community of growers that kept planting them and replanting them in return for the sustenance they provided. Every place on Earth has its own bean: No wonder they all wear different faces. And because the beans you eat are the seeds you save to plant next year's crop, it's easy for you to perpetuate your own favorite bean varieties and let them acclimate to your weather and your soil—as long as they are open-pollinated varieties that grow true to seed.

Moving through the fair's crowds one year, I came upon several bushel baskets at the Fedco Seed stand half full of dry beans marked "Bean seeds for children to play with." A small boy was sitting in one of the baskets while his sister sprinkled beans over his head. After that she started choosing beans by color and arranging them in patterns on a nearby chair.

For a gardener, growing dry beans for winter eating, and saving them from year to year, is so simple that you might honestly call it child's play. The beans do the thinking for you. Unlike the beans of summer that require a regular picking, beans for winter eating are just left on the vine until the pods turn tan and crisp, and the seeds inside mature to their final coloration. You do need to check the pods and catch them before they split open and scatter their precious contents on the ground. If the weather's wet enough to make the pods turn moldy, or if frost threatens before all the beans are ripe, you'll need to bring them indoors and let them finish drying there. Just cut the vines at ground level, tie them together in bunches, and hang them upside down in a shed or other dry spot, with a sheet below to catch any that fall. Or just lay them on a sheet to begin with.

To empty the pods, put the whole business in an old pillowcase, tie it shut, and beat it against a hard surface so that the beans fall to the bottom. It's also fun to stomp on a pillowcase with your feet or rattle it against the inside walls of a metal garbage can. After sorting out the beans that fall to the bottom, you can clean them of any remaining chaff by pouring them from one bowl to another on a windy day, or in front of a fan. Store them in tightly closed jars after they are completely dry and can no longer be dented with your fingernail. Line up your bean jars in a place that's out of the sun but enough in view that you can admire them every time you walk by.

If you have a small garden and wish you could grow lots of different beans, start a bean club. Give each of your friends a different packet to grow, then you can all meet later and divide up the harvest. Convince them with cassoulet and minestrone. Show them your jars. Then take them to the fair.

Life Stages of Bean Cuisine

The beans were coming in fast and it was hard to keep up with the picking. Granted, I'd stacked the deck in my favor by planting a most forgiving bean, an heirloom called Garden of Eden that Eliot and I came upon in the Johnny's Selected Seeds trial beds. Not to be confused with the Lazy Wife bean, named for the ease with which you can open the pods, this one might be dubbed Overextended Gardener, because, conveniently, the whole pod is good to eat at any stage, from small and flat to big and lumpy.

There are four phases in a bean's useful life. During the first, they are young and slender, the way they are often served in France. These skinny beans are not a different species or variety (although some have been selected for good flavor at a tender age). They eventually grow fat as the seeds form and the pods develop a tough string along one side. That string is useful if you want to zip open an older bean's pod to remove the seeds but is not pleasant to eat.

Nowadays you can avoid the unwelcome strings by growing stringless varieties, which brings us to the second life stage in which they were formerly called "string beans." Now, "snap beans" is preferred. They are still

Annelino beans are fun to grow.

young, the width of a pencil, with the seeds too small to be felt but the tender pods firm enough to briskly break in two. Most of our old favorite "green bean" varieties, such as Kentucky Wonder, fall into this category. I've also enjoyed growing certain Italian ones, such as the Romano, which has large, flat pods and are wonderful at this stage and even a little beyond. (I suspect Garden of Eden is one of these, and that others of that type will behave like it.) I also like the curly "anellino" beans sold by the Italian company Franchi Seeds, available in the U.S. via Seeds from Italy. I like to grow three at once: Two bush beans—Yellow Anellino and the green Anellino Verde plus the pole bean Anellino di Trento, which is green, marbled with purple streaks. They're gorgeous mixed together, but since the purple disappears with cooking, I serve the three raw, surrounding an aioli dip or garlicky vinaigrette. For this they must be tender—not so young that the flavor is undeveloped, but young enough that the toxins contained in mature bean seeds are absent. It's important not to eat any bean seeds raw if they are past the snap bean stage.

When you can feel the seeds in their pods, your beans are at the third stage, the shell bean stage, a brief moment in time when the pods of most varieties have lost their succulence, but their seeds are tender enough to be pierced with your fingernail. Sometimes called "shelly beans," these are wonderful for cooking, especially with sweet corn in a summer succotash. It's a moment that many people never experience unless they grow their own, since the shell beans in most stores are limited to frozen limas. Fresh or frozen, shell beans take only about twenty minutes to cook. Among the most popular traditional shell bean varieties are purple-streaked ones such as Rattlesnake and Vermont Cranberry, because their pods are especially easy to open for shelling. But don't overlook the great old kidney beans (so good in chili), white cannellini beans from Italy (perfect with garlic), and creamy, pale green flageolets from France (best paired with lamb).

After that stage there's the final and fourth one: dry beans, a mighty staple for the larder. Because they keep well for up to a year, they're a great survival food—filling and rich in protein. They usually need at least an hour of cooking to be tender. But they are not immortal. Keep them much more than a year and they'll take progressively longer to simmer to softness until they are finally uncookable, a stage at which I considered them has-beans.

Managing Beans

If pole beans are allowed to get into trouble, they will. Early on, they are like a "good" baby that sleeps through the night. Since they are a warm weather crop, you wait until there is no danger of frost, then poke the conveniently fat seeds into fertile soil rich in organic matter, letting the warmth and moisture of late spring nudge forth the big, healthy-looking shoots.

Most of the beans Eliot and I grow are the vining type, and vines by their nature lift themselves up into the sunlight by twining around or clinging to more stout-stemmed specimens such as trees. With nothing to climb, but plenty of sun, they will happily crawl around your garden, producing pods, ensnaring other crops, and wrapping themselves around any trowel, watering can, or glove left in their path. So up they must go, under your strict command.

There is a number of clever ways to support beans, but you must still be on guard. I've grown them successfully on a lattice deer fence, but they overwhelmed some nearby sunflowers. I once tried the ancient "three sisters" approach, where beans were allowed to climb cornstalks, with a weed-smothering mulch of horizontal-growing winter squash vines covering the ground below. But my beans were clearly not the Genuine Cornfield Pole Snap Bean variety, designed to climb gently up cornstalks, which themselves must have been more robust than mine. The entire corn planting fell to the ground.

I have often built teepees of three or four bamboo poles tied very firmly together at the top, letting two or three vines grow up each pole. That works quite well, distributing the weight of the vines in such a way that it is harder for a strong wind to blow the structure down. I find that a row of simple beanpoles works too, as long as the poles are very stout ones, buried eighteen inches in the ground and separated thirty to thirty-six inches apart. Each will support three vines at this distance without them getting together and forming a wall. Don't make them any taller than you can reach to pick. I prefer saplings cut from the woods for this purpose, trimmed to leave an inch or so of the cut branches. These form hooks for the vines to catch on, rather than slide down the poles when heavy with foliage and pods.

You can also, of course, plant bush beans, the type the Omaha tribe called "beans-not-walking." Unlike pole beans (which the Italians call *rampicante*), bush beans grow a couple of feet at most, then form a terminal cluster of pods. Because pole beans form pods all along the stems as they elongate, stretching out the harvest until frost, they give you a steady supply of beans throughout the season, as long as you keep picking them. With the bush type, you get one big harvest all at once—which is great if you want to freeze them for winter use, or put them up in jars as dilly beans, with vinegar, water, garlic, mustard seed, hot pepper, and dill. The only thing that can run away from you is the sudden abundance of your crop. Ignore the plants for a busy week or two and you might find the seeds swelling in their pods. At that point you might freeze the seeds as shelly beans instead.

Bean on the Run

If there was a prize for the most versatile legume, it might well be the scarlet runner bean. Best known as a children's plant, it's the perfect cover for a teepee hideout of your own creation. The seeds are easy for a small gardener to plant, and fast-growing, so by midsummer a tent of dark green vines has magically appeared, adorned with bright red flowers.

Because of its beauty, the plant has caught on in the adult world too. It makes a stunning screen for privacy, for camouflage, or as a leafy ceiling over a patio or deck. It gratifies almost instantly, while you wait out the three years it takes for your clematis to ascend, or five for your climbing

hydrangea. It doesn't close its blooms on cloudy days the way morning glories do.

If you don't find this bean in the "vegetable," "flower," or "ornamental vine" section of a seed catalog, check under "hummingbird plants." It's sure to attract these hovering bits of living jewelry, drawn to the red blossoms. Hummingbirds, along with bees and hummingbird moths (insects often mistaken for hummingbirds), are important pollinators of this and other runner beans, which, unlike most garden beans, are not self-pollinating.

Most American gardeners don't realize that runner beans are edible, even though they are culinary favorites abroad. The 1969 *Oxford Book of Food Plants* described the runner as "by far the most popular green bean in Britain." They can be eaten at any stage. Though the pods are green, I was enchanted to find the seeds of my scarlet runners a brilliant pink, turning purplish-black streaked with magenta as they matured—a display that, alas, fades with cooking. They were fine as a baked bean or soup bean cooked with bacon, but the best surprise were the red flowers as an edible garnish in salads. If you can imagine a flower tasting slightly beanish, these do. It's possible that you already have some growing for your kids, your hummingbirds, or yourself, and while you might not have planned it this way, the kitchen awaits them.

Choose a Pea, or Grow All Three

Peas are not for the absent-minded gardener. Into the ground the seeds must go, as soon as the soil has lost its winter sogginess, so they can make their growth during cool spring weather. Hot weather is the enemy of a good pea. If you miss the boat of early spring, they will survive, but struggle. It's tricky. Preparing a bed when the spring soil is wet will compact it and ruin its structure. Eliot and I find it pays to ready the pea patch in fall, so that it's set to go in spring, applying lots of manure or other organic matter, raking it in a little, and firming the soil lightly with the back of a rake. We might even make a shallow furrow so that we can just drop in and cover the seeds when the right time comes.

As climbers, peas need a structure to support them. Even the shorter bush types benefit from being kept upright, clean, visible, and easy to pick. We have used nylon or plastic netting supported by metal poles, but any mesh—or even leafless birch branches stuck in the ground—will do. The peas will need an inch of water per week to keep growing.

The second boat you must not miss is harvest time. With many crops you can be a little casual, picking a few outer leaves of a kale plant, pulling off a stalk of celery, and even raiding a hill of potatoes for new little spuds. Fruiting crops, on the other hand, have a time window—a month for an apple, a week for a tomato, and a blink of the eye for a pea. As with vining beans, the more pods you pick, the more will follow. And since you have a choice of several types of peas to grow, you'll need to recognize exactly when the pods of your chosen one reach their perfect moment.

The classic green pea (often called English pea or garden pea) is picked when the seeds have fully formed inside the pod, which happens twenty to thirty days after flowering. Look closely at a pod with its inner seam facing you and you'll come to know just how fat and rounded it must appear before the peas inside are full grown but still tender. This stage lasts, at most, two days before they toughen and lose their sweetness. You can confirm it by tasting, but the eyes and fingers tell a quick tale. If a pod feels rough and is no longer a shiny, bright green, it's past its prime and should be picked and discarded so that production does not stop. Fortunately, not all the peas in the row will ripen at the same time, and you can stretch the harvest for several weeks as long as you keep picking, preferably every day. They're best eaten right away but will keep their sweetness in the fridge for a few days. For me, the first sign that the peas are ready is empty pods in the path, where Eliot has grazed on them and kept the matter a little quiet.

For the Asian peas called snow peas, you do not let the seeds get round. The pods are edible, but only when very flat, so that you only feel the slightest bump of seeds inside. These are great in stir-fries or raw in salads, and if you've ever bought them at a store and found them limp and tasteless, you'll see how much better they are when freshly picked.

The snap pea is a more modern addition that was created by crossing the other two. Known as sugar snaps (the name of the seminal variety), they're eaten pod and all, even after the seeds have swelled. Busy cooks love them because they don't need shelling, and everybody loves their

These spring-planted peas benefit from a hay mulch.

juicy, sweet crunch. A simple bowl of them set on a table is a celebration. But when it comes to picking, they wait for no one.

Encore with Fall Peas

Fall brings temperatures cool enough for peas but, as in spring, timing is important. You'll need to start them anywhere from mid-July to early September, depending on how late the first frost is expected in your zone or microclimate, and how many days to harvest are noted for any given variety. The vines might tolerate a few below-freezing nights, but the blossoms and pods will not. And sowing in summer's heat is a challenge too.

Give it a try. Lots of empty spaces appear in the garden in late summer. Spreading some hay or newspaper on one of them will make the soil cooler and moister for sowing peas. After fall arrives, we start the seeds indoors. They germinate happily in our soil blocks, but you can use plug trays, or any little plastic six-packs left over from spring-purchased annuals. Look for quick-growing, heat-resistant pea varieties.

As days grow cooler and shorter, growth will slow down a bit. If frost threatens, drape some floating row cover on your pea trellis to form a tent. Dwarf, ground-hugging vines will be less exposed to the cold, but these too might need a cover on cold nights if you're racing with frost. I find a lightweight blanket works fine, as long as I remember to remove it promptly in the morning.

CHAPTER 21

Earth Vegetables

L et's call them that because the name "root vegetable" doesn't always quite fit. A potato, technically, is a tuber—that is, an enlarged underground stem. A kohlrabi, on the other hand, is an enlarged stem that sits just above ground level. Beets, carrots, parsnips, turnips, and rutabagas are all true roots, of a type called a taproot. And a celery root is actually a swollen hypocotyl, the embryonic stem that first lifts a plant upward. What's important about this motley clan of food storage organs is that they make great winter fare.

All of them grow either in or within close contact with the soil and are comfortable there. So when fall comes and you're wondering when to harvest them, think about how long you can keep them exactly where they are. The approach of winter brings out the best in these vegetables, and their flavor will only improve while they're sitting in the garden. Parsnips don't need to budge and can be harvested in spring. Most of the others will keep all winter in the ground in a climate where freezing is not severe. But otherwise, you must look for a cold, dark, freezeproof place to keep them, where you can splash water around from time to time to keep the air moist. In other words, just like the ground.

Potatoes: Buried Treasure

"This is called deadly nightshade," my father announced, pointing to a trailing vine with small purple flowers. My sisters and I were thrilled to have a death-causing plant in our humble yard. Later, it proved to be the less lethal bittersweet nightshade, but no matter. He could have also caught our attention in the vegetable patch, where we would find the foliage of the common potato. The tubers are the only parts of a potato plant that do not contain toxic levels of poisonous alkaloids and even they are off limits if green-tinged or spoiled. Eating raw potatoes, though less dangerous, can give you indigestion, and a prudent cook removes any sprouts that form and may even gouge out the "eyes" from which they grow.

Poison runs in the family. Known scientifically as the Solanaceae, plants in the potato family are famous for containing those powerful alkaloids. Some of them are used as deadly weapons, others as life-saving drugs. One family member, in the hallucinogenic *Datura* genus, is the common and dangerous jimsonweed. Henbane, mandrake, and the true deadly nightshade (*Atropa belladonna*) have similar profiles. The petunia is a relative too (not a flower to use as an edible garnish, perhaps), as is tobacco, which boasts a strong toxic alkaloid called nicotine, which people alternately spray on garden plants to kill insects and inhale into their lungs.

Historically, though, the potato is far better known as an important survival food that has seen humankind through times of war and famine—and, of course, as a source of Russian vodka, German schnapps, and Irish poteen.

And yet, how many home gardeners grow a crop that is so humble, lumpy, and cheap to buy at the store? There is an old saying, "It's time to plant potatoes when the grass starts to grow." But when the grass starts to grow, most people go out and mow their lawn.

The answer is that unless you have ever reached into the soft earth of the potato bed and stolen a few of the first little tubers to form, you have no idea how delicious these early treasures are. As soon as you see purple, pink, or white flowers on your potato plants, it's time to turn on the stove,

get out the butter, and celebrate one of the "firsts" of the season, every bit as good as that first tomato, first pod of peas, and first ear of corn.

The most important thing I ever learned about potatoes is that they need ample water. Never mind that their fleshy leaves show little sign of wilt in dry weather, a potato plant stressed by drought will consume itself, drawing moisture from some of the tubers already formed, so that fewer of them swell to a good size by harvest time. Not only that, the plant will be less able to fend off the pests and diseases to which potatoes are prone.

To be sure, rotating potatoes' growing spot will help forestall many problems, and so will giving them a fertile soil, rich in organic matter. They like slightly acidic conditions, so adding lime is not advised, and, as usual, a fertile soil will take care of most pH issues. The real key is consistent water. In a muddy, mosquito-ridden year in which it rained all summer, we had the most perfect potatoes ever, and any Colorado potato beetle that showed up must have crawled clear back to Colorado.

This might seem surprising when you consider that Peru, the potato's chief country of origin, is a relatively dry country. But the Andean heights, where thousands of potato varieties were born, have a long rainy season. Alas, both this botanical richness and the rains that nurtured it

It's easy to pull up a hill of potatoes when your soil is loose and crumbly.

are threatened, the former by the rise of global agriculture and the latter by global warming. But here is a hopeful fact: according to the Food and Agriculture Organization of the United Nations, a potato yields more food per unit of water used in growing it than any other major crop—as well as twice the protein of both wheat and corn, and four times the calcium of rice. So despite its water needs, the potato is a relatively sustainable crop. Clearly, when the conquistador Pizarro sailed to Peru in 1531, he was after the wrong kind of buried gold.

To grow potatoes, buy new seed from a grower of certified disease-free stock. By "seed" I mean small potatoes you bury in the ground, from which potato plants will grow. In future years you will have seed potatoes you have saved from your own harvest. Currently our favorite varieties, both for the farm and for the home garden, are Rose Gold, for the early "new potato" planting, and Charlotte, for the storage crop, both available from Wood Prairie Farm in Bridgewater, Maine.

Our potatoes go in two weeks before the last frost date, and before doing this we sprout them, a time-honored practice known as "chitting." This gives them a head start and results in a better harvest. We spread out the seed potatoes in a pan, in a single layer, in a spot with good air circulation and bright, but diffused, lighting. A temperature of 70 degrees Fahrenheit seems to encourage the growth of multiple shoots, which is what you want if your goal is to have lots of small early potatoes rather than the large late ones that you'll get from a fall storage crop. Notice that a potato's eyes are more or less clustered at one end, called the crown. Set the potatoes on the pan with the crowns pointing up and spray water on them daily. Chitting not only gives you an earlier crop, it also allows you to throw out any that don't sprout, so that there will be no gaps in the row.

We plant the potatoes whole, a foot apart and about three inches deep. (You can also cut a seed potato into pieces, to make it go farther, as long as each piece has an eye.) When little clusters of muscular stems and crinkled foliage poke up, we apply a hay or straw mulch, to retain moisture and prevent the sun from reaching the spuds and turning them a toxic green. This is also the time to lay down a soaker hose or drip line if needed for irrigation, and a sheet of floating row cover if you foresee damage from potato beetles.

We harvest our "baby new" crop whenever we're hungry. For a storage crop, after the foliage dies down and up until the first hard frost, we leave the potatoes in the ground, but make sure they are all out by mid-October. Once dug, they keep best in a root cellar, but any dark, cold, frost-free place will do. In a climate where the ground doesn't freeze, you could simply leave them be and dig when needed.

Even if your potato farm is just a city backyard, you could end up with a crop so fine you'll think your goose just laid a bucket of golden eggs.

Medley Time

It's dark in our root cellar in wintertime. It's a bit clammy down there too, as the temperature hovers around 33 degrees Fahrenheit with a humidity of 90 percent. It smells earthy and maybe a little cabbagey—not the kind of place to hang out in. But grab a bucket or basket, collect something from every bin, bring it all up into the light, and let's have a look.

Compared with frilly heads of lettuce or the dribble-down-the-chin juiciness of watermelons and tomatoes, there is nothing very sexy about the lumpy tubers we wrest from the soil. But when you hose them off, they become more appealing, and you can see why they're the Cinderellas of the produce world, loved by garden-inspired chefs.

Some relatively new ones, such as golden beet, win fans because of their bright colors. A golden beet is red-orange on the outside and yellow within, gorgeous on the plate. Andean potatoes that are purple both inside and out are the underground counterparts of those "black" tomatoes everyone talks about. And how about that Red Meat? I'm not talking about the beef course, I'm talking about a variety of Chinese radish also called Beauty Heart or Watermelon. Sometimes pink on the outside, sometimes a drab off-white, it's a fireworks display when cut, suffused with magenta in a starburst pattern. Even the common beet, with its brilliant redness, would dazzle us if it were not so common.

Scrub off the earth
and these vegetables
glow in your kitchen.

But look, it's flavor that counts, right? Oven-roast a medley of these together in a pan with olive oil and garlic and their natural sweetness will intensify as the fibers soften and the stored sugars caramelize. There's not much to roasting roots, aside from giving them an occasional stir to coat them with the oil and make sure they don't stick to the pan.

I have even more fun with mashes and purees. A pureed root vegetable is very smooth and silky, unless it's a potato, which will turn to glue. Mashed potatoes are hand-mashed for a reason. Truthfully, any root vegetable can be hand-mashed. Use power equipment if you like, but an old-fashioned potato masher does a perfectly good job.

Mashing two roots together can yield great results. The flavor of parsnips, for instance, is too strong for some tastes, but a half-and-half mix of parsnip and carrot tastes just right and is a pleasing pale orange. Combine kohlrabi with turnip, or with parsley root and some finely chopped parsley foliage for color. Steam Beauty Heart radish briefly and gently to retain its color, marry it with golden beet, and see what kind of sunset you can paint with that.

Celeriac Explained

Celery root, also known as celeriac, grows in a tentative way, half in and half out of the ground, as if trying to decide whether to be a root or a stem. Strictly speaking, it's a swollen stem base, a celery plant bred to bulge below ground rather than make succulent, extra-tender stems above. It's certainly no beauty, with its scruffy tan shoulders, rough-skinned knobs, soil-filled crevices, and gnarly tangle of roots. If oranges evoke Matisse and apples Cézanne, then celeriac evokes Hieronymus Bosch. But it's delicious, as more and more cooks and gardeners are finding out. Though entirely unrelated to the potato, it is like a potato with a mild celery taste and a less starchy texture. It has fewer calories than does the potato, or carrot, and is rich in potassium and calcium. Seed guru C. R. Lawn once called it "the frog prince of vegetables."

In 2013, inspired by the crop's recent spurt of popularity, we planted lots of it at the farm, and gave it star status. It occupied the most fertile beds we had, amended with lots of well-composted manure and a full complement of micronutrients, especially the boron in which our soil is sometimes deficient. We watered the heck out of it in dry weather. It's not as fussy about water as its stemmy sister, but it's still a thirsty plant.

We now grow it every year. We aim for orbs the size of softballs, which become somewhat smaller when peeled and shorn of those tangled roots. Some years they've been more like baseballs, other years they're huge and magnificent. One champion weighed eight pounds. As for keeping in the root cellar, they are superstars, often as perfect and solid in May as they were in October when we put them in.

When you first encounter one, it is rarely love at first sight. Shoppers at our farm stand will hold one up and ask, "What do I do with this thing?" I explain that the first thing to do is hack off all the grubby knobs with a large knife until the whole thing is snow white. You might then boil and mash them half-and-half with potatoes, for a lighter version of this well-loved dish. But I think they are even better cooked and pureed by themselves, with a little cream. Because they are low in starch, the cream is not fully absorbed, so that a mound of this mash tends to seep a bit at the edges. If that spoils your presentation, just add a bit of potato and it will weep no more.

The celeriac is a celebration of ugliness and wonderful flavor.

I find myself using celeriac in more and more dishes where potatoes would be customary, such as soups, stews, gratins, fritters, and fries. A big winner has been shepherd's pie. This economical and fortifying casserole dates back to the time when potatoes first reached the British Isles. Instead of making a pastry crust to top or encase chopped meat (lamb or beef), a potato crust was used. In my version there are a lot of vegetables mixed in with the meat—carrots, onions, corn, peas, or whatever I have— as well as herbs and a wee bit of flour and wine to bind it all together. I also scatter coarse, buttery bread crumbs on top of the celeriac crust that is now substituting for potatoes. It's a full meal in itself and a hearty one.

Another favorite is celeriac cutlets, which I learned about years ago from a German friend named Rainer Bergmann. The tubers are parboiled, then cut into ½-inch-thick slices, dipped in beaten egg, dredged in bread crumbs, fried in butter, and sprinkled with parsley and lemon juice.

Celeriac can be eaten raw, as in the classic French *céleri rémoulade*, where it is grated or cut into matchsticks and dressed with a mustardy mayonnaise or vinaigrette. It has a marvelous ability to absorb dressings, especially if refrigerated overnight before serving. Raw, it has a tendency to brown slightly, but will stay white if placed in water made acidic with a little vinegar or lemon.

Much easier to grow than stem celery, celeriac is more tolerant of heat, cold, and drought. We sow it indoors in early March, keeping the flats well moistened (like parsley, it's slow to germinate). We transplant it into the garden when the soil temperature stays above 45 to 50 degrees Fahrenheit. A cold snap can make this biennial think it has entered its first winter, causing it to bolt to seed rather than form yummy tubers. We plant the seedlings ten inches apart along three rows, with ten inches apart between rows. The plants like a neutral, fertile soil, rich in organic matter. Digging in well-made compost before planting will compensate for any deficiency of boron in your soil, but if your orbs still have brown hollows in the center, a simple remedy is 20 Mule Team Borax from the supermarket. One tablespoon dissolved in four gallons of water is the dose for 100 square feet of bed.

Over the years, celeriac breeding has aimed for smoother, less lumpy globes, with alabaster flesh that resists browning. But I'll take mine, lumps and all. Even browning indicates the presence of anthocyanin, an antioxidant that is beneficial to human health.

Candy Carrots

When you eat from the garden, there's always a daily blue plate special, the season's best. On an early summer day it might be the first fully ripened peapod, and on a gray November day it's a carrot, one that you pull up, hose off, and chomp like a rabbit. After a few no-nonsense frosts, the late-sown carrots have sweetened up, and the longer they stay in the ground, the more they are vegetable candy. Even the tender young carrots of spring don't have this quality.

As with most garden produce, carrot flavor is a complex thing, a balance struck between mildness and sweetness on one hand, and on the other the assertive notes that give a vegetable or fruit its identity. With only mildness, the taste is bland, but too much of the opposite is unpleasant. Naturally, it's a matter of opinion. Many people prefer the character of an acidic apple or tomato, unmasked by sweetness. In carrots, chemicals called turpenoids are part of their flavor complexity, but too much can remind the taster of turpentine. In the end, the best trick to getting carrots that are very sweet and crunchy is simply to harvest them from cold soil. According to Ed Behr, the insightful author of *The Artful Eater*, carrots are more able to store sugars in cool weather because less oxidation takes place.

Since varieties differ, it may take a few tries before you find your favorites, and it also depends on how you are using the crop. Garden moments of culinary ecstasy don't happen randomly. They happen when a gardener has made plans and sown seeds at the right time. For storage carrots, we currently prefer a variety named Bolero, which we plant in June, harvest in fall, and then store in our root cellar. For carrots planted in August to be harvested outdoors in early winter and in greenhouses for winter-long

harvest, we have had best results with the slender, sweet Napoli and Mokum.

The carrots you plant must also like your soil. Provide a soil without excessive nitrogen fertilizer, but adequate potassium. Avoid agricultural chemicals, especially oil-based herbicides, which can impart an "off" taste. The varieties we grow are fairly short, fairly slim, and appropriate for most soils, but we still put a lot of extra effort into preparing their bed. A carrot crop is as fussy as the heroine of *The Princess and the Pea*. What we call "carrot soil" will have as few obstacles as possible that might force the tapered roots off the straight and narrow path. There must be as few rocks as possible, and none bigger than a golf ball or, at most, an egg. No soil compaction. No crust on top. No fresh manure, to make them fork. The bed should be as soft, loose, and fluffy as a Swiss eiderdown—ideally a sandy soil rich in organic matter. If it's too sandy, and typically low in potassium because it lacks enough clay to keep potassium from leaching out, adding well-composted manure will make the soil more retentive.

Sow the seeds as thinly as you can and moisten the planted rows thoroughly with a gentle spray. Do this every single day—even several times a day if it is sunny and dry—until the carrots have germinated, and fairly often even after that. Thin them to an inch or two apart in the row, as needed, then keep the bed meticulously weeded.

As fall approaches, they'll embrace the cool days, turning that deep, beta-carotene orange and stocking up on sweetness. A taste test will tell you when they're ready to dig. Most carrot varieties have been bred for a strong attachment of stem to root, and can be pulled up by the leafy tops, but sometimes it helps to carefully loosen the soil around them with a digging fork, then pull them, grasping their shoulders with your fingers as needed. We cut off the tops right after harvest to diminish moisture loss but leave an inch or two of green to highlight the freshness of these just-dug beauties. What a great snack food they make, stashed in a bag for trips or piled into a big wooden salad bowl for meetings and potlucks! We rarely have a meal without some of them on the table.

You can leave carrots in the soil for a good part of the winter to dig as needed, covered with a sheet of plastic or a layer of straw. Placing a cold frame over them is an even tidier solution; harvesting is more pleasant with no snow or ice to brush off the crop.

If you have not dug every last one of them for the winter holidays, this digging for gold can go on until the tops start to grow again—a date which has more to do with lengthening days than it does with a change in temperature. As soon as the ten-hour day returns, new emerging foliage will start to draw on that stored sugar, and the roots won't be as much of a treat. By then you'll have other things on your mind, like deciding where to plant those exquisite early peas.

Good Old-Fashioned Beets

The ancient gardeners of the Mediterranean region were happy to find the beet. Or, I should say, its ancestor. Gathered in the wild, its leaves were tasty and tender enough to make their way into cultivation. Thus protected and nurtured, it used its long taproot to store some of the nutrients lavished on it, and so it was guided by its cultivators, who selected the most tender-fleshed plants and saved their seed, to become the beet of today.

Beets are unusual because they are multigerm plants. Their seeds are formed as clusters, with several seeds inside a casing. Monogerm (single-seed) beet varieties have been developed to eliminate the need for thinning the seedlings, but I have not found it necessary to grow them. I've never minded thinning crops that have a use at so many different stages. Direct sowing, then thinning at the small seedling stage provides tasty leaves to toss into a salad and, as the roots grow, you can pull individual ones at marble size, then others at golf-ball size, and eventually you have bigger and bigger beets, widely spaced so that they are easier to weed with a hoe. By the time they are a foot apart in all directions, they are also easier to protect against the voles that they attract in our garden, drawn by all that sweet flesh. The little rodents are better exposed to the hawks and other birds that so helpfully prey on them when they cannot hide under a thick forest of beet leaves. In fact, our current practice at the farm is to sow beets in soil blocks, three seeds to a block, and set them a foot apart in the row, so that the generous spacing is immediate.

I'm fond of old standard beet varieties such as Red Ace and Bull's Blood, which has beautiful deep red leaves in cold weather. Bull's Blood roots sometimes have a slight tendency toward bull's-eye markings: pale concentric rings. This is normally considered a defect, called zoning, that results from fluctuating water stress, but it is harmless. There's even a variety we've grown called Chioggia (named for the northwest Italian city of radicchio fame) where the white-ringed pattern is bred deliberately, as a decorative feature. We grow golden beets for their orange exterior and yellow interior. That oxidizes quickly when raw, and turns a disappointing brown color, but it holds the golden color well when cooked.

Beets do fine in cool spring, and we plant them as soon as the soil temperature is at least 45 degrees Fahrenheit, three rows to a thirty-inch-wide bed. They grow quickly and, even with our short summers, we can get several plantings, filling in with a beet crop when an early crop such as peas comes out. They can take frost in fall, but we dig them well ahead of a hard freeze and store them in the root cellar with their tops cut back to ½ inch. There they will keep for a long time, but, of all the storage crops, they require the most moisture. We sprinkle them frequently with a hose or a watering can and at times we have even set up a hose with a fine-mist nozzle to give them the 90 percent humidity that makes them keep well and stay firm where they are stored. Nevertheless, even slightly soft beets can still be used in cooking.

In the ancient days of my childhood we ate beets boiled, sliced, and served in a gooey sauce made of sugar, vinegar, cornstarch, and butter. This popular recipe was called Harvard beets, possibly in reference to the deep maroon color emblematic of that famous institution. Perhaps that recipe was a well-intentioned effort to tame the strong, earthy flavor that some find off-putting in beets. Beets do, in fact, contain a substance present in soil called geosmin, whose aroma is released after a soaking rain.

Gardeners have always liked beets, but they've acquired a wider following among eaters in recent years. Chefs eager to source more produce from local farms are turning to root vegetables in those months when fresh greens are scarce and tomatoes absent. Health-conscious diners love beets for their vitamins, minerals, and dietary fiber. As for antioxidants, beets announce in a blaze of color their stores of betaines and betalains, phytonutrients similar to the anthocyanins found in foods such as red cabbage, amaranth, and razzle-dazzle purple cauliflower.

Beet cookery has also become better and more varied. In the 1970s there were a lot of beet salads in which the roots were grated or shredded, sometimes along with carrots. Currently you're more likely to see cooked beets in a restaurant salad, sometimes with greens and often with feta cheese. Raw beets don't release their natural sweetness as well as carrots do. They're almost woody in their texture, thanks to phenolic compounds that reinforce their cell walls, and they are almost unique in the way they retain their structure during cooking. That can be an asset, because no matter how long you cook a beet, it will never turn to mush.

Beets that are boiled or steamed release a lot of their color, along with their nutrients, into the water. Cooking them slowly until all the water evaporates, then stirring butter into the pan and tossing the beets in it, is one way to overcome that flaw, but there's another solution. Baking beets in a way that releases as little moisture as possible is so satisfying that it's now my favorite technique. It requires little vigilance. I simply wrap foil around whole unpeeled beets (or large chunks if the beets are huge) and put them in a covered casserole in a 325-degree-Fahrenheit oven for two or three hours; the beets come out dramatically softened, almost caramelized, with their flavor and sugars concentrated. They are easy to peel, with their skins slipping off once they're cool enough to touch.

Then what? I slice and butter them. I add them to a hearty borscht with cabbage, onions, and maybe some beef or pork, passing sour cream at the table so everyone can add a dollop. I keep baked beets in the fridge, ready to be sliced or grated quickly to add substance and rich color to a salad. Sometimes I make what I call "beetsteaks": thick slices of large baked beet, served with a sauce made of horseradish, mayonnaise, and sour cream.

Don't forget the greens. How could you, when every time you pull a beet out of the ground a fistful of lush tops comes with it? As greens go, they are particularly sweet and tender, excellent chopped and simmered in a little water and butter until the water disappears and all that's left is a perfect side dish for any meal. When very young, beet greens are tasty and very nutritious in salads.

When you bake beets, sauté the greens for a great pairing.

Just for fun, you might take an odd bit of inspiration from French chefs of the Renaissance, who would cut up thin slices of cold cooked beet and trim them in the shapes of crescent moons or stars, as decorations to top a salad. A lofty purpose for a root of the earth.

Sweet Potatoes for Hire

Spring, so eagerly awaited, can outstrip your reserves of time and energy. There the garden awaits, a blank brown canvas, ready to be filled with the usual favorite foods. Leave it unplanted, and weeds will happily fill it for you.

One year, in June, spring had galloped even faster than usual, with summer's hot breath close behind. It had left me in the dust, so to speak, and I was looking for a quick filler that would consume some of the space, smother the weeds, and yet give me a bountiful harvest.

Sweet potatoes saved the day. They could have gone in a bit earlier, but it was still not too late. Given plenty of water, they got off to a great start as the days warmed, and before long they had blanketed their allotted space with glamorous vines.

The sweet potato bears no relation to the regular "Irish potato," nor to the yam, although they are sometimes sold under that name. Their vines, closely related to morning glories, have heart-shaped leaves, often tinged with purple. It's not surprising that ornamental varieties have been bred, in striking shades such as chartreuse and black. But the swollen roots are the main thing: delicious, rich in vitamin A, and a great winter food, brightening the table with their orange-fleshed, carotene-rich tubers. (There are white-fleshed ones too, but what's the point?) Cooking them is a simple matter of sticking them in the oven and turning it on.

The first sweet potato I ever "planted" was stuck in a glass of water, pointed-end down, supported by toothpicks. I set it in the sunny bathroom windowsill of my college dorm, and over spring break its vines grew so fast that they covered the window, becoming a sort of dorm pet.

Although that was just for fun, it also illustrates a perfectly good way to start off a crop, as long as the tuber has not been treated with something to prevent sprouting. (Organically grown ones rarely are.) To obtain "slips," just twist off the young shoots when they are about eight inches long. You can also buy rooted slips by mail from a grower, timed to arrive when the danger of frost has passed. When they arrive, they will look a little sad from their travels, but if you poke them into the ground right away, they will soon spring into lively growth.

Eliot and I plant the slips a foot apart in the row, with rows three feet apart. We give them ample water at first to help them set their storage roots. Thereafter, they need less and less as the summer wears on. Heavy, cold, waterlogged soil is their worst enemy. If your soil is clay, plant in raised beds or ridges, well amended with organic matter. Avoid excess nitrogen, which can lead to a crop that is all vine, with only skinny little tubers below. Harvest them when the leaves turn yellow with age or black from frost, whichever comes first. Cure them in a warm spot for a week or two to harden the skins, then store them in a cool room, ideally 55 degrees Fahrenheit. No root cellar needed!

My June planting, by August, had confirmed the sweet potato's worth as a handy ground cover. I even let mine wander among some newly planted fruit trees that were too small to shade the ground; the sweet potato foliage blanketed the soil like a living mulch. Few weeds dared to compete.

If there were ever a year when I decided to travel in summer instead of garden, I'd grow masses of sweet potatoes as a babysitter crop, letting a neighbor water them weekly in exchange for a share of the harvest. If you have a small plot, you might want to choose a bush variety such as "Vardaman," which doesn't wander. But if there is a time when the garden seems too large, go with the vines. Before you know it, that brown expanse will have turned to green, and how sweet that will be.

A Tale of Turnips

I call them Cinderella vegetables—so earthy only a vegetarian will eat them until a cook with a deft hand resurrects and prepares them with love. Then suddenly they are chic. It happened to celery root, it happened to rhubarb, and it could happen to rutabaga.

Most people, if they think about the rutabaga at all, would describe it as "sort of like a turnip." That's a good start. Picture a turnip that is bigger and firmer, with a swollen neck, purple shoulders, and yellow flesh. Its flavor is sweeter, especially if harvested after a few frosts. Like the turnip, it is a brassica, and therefore a cabbage relative. When cooked, its color deepens and its flavor mellows. The leaves, bluer than those of a turnip, are eaten too as cooked greens.

A history of overcooking the greens has not helped the rutabaga's status. Nor has its history, in which its use as livestock feed looms large. Like other earth crops, rutabagas store carbohydrates and protein in an enlarged root-level mass. In spring they use these nutrient reserves to make fresh foliage, seed stalks, and seed. Rutabagas have therefore been immensely useful for feeding farm animals, either as fall fodder, munched in the field, or gathered in for winter use. They increased a farmer's ability to keep more animals through the winter rather than slaughtering many of them in fall and salting the meat away.

Being tasty and nutritious for humans as well, they fed the farmer in the cold months too. Rutabagas' firm flesh makes them splendid keepers, lasting as much as a year if stored in a place sufficiently moist and cool. Rich in beta-carotene, calcium, potassium, phosphorous, and vitamin C, they kept many a family going until spring crops appeared. If all you ate during February and March were rutabagas, you might tire of them. I certainly did the first year I spent as a writer/subsistence farmer in rural Connecticut. Had I known how good they are roasted with garlic and oil, glazed with honey, mixed with caramelized onions, or pureed with nutmeg and cardamom in a creamy soup, I'd have loved them more.

Rutabagas are most notably a crop of northern Europe, the northern United States, and Canada. The name comes from the Swedish *rotabagge*, and it was from Sweden that they reached the British Isles. The English call them Swedes. In Scotland they are neeps, traditionally mashed—as in "bashed neeps"—and served with haggis. If you are introducing your family to rutabagas for the first time, try bashing them with an equal amount of potatoes, a little cream, and some butter. As for haggis, its ingredients include the stomach, heart, lungs, and liver of a sheep. A future Cinderella dish if there ever was one.

It doesn't have to be cold where you live to grow a good rutabaga if you time it right. Southerners plant them in fall for a winter crop. In the mid-Atlantic states, late summer is best, on whatever date will give a fifty-day stretch of gradually cooling temperatures before the first frost. (Late planting also enables you to avoid spring pests like flea beetles and root maggots.) Direct sow them in soil that is loose, well dug, and lightened with organic matter. A good application of compost plus some boron will guarantee good health, although too much nitrogen, just as with sweet potatoes, can make the plant go all to leaf.

A mulch will help the roots stay cool in hot weather and keep longer into the fall in the ground. Provide consistent water, especially when the plants are young. Thin them to a spacing of six inches, eating the little extras in salads. Harvest at any size, using a digging fork as needed.

As for the relationship between rutabagas and turnips, I treat them as different varieties of the same plant. I grow them the same way but, because they are larger, rutabagas take longer to mature.

There is, however, one type of turnip that is a different creature altogether. Gardeners these days naturally favor fresh-dug crops over ones grown for long-term storage. (How often do you see a house advertised as having a "washer, dryer, and root cellar"?) Thus it seems only natural to embrace the small, white, round Japanese type of turnip, as crisp as a radish but utterly sweet and mild to munch on. Their leafy tops are milder and more tender than other turnips' greens as well. We grow a variety called Hakurei, which can be harvested when no bigger than an inch in diameter. I slice them thinly to put in salads raw or to toss into fried rice for the final minute or two of cooking. They've taken the place of the water chestnuts that once gave my stir-fries an appealing crunch. (I may never open one of those little round cans again.) A brief sauté is better than roasting, since so much of their content is water, easily lost.

Although these make a good spring crop, sown as soon as the ground can be worked, they are even better in fall. Sown in late summer, they can be ready in thirty-eight days. You can keep resowing for a succession of harvests throughout the fall and winter. Late fall sown ones tend to go to seed after the golf ball stage, but they taste best when that small anyway. I can see cooking up a bunch of them for Thanksgiving dinner, with a squirt of maple syrup added to the pan at the end and drizzled over them. But truth to tell, I might feel some nostalgia for a buttery bowl of good old Swedes: hearty, deep flavored, and thoroughly satisfying.

Hakurei turnips picked at golf ball size are easy to grow and easy to love.

Radishes on the World Stage

Crisp, crunchy, tangy, zippy, zesty, snappy, peppy, pungent, sparkly, and piquant. These are some of the adjectives that the United Fresh Fruit and Vegetable Association, in a 1977 pamphlet, proposed to radish growers for advertising their product. It seems like a pitch aimed at the snack food market. The radish: better than a spicy potato chip.

We rarely give the radish its due as a peasant food. Its name in most languages simply means "root," which gives a good clue to its importance. In France it's a breakfast and supper dish; there's even a variety called French Breakfast, a petite elongated red type with white tips, sold in beautiful bunches in every market. Munich is famous for a large white turnip-shaped radish called Münchner Bier. Sliced and buttered, it is the standard accompaniment to a dark brew. Round Black Spanish is among the standard winter keeper radishes, black-skinned with crisp white flesh and just enough heat.

In Asia radishes win the highest honors. If the tomato rules southern Italy and the eggplant Greece, the long white daikon is king in Japan,

Crunchy, zesty little
French Breakfast
radishes are a cool
weather treat.

where it is sliced, grated, shredded, boiled, and stir-fried. A glance through the offerings of Evergreen Seeds is a good introduction to Asian radishes. Some are great for pickling. Some are suited to the popular Korean dish kimchi. Others have green shoulders and green flesh. And while all radish leaves are edible (they are brassicas, after all) some were bred just for this purpose. Baker Creek Heirloom Seed Company has an enticing selection of radishes from all over the world.

Try the beauty heart types, white with red-streaked centers. Sliced, they are stunning in salads and glamorous in stir-fries. I also love the little finger-shaped White Icicle, crisp and sweet, which even stands up fairly well to warm weather. If you explore radish territory, you'll find that certain ones work for different times of year and different soil types. For example, there are Asian ones suited to heavy clay soil, which don't mind growing with most of the root aboveground. Joy Larkcom's book *Oriental Vegetables* will give you an excellent introduction.

If you've had a bad radish experience, your best bet is to try a number of types and planting schedules to see which suit your garden. And keep in mind a few basic facts about radish culture. In general, hot weather leads to hot radishes. The small ones are planted in spring or fall and harvested as soon as they look and taste ready (a series of quick crops in succession works best). Larger ones are started in mid- to late summer for harvest before severe frosts. Do everything you can to grow the roots quickly, because spending a long time in the soil can also lead to excessive heat. This means giving them fertile soil with well-matured organic matter (deeply dug in for the long types) and plenty of moisture, especially in warm weather. Floating row covers will protect early crops from flea beetles and the root maggot fly.

Another trick is to use them as a nurse crop, sowing them along with a row of slow-to-germinate crops like carrots. This has four purposes: to mark the row, to break the soil's crust so that the spindly little carrot seedlings can emerge, to shade them, and to console you if the carrots never come up at all.

CHAPTER 22

The Onion Tribe

Most things I cook begin with an onion. Soups, stews, stocks, stir-fries, sometimes sauces. Often they are joined by chopped celery and carrots, to be sautéed together as an aromatic base. Cooking them tames their pungency, and their sweetness cancels out bitterness in other vegetables. Best of all, the earthy smell of onions cooking, along with their allium cousins—garlic, leeks, and shallots—is a sign that a cook means business, and a kitchen that says: "Make yourself at home."

I don't feel secure unless I have a working stash of onions, garlic, and shallots within easy reach. In the kitchen, there's always a bucket, bin, or basket for them—anything that works, but never the fridge, where too much moisture would make them rot. (Leeks, on the other hand, like the fridge and need cooling.) All the alliums are outstanding when eaten fresh after harvesting. But their main convenience is that they last many months in storage. An ideal space is dark, cold, frost-free, and dry.

Growing Onions

A good onion soil must be light and loamy or sandy, with high fertility and plenty of organic matter. It is also important to choose the right onion for your area, and to properly time your plantings.

There are three general types of onions, named according to the number of daylight hours per day that will give each one the signal to form full-sized bulbs. Short-day onions make bulbs at ten to twelve hours, and therefore do best in the American South, where summer days are shorter, but the long, warm season gives them plenty of time to mature. Generally, they cannot survive temperatures below 20 degrees Fahrenheit. Long-day onions don't form bulbs until the summer days are fourteen to sixteen hours long, which only happens up north. These are much more cold hardy and store better than the southern types but are not as sweet. The third type of onion, known as intermediate, sets bulbs at twelve to fourteen hours and is suited to regions such as the mid-Atlantic states. Most sellers of onions will specify the day-length category of the varieties they offer.

There are also three ways to grow onions: from transplants you buy (most southern onions are grown this way), from "sets" (tiny dormant bulbs often used up north and only available in a few varieties), and

Onions planted four to a block

from seed. Typically, onions are a spring-planted crop, sown for harvest in late summer and then stored. The young plants need regular watering and regular weeding, since the slender foliage casts little shade and can't crowd out competitors. We sow the seeds indoors, four seeds to a soil block, and transplant them out in a grid twelve inches apart each way. This gives us space to cultivate the soil between the groups regularly with a draw hoe to keep weeds from germinating. But you can also direct sow them (with easy-to-handle pelleted seeds if possible), thinning them to three or four inches apart and eating the delicious little pulled plants in salads. Either way, it's best to harvest the bulbs by running a sharp knife just below their base to cut the roots, rather than yanking them. That way you avoid disturbing the ones left in the ground and leave the roots to decompose and add nutrients to the soil.

The best plan is to have fresh-picked onions almost year-round by planting a fall crop as well, and letting it stay in the ground over the winter. Choose a variety well-suited for this, such as the day-neutral Candy, the cold-hardy Bridger, or the ever-popular Walla Walla Sweet. Wait until the weather has started to cool, then direct sow them, giving them winter protection in USDA zones 6 and above. The trick is to time your sowing date so that the plants are no more than ¼ inch in diameter before cold weather sets in. Any bigger and they'll consider themselves two-year-old plants in springtime and go to seed rather than make bulbs.

Overwintered onions are not keepers, so use them up. Cut them in half and roast them, basted with olive oil and herbs. Pair them with asparagus, then green peas, then young zucchini in a progression of early garden soups, light but a little creamy. Cook them down by themselves into a jamlike relish and bury burgers under it. Do not stint or hoard. The summer crop will soon be ready for stealing.

If your onions are not as sweet as the much-touted Vidalia (grown in a part of Georgia in which the sandy soil leaches sulphur downward), don't disparage them. I hope that onions will always have a bit of hellfire and brimstone about them because therein lies not only their distinctive flavor but also the antioxidant and anti-inflammatory qualities they are

known to impart. If onions were meant to taste like apples, they would grow on trees.

The Power of Garlic

A garlic clove is an intense little piece of living matter to which few people are indifferent. Some are addicted to its aggressively rich flavor, others flee. Love affairs may have been aborted by its penetrating scent, but more are launched by a cook's skill in harnessing the charms of the "stinking rose."

Strangely, garlic is not in everybody's garden, despite being a tidy, space-saving, easy-to-grow crop. Perhaps it's because planting garlic usually lies outside the spring routine of sowing and planting. It helps to think of it as part of fall bulb-planting, along with tulips, daffodils—and the lilies to which garlic is related. All are set into the ground while dormant, in midfall, just early enough to make some root growth during the cool weather they require but not so early that top growth can begin. Later plantings, right up to hard freeze, will overwinter fine and sprout in springtime, but they will have made less growth by midsummer when they mature. The same is true of early spring planting, which is the norm in some areas. Spring-planted garlic heads will mature a month or so later than ones planted the previous fall (with the daffodils) and keep longer in storage. But fall planting gives you larger heads.

Take your pick. And rejoice in the fact that planting garlic is such a simple matter. Just before planting, you "pop" the cloves by prying them gently from the head, taking care not to puncture them or break the growing plate at the base. Poke them pointy-side up, two inches deep and four inches apart in a well-drained seedbed rich in organic matter. Rows can be set a foot apart.

A loose winter mulch of hay or chopped leaves will keep garlic cozy in winter but push it back in spring to allow the ground to warm up. Then push it back around the plants later on to conserve moisture. A drizzle of compost tea or manure tea (a five-to-one mixture of water and compost or manure steeped in a watering can) or liquid fish fertilizer will spur on growth. Eliot and I have good luck with a winter mulch of seaweed, gathered when a storm washes it up onto our road.

We hold off watering the last two weeks before harvest. We pull the plants gently from the ground once the tops have started to brown but there are still about six green leaves left. (Don't wait too long because each of those leaves is connected to a protective covering below that must remain intact for the sake of the lifted bulb.) We cure the garlic indoors or out in a dry, warm, airy place, then store in a place that's dry and cool—just above freezing if possible—setting aside some of the firmest and largest cloves for next year's planting.

There are two basic types of garlic. The ones you buy in the store are usually softneck types, which form large heads with lots of tiny and fairly

useless cloves at the center. Skins that stick tightly to the cloves make them great for long storage, but hard to peel. They are the kind to grow for garlic braids. Hardneck garlic, which is more cold hardy, forms a single circle of large, easy-to-peel cloves around a stiff central stalk. They also have great flavor, so it pays to sample these types. Try the Porcelain hardnecks such as Music if you like extra-fat cloves for roasting.

Hardnecks also send up scapes, which look like flower stalks but actually support topsets—clusters of tiny garlic cloves. Some experts say that removing the scapes forces the plants to put more energy into the underground bulb. I cut them anyway because their tenderest parts are so good to eat, slathered with olive oil and roasted until they're chewy-crunchy. I especially like the scapes from hardneck garlics called Rocambole, which taste good and grow with a comical loop to them. I once thought these loopy garlics were the source of the French word *rocambolesque*, which means incredible or fantastic. *Non.* That comes from the outrageous adventures of Rocambole, the roguish hero/villain of a popular series of nineteenth-century French novels by Pierre Alexis Ponson du Terrail. This Rocambole was a gentleman outlaw who used his great powers to aid the weak. For both, a name well-shared.

Above left: Curing hardneck garlic on the screened porch

Above: Loopy garlic scapes in the garden

Vegetable of Champions

"Oooh," our dinner guest murmured. "Where did you get these lovely little leeks?" In June it would have been a compliment, but this was November and, thanks to a delayed planting, our leeks were a pitiful size, lovely or not. With winter varieties, size counts. You want a beefy leek, a stout-hearted leek to hold in the ground until spring. The old variety names tell the story—Giant Musselburgh, Elephant, Winter Giant.

Leeks are never a quick crop. Even "baby" leeks—sweet, tender, and perfect for summer grilling—might take two-and-a-half months after a direct sowing in the garden. A summer leek such as King Richard might take three months. Some of the superstocky types take even longer than that to reach full size before cold weather. St. Victor, a purple-leaved beauty, needs 145 days. It's a strain selected from the old French heirloom Bleu de Solaise, which, like most hardy leeks, is blue-green.

If you are Welsh, you take leeks seriously. The English have a rose as their emblem, the Scots a thistle, the Irish a shamrock. For the down-to-earth Welsh it's a leek. Many old Welsh recipes feature leeks, such as leek pie or cawl, a meaty soup. As legend has it, leeks won the day for the Welsh in a battle with the Saxons in 640 AD. Each Welsh warrior donned a leek in his headgear to distinguish himself from the enemy. Shakespeare, in a caricature of Welshness, had Fluellen, a scrappy Welsh soldier in his play *Henry V*, sport a leek in his hat. And to this day patriotic folk wear the pungent symbol on the Welsh holiday St. David's Day, March 1—this despite the daffodil's ascendency as a buttonhole ornament. Saint David himself, a learned missionary, lived an ascetic life, with a diet of bread, water, and fresh greens.

By St. David's Day, it's wise to have already sown your leeks indoors or in a cold frame to get pencil-sized transplants ready to go into the garden by April. This should give you a twenty- to thirty-day jump on the harvest. For an almost continuous supply, start three varieties—say, King Richard for summer, Upton for fall, and Tadorna for winter. In areas where the ground freezes, you'll need to protect winter leeks with a cold frame or a plastic A-frame tent to keep the ground diggable. Come spring, tough flower stalks will start to arise from the plants' centers, so there's a short "leek gap" before summer varieties are ready.

To sow leeks indoors, we use three-inch-deep flats filled with a soilless potting mix, set in a sunny, warm spot or under grow lights. We sow the seeds ¼ inch deep, one inch apart, in rows two inches apart. When it's time to move them to the garden, we choose a cloudy day, setting them in deep, loose, fertile soil, one to two inches apart for baby leeks, six inches apart for large ones.

For a cook, having leeks with long, white shanks is more important than having big fat ones. The green leaves can add flavor and nutrients to a simmering stock (to be strained out later), but it's the soft, creamy white part that braises so beautifully and thickens a soup with its satiny richness. The only way to get a long, white shank with direct-sown leeks is to blanch them, which means drawing soil over the bottom parts as they grow. But Eliot taught me a better method. We plant leeks by making a nine-inch-deep hole with a dibble or trowel and dropping a seedling in, leaving the hole unfilled. The roots have been trimmed to an inch long and the tops to ten inches, so that about an inch of green sticks out of the holes. As we cultivate with our hoes all season long, the holes gradually fill with soil. We then harvest the leeks by loosening the roots with a digging fork and pulling them by grasping the base. The roots and tops can be trimmed right there in the garden. Before I cook the leeks, I split and rinse them thoroughly to get rid of soil lodged inside the many layers.

During the year of puny leeks, just for fun, I bought a copy of Bernard Lavery's book *How to Grow Giant Vegetables*. On the cover is a picture of its Welsh author, proudly holding an exhibition leek he grew. The white part alone reaches from his waist to the top of his head, mighty enough to take down a murderous Saxon with one blow. Try doing that with a daffodil.

Leek seedlings set into deep holes with tips showing will gradually be blanched as they grow.

Scallions Forever

Fine as it is to eat only what's in season, there are some vegetables that a cook always wants to have on hand, and the scallion is one of them. Whenever a dish looks or tastes a little boring, all you need do is grab a scallion and a pair of scissors and snip away, letting the pieces cascade over the surface. Your creation will instantly look fresh and appetizing, whether it's a salad, a bowl of chili, or borscht.

To grow scallions properly it's best to sow them in cool weather, when the soil is about 50 degrees Fahrenheit. So if I haven't put any scallions in our summer garden, I'll have to wait and plant them as a fall or winter crop. This means no scallions in summer salsas, and no scallions to scatter over that oh-so-white potato salad.

I find that by broadening the definition of a scallion, I can extend its season. Scallions, also known as green onions or bunching onions, are a distinct species (*Allium fistulosum*). They never form a bulb at the end but remain straight and slender from top to bottom. However, you can get those long, green, oniony leaves from any plant that is, at the moment, exhibiting scallionaceous behavior. Viewed this way, scallion season might start with the onion bin at winter's end, when your storage onions have reached the end of their shelf life. The bulbs have softened and are sending out long shoots from the tops. These are firmer than classic scallion foliage, yet still good to eat. If they're pale from living in the dark, just set them next to a sunny window and they'll green right up.

Regular bulb onions, on their way to maturity, can have their tops robbed prematurely at those times when a scallion must be had. Occasionally bulb onions don't get around to bulbing at all. Don't call them a crop failure, call them scallions.

Perhaps you intended to plant bulb onions and never got around to it. Visit the garden center and see if there are any leftover little onion sets that nobody bought at planting time. Plant them now, keep them watered, and they'll yield green shoots, ready for snipping as garnish material.

If you have garlic growing, steal some of its green tops too for instant "green garlic," an excellent by-product of that praiseworthy bulb. Then, later, when you're sorting out the biggest garlic cloves to save for next year's crop, sow the puny rejects. They'll make green garlic too. And when your chives get fat and mature in summer, they'll be a good enough imitation to tide you over until cool, scallion-planting weather returns.

CHAPTER 23

Cukes, Zukes, and Beyond

The Cucurbitaceae (more simply known as cucurbits) is a fascinating family of vegetables. Most of the ones we eat are either cucumbers or squash, with the squash being the largest, most varied division. (Gourds too are members of the clan but are rarely edible and fall more under the categories of storage vessels and tableware.) In size cucurbits range from the tiniest French pickles called cornichons, made from cucumbers picked at only an inch or two long, to giant pumpkins, which are less a food and more a competitive sport.

All of them are good for you. I regard squash, especially winter squash, as one of the best ways to eat complex carbohydrates, loaded with excellent fiber, as opposed to simple carbohydrates such as sugar, and bread or pasta made from refined white flour. If I want to add a healthier carb to the dinner plate, odds are I'll pick a winter squash. They are also among the most beautiful foods you can eat.

A gardener about to grow a cucurbit crop will be cheered to hear that they are vigorous, prolific, and easy to grow. But this is a bit like having a teacher praise your "energetic," "enthusiastic," and largely uncontrollable child. These are the overachievers of the vegetable world, so get ready, get set, go.

Zucchini Explosion

If growing a giant pumpkin makes a gardener look like a hero, why does growing a giant zucchini make her look like an idiot?

This tasty squash is a crop that catches gardeners off guard. It is too easy, too bountiful, too quick on the draw. Direct sow a few seeds after the soil has warmed up and very soon you will have beautiful healthy plants, bursting with huge golden flowers. It takes a mere four days or so after a female flower blooms to produce a fruit of edible size. The name zucchini means "little squash." Grow more than one plant and you may soon have zucchini piling up on the kitchen counter, way more than you can eat. And they will not be "little" unless you watch them carefully and pick them nearly every day.

Summer squash are best picked when small.

The hotter the weather, the more rapidly each one grows. Because zucchini are green-striped cylinders that look a lot like the stems that bear them, it's easy to miss them, becoming quietly enormous under huge mottled green leaves. Lose your focus for a week, and long green shapes will be deployed in the shadows, like submarines.

One summer I was distracted by the need to groom my flower beds for a garden tour. I thought the vegetable plot was in good shape, but I sent my young helper Kim into it for a last-minute sprucing up. "Wow!" she exclaimed. "I've never seen a zucchini so huge. Oooh, there's lots of them!" As visitors' cars swept up the driveway, Kim and I staggered across the lawn, arms loaded, to bury the evidence of my neglect in the compost pile.

Faced with an explosion of zucchini, a gardener may consult one of the numerous cookbooks devoted solely to this overzealous vegetable. Only desperation could make human beings come up with zucchini pizzas, zucchini martinis, and zucchini chocolate chip cookies. But you will find that zucchini are delicious simply steamed or sautéed with onions and then tossed with butter and fresh herbs. With their mild flavor, they're a great background for assertive summer herbs such as tarragon, basil, and sage. Bright edible flowers such as calendula, nasturtium, mint, and even lavender florets are fine companions too. Try a creamy soup combining zucchini and corn off the cob.

Too big. Too many.

They keep on coming. You vow to be vigilant. Post-its go up on the fridge, the medicine cabinet, the steering column of your car: "Pick zucchini." As summer goes by, other pleasures compete for your time. The plants are now huge nests of prickly stems and leaves into which you must wade with the pluck of Indiana Jones, wearing long sleeves even if it's 100 degrees Fahrenheit. As the plants grow older, the heavy stems elongate and sprawl along the ground, pinning some of the delicate-skinned fruits beneath. You must lift the plant to cut and remove them carefully, like victims of a logging accident.

And yet, how can you not love something that grows and bears so eagerly, whatever the color of your thumb? Here are a few ways to take charge of it.

- Don't plant too many. Often a single plant will feed the whole household, though I can rarely resist growing one each of a few separate types. Besides the classic green-striped version, there are the extra-nutritious near-black zucchini, the beautiful deep yellow ones like Gold Rush, the flavorful Cocozelles, as well as the other (and equally prolific) summer squashes such as yellow crooknecks, round ones like Ronde de Nice, and the disk-shaped pattypan.

- Pick early in the day, when a shirt and gloves are more comfortable, or grow a nonprickly variety such as Spineless Beauty or Gentry.

- Pick fruits while very small, with shiny skins. Those two to four inches long are the tenderest, and I discard anything over about eight. This way I consume them at their best and also keep pace with the supply. If I hoard them in the fridge, they deteriorate at the same rate they do everything—fast.

- Practice squash birth control by picking some of the flowers and using them in soups and fritters.

- Grow varieties described as "compact," "upright," "open," "with fruits carried high," and "easy to pick," among them Condor, Gold Bar, and Elite.

- Plant a second crop. "*Grow more zucchini?*" I can hear you saying. "*Are you crazy?*" But even if the current crop is still producing, remind yourself how much nicer the plants were to deal with when they were smaller and younger. Since summer squash only takes about fifty days, there is still time in midsummer to start plants that will mature and bear until the first frost. The earlier planting can be composted to make room for other fall crops such as kale, carrots, spinach, and broccoli. It'll be time to start thinking seriously about fall crops anyway. And this one is so easy.

Blossoms for Breakfast

There are moments you can savor only as a gardener-cook and picking zucchini blossoms for Sunday breakfast is one of them. When I went out on a recent sunny August morning, dew was sparkling on the golden petals. By afternoon they would be closed and starting to wilt, but now the huge, upward-facing cups were open to the sun's rays. Harvested early, they would stay open all day if kept cool, but it was still best to eat them while fresh and crisp. Hence breakfast.

A squash plant bears both male and female flowers. The male is held upright on a long, slender stem, while the female has a bump—the beginning of a tiny squash—at the base. I usually choose the males for cooking, leaving the females to produce fruits.

I first tasted squash blossom fritters in Rome, years ago, and have been working to perfect them since. I gently poke a cube of cheese into the base of an open flower, which I swirl in a thin batter of flour and water, then fry in olive oil until crisp.

The first step is to make sure the flowers are clean and to evict any wildlife still at work. On Sunday, my blossoms had been full of bees when harvested, but those had flown, leaving only a few ants and striped cucumber beetles to be brushed off. Next, I removed the flowers' reproductive parts—a single pillar for the males, a shorter, bulbous mass for the females. These are difficult to pinch out with your fingers without tearing the petals; needle-nose pliers with blades bent at the tips do a better job. The organs, as golden and no doubt as carotene rich as the blossoms themselves, are fine to eat raw or cooked and can be saved for a garnish but removing them creates a more secure pocket for the cheese. I use a firm cheese, such as cheddar or Monterey Jack, that will melt just enough during frying but not ooze out before the job's done.

A shallow bowl is the best shape for swishing the flower in the batter. The male stem makes a good handle, but so does the little squash on the female, if left on, and it will cook right along with the flower. Twisting the flower while you're rolling it in the batter helps to close it up and seal

in the cheese, but this still takes care and patience. Holding the petal tips closed with the other hand is a help, especially when transferring the batter-coated flower to the pan of sizzling oil. After that delicate move, you're home free. The fritters crisp quickly and can be easily flipped over to brown on the other side, then salted and drained on a paper towel, to be eaten as soon as possible. With a bowl of fresh blueberries to follow, there is no better way to start a day.

A Squash Built for Speed

We try to keep the door closed between our little home greenhouse and our utility room, to exclude rodents, but the other day a squash plant wandered in. Or leapt in, gaining (or so it appeared) a foot of floor space per day. This particular zucchetta rampicante is favored in the Ligurian region of Italy, especially the town of Albenga. In fact, one of the plant's common names is *tromba d'Albenga*. Others include *tromboncino, trombolina*, and trumpet squash, all of which refer to its fruits' trumpetlike coiled shape.

Two young friends have fun with zucchetta rampicante.

Rampicante simply means "climbing" or "creeping" in Italian, but an assumption of "rampant" in this case is more than justified. According to *Cornucopia: A Source Book of Edible Plants* by Stephen Facciola, it can grow thirty to forty feet in one season. Surprisingly, it's a variety of *Cucurbita moschata*, the species that includes most winter squash, as opposed to *Cucurbita pepo*, which comprises most summer ones. In fact, you can mature it to store as a winter squash (a bit like the butternut type). But it is most prized as a summer treat.

I'd grown this plant some years ago and wanted to see if it tasted as good as I'd remembered. I got the seeds from John Scheepers Kitchen Garden Seeds, a specialty seed company.

True to its name, the plant rewards me with hilarious loopy fruits. They dangle more vertically when trellised, but I love the twisted coils they make when grown along the ground, hiding under the huge leaves, like serpents. It's fun to roast these whole on a rimmed baking sheet, tossed with olive oil, garlic, and some favorite herbs. I also tried a taste test along with regular zucchini, steaming each separately and tasting them without butter or seasoning. The zucchini was sweeter, but the zucchetta rampicante was still full flavored, with a much more versatile texture. When cooked it's tender but a bit firmer than a zucchini and does not get mushy or watery. I started out cooking just the young fruits but found that even three-foot wonders were tasty. Nearly seedless, too.

Don't be scared off by this force of nature. It will win you over with its resistance to squash vine borer, its heat tolerance, and its outrageous vigor. Train it on a very stout trellis or allow it to wander along the ground in a spot where you'd just as soon not weed. Didn't Sister Squash play that weed-smothering role in the "three sisters" trio of squash, corn, and beans? There are currently no weeds in our greenhouse, where squash vines now cover the soil. We head them back down when they try to climb the trellised tomato vines with which they share the space. And we remember to shut the door.

Squash Slayer

King Arthur would have known just what to do. My heftiest knife was plunged to the hilt in a Blue Hubbard squash twice the size of a turkey, and only a heroic effort would remove it. By drawing the handle toward me as far as it would go, then thrusting it in again, I could waggle it back and forth, creating a cleft just wide enough to pull the blade free. With repeated thrusting and waggling, the great squash finally split in two.

By no means as hard as the king's stone or the famous sword he found lodged in it, Hubbard squash are still intimidating. When it comes to winter squash, today's gardeners are more apt to grow 4-to-5-pound acorns, kabochas, buttercups, and even smaller ones such as the merrily green-striped Delicata. "Portion control" is now part of our vocabulary, if not our daily practice, and food waste is the eighth deadly sin.

My giant specimen was from a young farmer who left it on my kitchen table as a surprise. The inside of her gift was a stunningly rich orange color. I scraped the seeds from the inner cavity and roasted half of it in a 350-degree-Fahrenheit oven, unadorned, in my biggest pan. After an hour the slate blue skin was bronzed and blistered, the flesh juicy, succulent, and delicious. Seizing my biggest spoon, I scooped it out easily, mounded it in a bowl, dotted it with butter, and served it up to the farm crew.

I have come to believe that roasting is the best thing you can do to a winter squash, because it concentrates and enriches its flavor. It also makes removing the tough skin very easy. After that you can make soup with it, make a pie with it, make red Thai curry with it, can it, freeze it, or whatever you like.

Winter squash, as compared with summer squash such as zucchini, are heavier and firmer. Most are, to a varying degree, "keepers." The fruits, if properly cured and stored, provide excellent winter food. But unlike hardy root crops, neither squash plants nor the fruits they bear will withstand freezing temperatures. The tops of the squash vines are often the first plant parts in a garden to show damage from the first frost.

Apart from giving them good fertile soil and plenty of space to grow, winter squash, like summer squash, are easy to grow. They are usually direct sown. You can start them indoors but they will not transplant well if they are more than two or three weeks old when they go into the soil.

With squash it is very important to find out as much as possible about what your plant is going to do. If the company that you buy the seeds from does not give you full descriptions of the varieties they sell, look them up online. In order to know how much space to give them, check to see if they are the compact type or have long vines. You also need to know how long they will take to mature, so that you can plant them early enough to get there. Otherwise, they will not taste as good. If "the frost is on the punkin," as James Whitcomb Riley put it, the punkin's grower has actually waited a bit too long. It's best to let the natural dying down of the vines signal picking time. To be sure, test the squash rind with your fingernail, which will not penetrate a mature one. Find out what it looks like when it's ready to pick. Many have interesting, very individual markings. Unless you've grown it or at least eaten it before, a picture will tell the best tale—or a visit to the vegetable displays at an autumn fair.

A winter squash seems tough, hard, and durable, but don't be fooled. It must be babied to avoid any nicks or scratches that let in bacteria and cause decay. Clip the stems an inch from the fruit with pruners, never yanking or tearing. Don't use the stem as a handle. Never throw the fruits into buckets.

Once they are off the vine, I can let them cure in the garden in what I hope will be a warm, sunny fall. Heat will not only toughen the skin, heal tiny cracks, and thereby keep them better, it will also make them sweeter because it boosts their sugar content. If the weather is cold and/or wet, I bring them inside and find a warm, dry place to cure them, like a sunny room, an attic, or even on top of the kitchen cabinets. Never mind if they collect a little dust; they can be tenderly rinsed off and dried with towels, the way you would fine china. Even three weeks is not too long for this curing process.

Winter squash vary as to how long they will keep in storage, but they all have similar requirements. One of their best features is that they do not need the cold, moist environment that root crops demand. The ideal is a well-ventilated spot where the temperature does not go below 50 or above 68 degrees Fahrenheit. The basement is out unless it's quite dry.

Pumpkins are a type of winter squash, and there are ones of all sizes sold chiefly as "carving" varieties. "Pie" pumpkins, on the other hand, are especially sweet and flavorful, with small inner cavities and thick, smooth, dense, nonstringy flesh. These are apt to be tall ovals, good for several Thanksgiving pies, but my favorite is a very large French heirloom called Rouge Vif d'Étampes, also known as Cinderella. Once a specialty item, it is now widely grown because of its beauty. *Rouge vif* means "bright red" in French, and so it is. Weighing in at ten to fifteen pounds, it is a stunning sight and makes fine pies and velvety pureed soups.

If I were to grow just one squash, it would be a good old-fashioned butternut. Some fruits flaunt their lusciousness. Purple grapes beckon from the vine, honey-dripping figs from the tree. But the orange flesh of butternut squash is clothed in beige, the khaki trench coat of food. Its plan is to keep itself unnoticed until spring. That plain, firm skin guards the fruit from predation and rot until it's time for the ripened seeds to sprout, nourished by the garden of its own decomposition.

A butternut's size and shape are kitchen friendly. The classic variety is Waltham, bred for a long straight neck. It ends in a rounded bottom, enclosing a small seed cavity. Individual fruits vary within a planting, some straight and club-like, others more curvaceous, with a narrow neck and a bulb-shaped bottom. I choose a straight one to use when I make one of my favorite dishes: rounds of the neck cut into perfect ½-inch-thick disks, like hockey pucks, and roasted in butter.

In the summer of 2008 I started growing a minibutternut variety called Honeynut, bred by Cornell University's Department of Plant Breeding and Genetics. A butternut was crossed with a buttercup, a dark green type similar to acorn, with very bright, sweet, rich flesh. Honeynut's was deep orange, flavorful, and nonstringy. Most weighed only a pound or so, as opposed to the usual four or five. I was thus able to train them vertically on the trellis fence surrounding the garden, where they dangled, looking very decorative, with skin that was more of a rich tan than beige.

Another reason to make a habit of reading seed catalogs is to keep abreast of how squash (and other vegetables) are being improved on. Much as I doted on Honeynut, it did not keep well. So now I'm in love with one unglamorously called 898, from Row 7 Seed Company. It's little, it's tan, it's sweet, and it will stay that way for at least five months if kept cool, dry, and dark. It makes great single-serving boats when cut in half lengthwise and the seeds removed. Put a pat of butter in the hollow, bake until very tender, and let the diners spoon out the rich, sweet flesh from the skins.

Spaghetti Squash Gets Real

I'm annoyed when a food pretends to be something it's not. The smug soy burger has no meat inside its bun. The charbroiled seitan steak, another beefless wonder, is composed of processed wheat gluten. "Sea legs" are cylinders of white mystery fish, tinted red to resemble crab. And Tofurky for Thanksgiving? Not for me. I might actually warm to tofu if it didn't spend so much time doing animal impersonations.

It's not that I'm antivegetarian. The more people eating vegetables the better. But I'm a stickler for authenticity. Because of this prejudice I was once deeply suspicious of spaghetti squash—then pleasantly surprised when I tried it. Once cooked, the flesh can be forked out of the skin in strands that look very much like what's inside a box of Ronzoni, though the taste and texture are definitely squash-like. And delicious. "Well and good," I said, "but this is not going to fool kids." I'd never been able to trick my son, Chris, into eating vegetables. But, miraculously, he ate this one. I had performed a magic trick, and turned a dish he expected to be strong-flavored and mushy into one that was mild, sweet, and slightly crunchy—and looked like pasta.

The spaghetti squash is a New World plant that originated somewhere in the Americas. No one knows how or why it evolved into an imitation of a vehicle for red sauce. When fully ripe, it looks like a pale yellow blimp about ten inches long. It belongs to the species *Cucurbita pepo*, which includes summer squash like zucchini and certain winter squash, including acorn.

Spaghetti squash reveals its inner self.

I've seen spaghetti squash listed as a summer squash—a category into which its flavor might place it—but usually it is considered a winter one because of its firm flesh, which tastes best when fully ripe. It is rich in fiber and folic acid. I wonder if its strands are an extreme version of the slight stringiness present in the acorn type. It keeps longer than a summer squash does—about a month at room temperature and as much as three months in a slightly cool cellar—but not as long as most winter squash and pumpkins.

Grow it as you would any squash, with plenty of space, full sun, and enough water in dry weather so that the fruits can form. (Some varieties grow on short vines, others on long.) Pick it when the skin is more yellow than cream and cure it in the sun for ten days before bringing it inside.

There are several ways to cook a spaghetti squash. You can simply pierce it a few times and place it in a 350-degree-Fahrenheit oven for an hour (less if it's small). When it's done, cut it in half lengthwise, let it cool a bit, scoop out the seeds, then perform the miracle of the strands, drawing a fork through what looks like solid flesh, and watching it become, I'd say, closer to vermicelli or angel hair. You can also boil the squash in water, whole, for about forty minutes, or slice it in half first and bake the halves—cut-side down—on a cookie sheet or in a baking dish with an inch or so of water in it.

How to treat it afterward is a matter of personal taste. Perhaps it's my aversion to ersatz food, but I prefer to treat spaghetti squash as squash. Bolognese and marinara are not words that go with squash. I love it with just butter, or butter that's been browned a little with some chopped fresh sage. You can also form the flesh into patties, binding it with egg, then frying them like potato pancakes. Or turn it into a gratin. Or just top a plate of it with olive oil and Parmesan cheese. That's about as Italian as I'm willing to go.

The hybridizers have gone to work on spaghetti squash and some of the new varieties are quite radical departures. One called Stripetti is a cross between spaghetti squash and Delicata, the popular small winter squash that is cylindrical and handsomely striped with dark green. The result looks like a large Delicata, with its better keeping ability and spaghetti flesh inside. A big breakthrough came in 1986 in Israel with the development of Orangetti, a bush version with orange skin and flesh— and a high level of beta-carotene.

Some people still prefer the old, primitive original, often sold as "vegetable spaghetti." They claim its flavor has been sacrificed with all this tinkering around. But it's fun to see what the breeders come up with. What's next? A beet-colored one called Purpletti? Maybe. As long as it's still a squash.

Catch and Release Cucumbers

I've never quite understood sport fishing—the kind where hooking a creature and throwing it back into the water is the goal. No matter how fun the day, I need to see a fresh-caught meal at the end.

The same goes for gardening. I won't grow anything I don't like to eat. Eliot, ever the adventurer, is different. As a serious market gardener, growing great cucumbers is not only profitable, it's taken on the fervor of a challenge, even though he doesn't like to eat them. It's a catch-and-release game.

It started in 1989 when he visited a French grower. In a greenhouse, this fellow had dug long trenches wide enough to hold rows of straw bales on edge and deep enough to bury them by two thirds in the ground. Once placed in the trenches, the bales were soaked with dried blood and other organic, high-nitrogen materials to get decomposition going and to heat them up. After they had cooled down to 80 degrees Fahrenheit, the farmer covered them with four inches of mature sheep manure compost and set out cucumber seedlings. The bottom heat provided by the bale beds produced quick growth and a spectacular harvest.

Our farm's program for growing flavorful cukes in the greenhouse is a bit less extreme, but we do enrich their deeply dug beds with lots of composted horse manure. The vines are trained to grow upward to a support bar seven feet above the ground. Fruits that form below three feet are removed, and above that one fruit is allowed to grow per node, where the leaf attaches to the stem. All suckers are pruned out as well to eliminate side shoots. When a vine reaches the top, it is allowed to develop a second stem, and both stems grow downward from the bar. They form a cucumber at each node all the way down.

If really vigorous, they can be trained all the way back up to the top again. The rows of mighty vines, with leaves up to seventeen inches across, look like a South American jungle organized by a German engineer.

Meanwhile, I'm over in the home garden training cucumbers up a wall of wooden latticework, though in a less orderly fashion. Because I've enriched the soil in the beds with manure, just as Eliot has, the vines are vigorous and the fruits are numerous, almost to a fault. And my mind, unlike his, is busy thinking of ways to eat them.

For some people, the only reason to grow cucumbers is to make pickles. I like pickles, but if I barely have time to pick all my cucumbers (which is necessary, to keep them producing), I definitely don't have time to pickle them.

In summer, simple dishes rule. A sandwich of sliced cucumbers with mayonnaise, salt, and pepper makes a great, quick lunch. Try it with cream cheese instead of mayo and add watercress.

Use cucumber slices in place of crackers, spreading them with goat cheese and dill. Make a dip out of something colorful like saffron aioli or pureed red peppers with feta cheese, and supply cuke rounds for dipping. Make dugout canoes by cutting them in half and scraping out the seeds. Fill them with a cargo of mustardy egg salad or finely diced chicken salad with mayo and seedless grapes cut in half.

A cucumber vine, trained upward, is attached to a string with plastic clips.

Eliot doesn't realize how much sliced cucumbers improve a green salad of lettuce, a little thinly sliced onion, and tarragon. Or how essential it is to have a cooling raita made of grated cucumber and yogurt to cool the tongue between bites of spicy Indian curry.

Thank heaven for his favorite soup, gazpacho, a Spanish-style cold soup I make from tomatoes, peppers, celery, scallions, garlic—and cucumbers. I like it chopped, rather than electrically blended, so that all the ingredients are noticeable, with a bit of olive oil and balsamic vinegar stirred in at the end. The ultimate soup from the summer garden.

Life Lessons for Cucurbits

Watch any plant of the cucurbit family in summer and you'll see a lively drama unfold. Bright yellow flowers open in the morning to receive bees eager to burrow deep within for nectar and pollen. In so doing, they transfer pollen from the male stamens to the female stigma—a little golden circlet that crowns the ovary, where a new fruit will form. All members of this tribe have both male and female blossoms on the same plant and, if all goes well, the ovaries of the female will soon swell and turn into something that resembles a tiny cucumber, melon, or squash. If you see a lot of bees going in and out of the flowers, it's a good sign.

It's also a good sign when the little fruits start to appear, but it does not guarantee success. Fruit-set can begin without pollination and—unlike a human mama—a female squash blossom can be a little bit pregnant if enough pollen has landed on the stigma to get the fruit going but not enough to create a vegetable worth picking. That takes numerous bee visits. For instance, you might have seen a little zucchini get off to a good start, then turn to mush at the flower end. It's not diseased, it's a poorly pollinated fruit that can go no further. If you get a small harvest of cucumbers or melons, inadequate pollination may be the cause there as well.

So along with giving your plants good soil and sowing them on time, you need to think about bees. It's worth keeping track of bee numbers. If there are few, think about what you could plant to attract more of them.

Blue salvia and catmint blossoms in our farm-stand garden are a delight for the bees.

Even if there are few honeybees around, many native bee species will be lured to a yard full of nectar-rich flowers. Observe which plants bloom when cucurbits are flowering, and which ones are quivering with active bees. Those that bloom in the purple range are their favorites, and it only takes a glance to see that catmint (*Nepeta*), followed by any of the purple-flowered sages, is bee heaven. From there, move on to liatris and bee balm in midsummer, and purple asters in fall. Hate the color purple? Get over it.

And don't use poisons in the garden. The evidence linking huge bee die-offs to chemical pesticides such as the neonicotinoids is not only a sad tale of furry little bodies lying dead. It could also foretell poor harvests for you and other growers.

With cucurbits, pollination is not the only thing to pay attention to. On a hot summer day, everything in the garden can look a little wilted, including the gardener. Come evening, or a welcome shower, everyone perks up. But now and then you'll see a cucumber plant that's down for the count. Within a week or two, the vine has settled into a permanent wilt from which it doesn't recover; sometimes the whole patch goes. The tomatoes are fine, the peppers and celery are fine. But these alone do not gazpacho make.

The problem is usually cucumber wilt, a disease in which bacteria clog the plant's stems and prevent the flow of water. (You can sometimes see the bacteria's stringy, milky ooze when a lower stem is cut.) It affects other cucurbits such as melons, but it is more serious in cucumbers.

There's no cure. All you can do is put the vines on the compost heap. But cukes are a quick crop, and if it's not too late in the season you can plant more of them, in a different part of the garden.

You can also practice prevention. Wilt bacteria are spread by cucumber beetles. (East of the Rockies they are yellow ones with black stripes; in the west they have spots.) Though these beetles can damage young cucumber plants just by eating them, the worst problem is the bacteria they inject into the stems as they chew. Keep an eye out for these beetles as the summer goes by. Hand-picking them is tricky, as they tend to fly away when they see you coming. Instead, become a morning person and go out at dawn with a shop vac, and vacuum them off while they are still heavy with dew. This works best if you use the slotted attachment, which is gentlest to the leaves. Knocking beetles off with water from a hose can help too.

Ultimately, the best way to ward off wilt, other than just giving the plants great fertile soil and consistent water to make them vigorous, is to cover young cucumber plants with floating row covers at planting time to exclude the pests. However, as soon as blossoms appear, you'll need to remove any pest barriers. By then the crop will need weeding and trellising. But even more, they will need the bees.

CHAPTER 24

Other Favorites

The list of vegetables that a gardener might grow is endless, so forgive me if I have omitted your favorite, whether it be the improbably productive tomatillo or the elusive but delectable cardoon. Here are a few, such as the thorny artichoke, that might not be the most practical because they require more space, time, or experience than most. Others carry with them extraordinary histories, demonstrate remarkable diversity, and hold deep secrets within. And some, like the pepper, have a mysterious secret power.

Corn Heaven

Sweet corn is not hard to grow but it is not always an obvious crop for the home garden. It takes up a lot of room for the food it yields and is a hungry feeder. A windstorm can blow it down. Its season is short. Raccoons always seem to know, the night before you do, when the ears are perfectly sweet and tender, and show up for dinner. Sometimes only such extreme measures as traps, an electric fence, or even a tall fence roofed like a cage will ensure protection.

But just like our furry masked marauders, we are irresistibly drawn each year to the prospect of freshly picked corn. In fact, the first corn of the season is already in my sights in April as I shuffle through the seed packets, noting which crops I can sow now and hurry along for earlier results. Traditionally, corn is not one of them. Direct sown in the ground, it will grow fine in soil as cool as 50-degree-Fahrenheit, but here's the catch: It won't germinate until the soil is at least 65 degrees. The solution is to sow the seeds indoors in nice warm soil mix, four seeds to a soil block or compostable pot. They will spring to life within four days and you can then plant them in 50-degree soil and have them grow.

If you've amended the soil with manure or compost the fall before, that's great. If not, do it now, preferably with manure that is well decomposed—not like the stuff in the cheeky French cartoon in the Paris newspaper *Le Monde*, in which a farmer astride a horse drops seeds behind him into each manure deposit the horse lets fall. Actually, that idea is not so far-fetched. Farmers have been known to lay down cowpats, mounded with soil, as a base into which they drop a few corn seeds.

We thin our four-seed clusters (known as "hills") to the strongest three, then plant them eighteen inches apart down the center of a thirty-inch-wide bed. Just one bed? One is often told to grow corn in blocks rather than long rows, to ensure good wind pollination. But pollination is assured if they are sown in hills. It's also easier to weed or cultivate them with this wide spacing.

Corn ears will not get more mature after picking so I wait until they are ready to eat. I get out a big pot when the tips of the ears feel more blunt than pointed when I pinch them. I'll peel back just a bit of husk to see if the kernels are full size and yield to a poke with a fingernail.

When my sisters and I were kids, we would gather up the ears and rush them into a pot of boiling water because everyone knew that sweet corn turned starchy if you waited too long to cook it. At markets, people shopped for corn by variety, looking for reliable ones, such as the yellow-and-white Butter and Sugar or the white Silver Queen. Farm stands sometimes used these names to market their ears, even if they

The colorful patterns in heirloom corns reflect their origins.

were something else. "Butter and Sugar," I heard one farmer say. "Lots of it sold. Not much grown."

With most present-day corn varieties, the garden-to-kitchen sprint is no longer a must. The discovery of sugar-enhanced and supersweet genes has led to corn kernels with a bigger percentage of sugar to start with and a tendency to stay sweet—more convenient for the cook. Progress has come at the expense of flavor, some say. Plant some and decide for yourself—if you can beat the raccoons.

Other Corns to Crave

They're as beautiful as jewels, and often just as precious and rare. The seeds of ornamental corn, lined up in rows on their cobs, explode with every known color, in fanciful combinations. Corn's color variability led geneticist Barbara McClintock to the far-reaching discovery that genes are not static, that controlling elements called transposons can jump from one gene to another, turning genetic traits off or on. Her work, published in 1950, eventually earned her a Nobel Prize.

To us, these seed mosaics seem like wondrous but random creations. But in fact, they encapsulate corn's history. Thought to have been developed from a plant called teosinte in ancient Mesoamerica, corn became the great foundation food crop of the western hemisphere. Millennia of planting, harvesting, and selecting by Indigenous growers gave it the strength of diversity—that is, the ability to survive by drawing on large numbers of well-adapted varieties. Corn's colors, which signal chemical agents that the ears produce for their survival, are like a secret code or a text that documents their evolution and their persistence. They are not embellishments upon what we regard as basic corn. In fact, many of those yellow or white ears we slather with butter result from the elimination of chance, randomness, and the power to adapt to their natural surroundings. Their parental kernels were born in laboratories that produce proprietary, patented seeds.

Hybrid corn, which does not reproduce true to seed, might seem like a David against this Goliath of history but, in fact, much of it carries its own ignorant weapon, the Roundup Ready gene, which could potentially infect every treasured open-pollinated variety with its onboard pesticide and also snuff out its genetic purity. And in nature, diversity is backup. Diversity is what saves you if the few hybrids that dominate world commerce meet an unfortunate fate.

You'll find Indian corn in many seed catalogs listed under ornamental corn. Companies that carry a better-focused selection, such as Seed Savers Exchange, Baker Creek, Victory Seeds, Southern Exposure, High Mowing, and Fedco, are drawing shoppers to these corns' culinary uses—for making cornmeal, corn flour, and hominy, or for roasting. Some are noted for their adaptation to specific regions of our country, such as Bloody Butcher from Virginia, Abenaki Calais Flint from Vermont, Ohio Blue Clarage, Nothstine Dent from Michigan, Mandan Bride from North Dakota, and Blue Hopi from Arizona. But many people still regard these ears as nothing more than fall decorations to tack up on your door.

Decorations are fine but consider growing an heirloom corn to make cornmeal with some year. We don't often think of our home gardens as sources of grains, despite the fact that some, such as wheat (easily threshed) and hull-less oats (even simpler), can be grown easily if you have extra space for them. And corn is the simplest grain crop of all.

Whenever I write about a particular food crop, I fantasize about eating it, even though the harvest might be months away. Popcorn is a joyous topic because there is always a jar on our pantry shelf. I am typing this with buttery fingers.

Recently I discovered a book by Andrew F. Smith, *Popped Culture: A Social History of Popcorn in America*. Smith follows popcorn's agricultural and entrepreneurial journey from a nourisher of Indigenous tribes to a strange growth swelling its foil package inside the microwave. It's the tale of a food long associated with fun, circuses, fairs, carnivals, and ball games, a snack we buy in a holiday mood. Preparing it at home is more play than work, and who ever outgrows the delight of watching, hearing, and smelling popcorn as its hard little kernels turn themselves noisily inside out? I love to imagine some ancient cook's discovery as an ear roasting in the fire suddenly burst. American popcorn popping even in the nineteenth century was often scarcely more controlled. There are descriptions of pans placed near the fire, blizzards of airborne kernels falling like snowflakes—no two alike!—a scramble to save them from the embers and ashes. My own memories of shaking a covered pot over a gas burner until the kernels lifted the lid seem just as magical.

The process by which popcorn pops is complex but, essentially, moisture turns to steam inside the endosperm (the starchy inner part of the kernel) until it suddenly explodes. This happens with other grains too—certain types of sorghum, rice, millet, quinoa, and amaranth—though with less drama. Quite apart from the fun factor, it's a handy quality to have in a stored crop. Popping doesn't impair the grain nutritionally and it creates an instant, fresh-tasting food with far less labor than it takes to grind meal and cook it until tender.

Growing your own popcorn is a great project for anyone but especially for children. As Smith notes, there's a tradition of farmers' sons earning pocket money by raising this niche product. Even the plants seem a bit childlike, with short stalks, small ears, small kernels. It makes a great beginner's crop, since the seeds are easy to handle and space regularly, the end result a food kids love to eat. Plant it as the soil is warming in earnest and there's still a long frost-free season ahead. Though some popcorn varieties mature in 85 or 90 days, others take up to 120. This can be a plus if you're growing sweet corn as well. But it's essential to prevent cross-pollination in corn if you are saving the seeds for next year's planting (a good way to round out the project), and it can even affect the quality of this year's crop, since, with corn, it is the seed itself you are eating. Crossing with popcorn can diminish sweet corn's sweetness, though popcorn's poppabilty is not affected. Planting the two crops at a distance from one another is one solution—difficult on a small property. Separating them by time, so that they shed their pollen several weeks apart, works best.

Many seed catalogs list popcorn. Essentially, there are two ways to go: the modern "gourmet" hybrids and the more eccentric heirlooms. The latter include the colorful Mini Blue, and Strawberry, which has cute two-inch ears. Many heirloom popcorns are great to bunch as fall ornamentals, and to grind as cornmeal too. The gourmet types will be forever associated with the charismatic Orville Redenbacher, a successful breeder who used the term "gourmet popcorn" to help justify the higher price he had to charge to make his improved varieties pay. Redenbacher and those who followed him strove for bigger, puffier kernels with fine flavor and less intrusive husks.

Popcorn requires well-drained soil, lightened with organic matter as needed to help the shallow roots take hold and keep the stalks upright. Sow the seeds in hills, as with sweet corn, then harvest it when the kernels are firm. Pull the husks back a bit and hang the ears in a warm, dry place to cure. The optimum moisture level within the kernels for popping is 13.5 percent. Test the kernels by popping a few, then store in sealed glass jars when ready.

Popcorn cookery has a long history, from popcorn cereal (eat it quick before it's soggy!) to gooey popcorn balls to modern popcorn snacks in odd flavors. It is often touted as a low-calorie snack, which it is until you add high-calorie fats and sugars. My favorite way to eat popcorn is doused with hot butter and a bit of soy sauce, then sprinkled with brewer's yeast—a delicious combination. Friends who do not embrace butterfat as confidently as I do claim that it is just as good with soy sauce and yeast alone. To them I raise my hand in a buttery salute.

Asparagus for the Long Haul

Nothing is forever, even a good bed of asparagus. But as garden investments go, this one pays off richly. One of the few perennial vegetables, an asparagus bed, well tended, might last half a lifetime. Every spring the little green missiles pop out of their underground silos with a payload of folate, fiber, and vitamin C.

Asparagus, as a permanent crop, requires more initial labor than other vegetables. Give it a deeply dug bed enriched with compost, and also some rock phosphate and lime if needed. A sunny spot is best, and a well-drained one is essential. Weeds and grass—especially grasses with long rhizomes—must be removed completely.

The usual practice is to buy dormant asparagus plants ("crowns") from a garden center, feed store, or mail-order nursery. An asparagus crown looks like an octopus with extra tentacles. To plant one, you dig a generous hole in the ground with a mound of enriched soil in the bottom, then spread the dangling roots over the mound. It should be deep enough that the top of the crown is several inches below soil level. Then fill in the rest of the dug soil. This can be done either with a row of individual holes, eighteen inches apart, or one long trench.

New plantings should be kept watered. An annual fall top-dressing of rotted manure and/or seaweed will keep them vigorous. A summer mulch of hay, straw, chopped leaves, or pine needles will help keep the soil moist and weed-free.

In recent years more gardeners have resumed the once common practice of starting asparagus from seed. It lowers the risk of bringing

For us, asparagus spears emerge in early May.

in diseases (although today's varieties tend to be more resistant) and it also allows seedlings to be segregated in a nursery bed until they declare their gender. Asparagus are dioecious—that is, they produce both male and female plants. The females bear red berries and are fecund to a fault, producing weedy little unwanted seedlings. Males, on the other hand, put their energy into growing spears, which are larger and more robust than those from females. There are all-male varieties, developed at Rutgers University in the 1990s, such as Jersey Giant. Practical as these are, you still may be tempted to plant some old-fashioned purple varieties such as Purple Passion. They are bisexual, but the spears are particularly sweet and tender.

If you go the seed route, order the seeds in January. Even after soaking in water for two days, they are slow to germinate, and you'll need to bring them on as seedlings at least eight weeks after germination and after danger of frost.

With either method, the plants should be spaced eighteen inches apart in rows four feet apart. You might plant a few extras in a separate bed in case you need to replace a few that don't come up the following year.

Establishing a productive bed also takes patience, because the first real harvest won't come for several years after planting. Take a few spears the first two years, but leave the rest to grow into fern, adding permanent vigor to the plants.

It's also crucial to keep the planting well maintained. That's the tricky part because it's easy to shift your focus to your annual crops. Long after spring asparagus with hollandaise has given way to summer tomatoes with vinaigrette, that bed still needs your attention.

I try very hard to keep our asparagus bed free of weeds, especially those with long tiller roots. My parents once lost a bed to orchard grass, with its powerful snaking rhizomes, and I lost one to the raspberry planting I thought I'd set at a safe distance away. It was impossible to remove the berries' underground stems without disturbing the asparagus crowns, and there was nothing to do but start over with fresh plants.

Watering the bed in dry weather is important too. Asparagus plants won't wilt in dismay the way lettuce will, but they'll be less productive the following year if allowed to dry out. So I have to keep it watered just like the rest of the garden.

If your site is windy, as ours is, the plants may flop, and it is worth running a length of sturdy twine, held up by stout stakes, on either side of the row to hold the stems upright. I use metal T-posts. In late fall we apply a top-dressing of hay, straw, and seaweed to keep the crop vigorous next spring. Since asparagus is relatively salt-tolerant, the salt residue in the seaweed is not a problem, but you can certainly use manure or compost instead.

If your asparagus seems to need a serious boost some year, stop picking it sooner than usual to give it a rest, and feed it with a liquid seaweed fertilizer. In the summer days ahead it will be easy to forget about a crop that has ceased to bear, when others are screaming for attention. Just remember what spring asparagus is like when picked and eaten immediately, sliced with butter. It's a taste that no amount of money can buy.

Celery Comes Home

Celery is a vegetable that everybody eats and hardly anybody grows in their gardens. We all love its crisp, mild taste, but we don't think of it having a season. It is simply there, in the crisper drawer, waiting to transport cream cheese or onion dip to the mouth, a sort of living cutlery.

Can you imagine cooking without it? Turkey stuffing without celery? Or chicken salad, potato salad, egg salad? There must always be a bunch of it handy, to sauté with onions and carrots as the base for a stock or a soup.

If you have ever raised celery and done it well, you know that the homegrown stalk is better than what comes in the plastic bag. For one thing, it always has leaves, which are good for the stockpot and also delicious fresh in a salad or in a ham sandwich.

Veteran celery growers also know that this is not something you plant casually—perhaps the reason it is not a present garden staple. It is fussy about moisture, temperature, and soil, and you can't turn your back on its needs. Consider yourself an accomplished gardener if you can produce magnificent celery.

Historically, celery is a marsh plant from the Mediterranean, noted by Homer. The original form, consumed for its strongly flavored leaves or used medicinally, was called smallage by the English, and sprouts up wild in damp places all over the world. The stalk celery we eat now was developed in England and first cultivated as a serious crop in America by Dutch farmers who settled around Kalamazoo, Michigan. Accustomed to working wet soils, and shod with stout wooden shoes, they grew celery in the region's rich, mucky fields. Before long the succulent novelty was being peddled to train passengers who paused at the Kalamazoo station. From there it spread by rail, as a snack food.

Those marshy beginnings are a clue to good celery culture. Though it won't grow in standing water, the soil must be kept continuously moist for germination, growth, and good flavor. It's also a hungry crop that will thank you for a bed rich in mature compost or well-decomposed manure.

You might find seedlings for sale at a nursery, but if not you can sow some of the tiny seeds indoors about ten weeks before the danger of frost has passed, in flats of well-moistened soil mix. Be patient, as they are slow to germinate. It's important not to transplant them outdoors too soon. Celery is a biennial that sets seed its second year. If you bring it outside while temperatures are still below 50 degrees Fahrenheit, it will think its first winter has arrived, and send up a tough flower stalk at the center when the weather starts to warm.

I suggest planting the heads in a double row, set a foot apart each way. Do it on a cloudy day to avoid heat stress. After that, the trick is to never let the celery stop growing. Make sure it gets a steady supply of water, and dose it with liquid fish fertilizer if growth is slow or the foliage is pale. I sometimes harvest a few of the outer stalks as I need them for the kitchen, but I make sure to cut any mature heads before the stalks can turn pithy.

For a fall crop, sow your flats, then set out seedlings in August. Celery likes the cooling days of fall and will even stand light frosts. It'll store a month or two in a cold cellar if you leave the roots on and cover it to keep it from drying out. Or use a spare fridge.

In the old days, celery was laboriously blanched in the field to make it tender. Then pale "self-blanching" varieties were developed. But they were less tasty and nutritious, and modern green varieties like Ventura, which need no blanching, make more sense. Despite these advances, it's still a Cinderella vegetable. You will rarely find celery in gourmet seed catalogs, although you might find something called "cutting celery," which is not far removed from the old smallage and essentially a leaf crop. Once known as "soup celery," it is easy to grow.

In the past, strongly flavored red varieties of celery were sold. A number of companies carry seeds of Redventure, a cross made by renowned Oregon breeder Frank Morton between Ventura and the old Giant Red. It's tender, without the stringiness of the old red celery, but with an assertive taste.

I am sometimes amazed at how we take our staple foods for granted, how we stroll by them in the market, or toss them into the cart with so little awareness of what kind of trail led them to us. Next time you reach for a celery stick, don't dwell on the fact that it's not a doughnut or a cookie. Imagine it's 1890 and you're on a train pulling into Kalamazoo. Someone hands you a green stalk. It's so crunchy and full of moisture, so alive, so new.

A Rainbow of Eggplants

"Eggplant is a color," my young friend informed me. "It's, like, a T-shirt at J.Crew. At J. Peterman it might have been Aubergine, It is not something that you would eat."

The girl didn't know what she was missing. When summer's heat ripens those purple-black beauties at our house, I celebrate. Out come the fresh herbs, olive oil, and tongs, up go the flames, and onto the grill go the eggplant slices as soon as the coals settle to a quiet smolder. Their smoky flavor, lush texture, and crisp-crunchy skin have turned many an eggplant hater into a fan.

Growing and eating eggplant are all about heat. From the minute you start the seeds indoors—about eight weeks before the last frost—until harvest time, our job is to make them think they are in Africa, Iran, or, at the very least, Orlando. The seeds germinate best at 80 to 90 degrees Fahrenheit, and the young seedlings are happy at 70 degrees. We wouldn't set them outdoors until it's at least 60 degrees and would sooner move them up to bigger and bigger pots indoors than risk a setback. A blanket of white floating row cover offers a bit of cold protection and, more important, a barrier against flea beetles, the one pest that has plagued ours. Later in the season these tiny hopping bugs, which turn the leaves into lacy skeletons, are less active.

The fruits are snipped off the plant before they are biologically mature, while the skin is glossy and the seeds inside have not darkened. Often they're picked at baby size, though I wait until they've softened enough to leave the imprint of my fingernail when poked. They're better tasting then and more digestible. It's important to keep up with the picking, even if you fall behind on the eating, so the plants will continue to produce. Eat them within a few days, without refrigerating them. Even after harvest they prefer warmth to cold.

In the kitchen, heat is always part of the picture because eggplant is never eaten raw. (Few fruits of the garden share this distinction, though okra, another heat lover, is one of them.) Most people know eggplant only in eggplant parmigiana, a dish in which it functions largely as a thick blotter for soaking up tomato, cheese, and oil. Its personality shines more in moussaka, that heavenly Greek casserole involving lamb and a rich cream sauce. Or the Middle Eastern baba ghanoush, for which it is roasted whole until soft and smoky, then peeled, mashed, and mixed with tahini, lemon, olive oil, and garlic. It can also be combined with yogurt in a smooth, garlicky dip. Caponata is an Italian version with capers, olives, peppers, tomatoes, and pine nuts. Perhaps you've discovered eggplant

in red Thai curries, or Indian curries with tomatoes and onions, or in a French ratatouille along with tomatoes, peppers, onions, and summer squash. To all of these it brings a rich body and just the hint of a pleasant bitterness.

Next to grilling, my favorite way to treat eggplant is to fry it in olive oil (with or without a breading), then sprinkle it with parsley and lemon. I use the traditional method of slicing and salting the fruits to draw out moisture, letting them drain on towels for a half hour. I find this works best if I then rinse the slices under running water, squeezing them flat with my fingers. This helps them to cook quickly and evenly, without absorbing too much oil. I think salting to remove bitterness from eggplant is a bit of a myth, since none of the varieties I know are bitter in excess.

Try growing several different eggplant types to discover their special virtues, not the least of which are visual. The big black ones are gorgeous, but so are skinny Asian varieties such as Orient Express, which bear early and heavily. Louisiana Long Green is mild and tasty. I once had fun with a luminous magenta one, aptly named Neon, and there are magnificent eggplants striped with violet or green. Others are pure white, like the small, round ones, firm-fleshed and thick-skinned, that gave eggplant its English name. There are even red-orange ones from Africa, but unfortunately, in a short season like mine, these would have to be eaten before they reached full color.

Not surprisingly, eggplant first came to this country as an ornamental plant, not an edible one. Quite apart from the old misconception that they were toxic and caused insanity (their Italian name *melanzana* translates as "crazy apple"), I can understand growing them for their beauty alone. The plants are compact, with handsome blue-green leaves and stunning purple flowers. I have sometimes grown them in my herb garden near the kitchen window, just so I can look out and admire them. (They also make good container plants.) Imagine a mixed eggplant border in which a rainbow of fruits hangs from the plants in high summer and are displayed in a bowl on the dining table. Like colored T-shirts, you can never have too many of them.

Quirky Cauliflower

Among the brassicas, cauliflower is the trickiest to grow, which is why you see it less often in gardens than you do cabbage, broccoli, or kale. But it has the mildest, most delicate flavor, a pleasant texture, and, besides that, unusual beauty. A cauliflower head, whether it is basic white or a trendy gold, purple, or lime-green, is like a jewel set in a corona of great green leaves. Watching a head grow is like watching a flower slowly open and bloom.

Cauliflower might seem like a giant flower cluster but, in fact, a cauliflower's curd, or head, is essentially a large cluster of dense, multi-branched, immature floral material whose development stops at a stage preceding bloom. An uncut cauliflower head may eventually produce flowers if it does not rot first, and leaves may sprout within the curd in very hot weather, but what you want to produce is one with a tight, smooth, hard surface.

Sensitivity to climate is what makes cauliflower such a princess in the garden. Spring seedlings, which should be started indoors, are a bit less frost hardy than those of other brassicas and should be no more than three weeks old when they are transplanted into the garden. They can go in before the danger of light frost has passed but must be protected with floating row covers if a hard freeze threatens. Plant them two feet apart (for good air circulation) in a fertile soil with a neutral pH and plenty of organic matter for good moisture retention. Once established, the plants themselves will happily endure both cool and hot weather, but proper head formation can be thwarted by extremes of either. Sometimes you just have to let cauliflower wait out a hot spell. When it eases off, heads may appear.

The crucial thing with cauliflower is never to let growth be checked. Keep moisture even and top-dress with a liquid seaweed or manure if the plants grow too slowly. In a climate where the window between last frost and first heat wave is short, an early-maturing variety is the best choice. You can also set out transplants in mid- to late summer for a fall crop, as long as there is plenty of time for them to mature before hard frost. Always keep them well watered.

The pristine whiteness of a cauliflower head can be as elusive as Ahab's whale. Hot sun will cause it to yellow, and you may have to fold or tie a few big inner leaves over the curd to shield it, even with the lush-leaved "self-blanching" varieties. Let a head sit too long on the plant and the smooth curd will start to open up. Dark, fungal smudges may appear as deterioration sets in. Think of cauliflower as a gorgeous white suit or dress, easy to sully and an effort to clean. But what would a summer be without it?

There is another quirky thing about cauliflower, though, quite apart from its smooth whiteness. Take a look at its most unusual type, Romanesco. Like certain more normally shaped varieties, such as Vitaverde (or "broccoflower"), it is a striking yellow-green color, but look even more closely at its structure. Its head is a spiral made up of smaller spirals that are, in turn, made up of even smaller spirals, and would go on with this self-similar pattern indefinitely if a hot spell, a freeze, or simple old age didn't put an end to this extraordinary fractal-like display.

Romanesco cauliflower (also known as Roman cauliflower or Romanesco broccoli), which seems to have appeared, either by chance or human effort, in the fields around Rome in the fifteenth or sixteenth century, is certainly not the only example of self-replication in nature (fern fronds and frost patterns being other classic examples). Biological geometry in general is one of those wonderful quicksands of knowledge that I could happily sink into, never to spend time in more practical pursuits again.

Sometimes I look at a regular cauliflower and see that it is trying to replicate its big head in all the smaller mounds on its bumpy surface, and maybe in the still smaller bumps on those. Why? And when a plant does produce a flower, why am I so pleased by the arrangement of its petals, their color, and their scent, I being neither butterfly nor bee, with no role in its survival?

I'll leave you to figure all that out. One of the comforts of being a kitchen gardener is a simplicity of purpose. As with any cauliflower, Romanesco is at its best cooked (although it looks spectacular raw on a crudité platter as well). I recommend separating the head into little tree-shaped florets, steaming them, then tossing them in bread crumbs and butter, to serve hot. Just don't be surprised if someone stops and gazes, with fork suspended, at a small morsel of infinity.

Gift for a Founding Father

It's been two hundred years since Thomas Jefferson's American consul in Florence, Italy, Thomas Appleton, sent him some fennel to plant at Monticello. Jefferson did, and the crop has thrived over here in peaceful obscurity ever since. In California, where the climate is something like the plant's native Mediterranean region, it has naturalized and is not unusual in cuisine. Easterners have taken longer to embrace it.

I tasted my first fennel as a child in an Italian neighbor's garden. It looked like a stalk of celery with a licorice flavor, but a mild one—not the strong, cloying taste of licorice candy, or the potent thrust of liquors such as ouzo, Pernod, and anisette. Many years later I ate a fennel salad in an Italian restaurant that was milder still—almost as subtle as the licorice hint you get in chervil or tarragon. This fennel had been sliced thin, doused with good olive oil, paired with oranges, and topped with curls of Parmigiano-Reggiano cheese. I was hooked.

This was Florence fennel, or bulb fennel, which looks like a celery plant that has stepped in front of one of those funhouse mirrors that widen your girth. It is a beautiful vegetable. The flattened base, when mature, can be as wide as your hand, the stalks wrapped in an overlapping pattern. A thin green stem projects from each, topped with ferny foliage a bit like dill's but firmer and greener, perfect for garnishing a plate.

Fennel's use extends through much of the world, but to me it always evokes the Mediterranean countries. In the south of France, it is as customary as saffron in bouillabaisse and other fish soups. In fact, to many minds, fennel is always associated with seafood. English fishmongers have traditionally offered the tasty fronds with fish to use in an accompanying sauce. It's great for stuffing a fish or as a bed on which to roast one whole. There is indeed something very pleasant about the way fennel balances a fish's flavor, especially the stronger, oilier ones like salmon and mackerel. It even makes them more digestible.

I often cook the bulbs by themselves, brushed with oil and braised until they caramelize. Raw, they can be used any way you would use

Above left: Cheddar is a cauliflower variety with an appealing golden hue.

Above: Eliot harvests a fennel bulb by slicing it off the roots at ground level.

onion or celery—raising a tuna or lobster salad well above deli counter status.

When Thomas Appleton recommended fennel to Jefferson, it was as a dessert.

Though fennel is now familiar in restaurants, and even produce markets, it is just starting to appear in home gardens. You do not have to go to Florence or Marseille in order to learn to grow it, fun as that would be. Many seed catalogs carry it, sometimes under its Italian name, *finocchio*, which rhymes with that of the famous long-nosed puppet.

The nonbulbing fennel, often sold as herb fennel, is also useful and attractive. There is even a purplish type called bronze fennel that makes a pretty foil for roses and other flowers but it can be invasive in some gardens. Herb fennel is allowed to bloom. It makes the same yellow umbels you find on parsley and dill, attracting beneficial insects such as lacewings and syrphid flies in heroic numbers.

Bulb fennel tends to bolt in hot weather, so it is most successfully grown as a fall crop. If you start it indoors, sow it in containers or soil blocks. (Because of its taproot, it can only be pricked out of a seed tray when very tiny.) But you can also sow it directly in a fine-textured seedbed outdoors, as thinly as possible, keeping the bed moistened. Soil should be fertile, well drained, and not too acidic. Thin the seedlings to several inches apart, then to about eight inches, eating the thinnings. Even if the bulbs never become supersized before hard frost, you'll be guaranteed a crop of the baby fennel so prized by chefs for its tenderness and elegance. If you're going for big bulbs, feed them every month or so with manure tea or a fish/seaweed fertilizer to help fatten them up. Harvest them before they turn woody.

Sometimes fennel will surprise you. Once, in late fall, I came upon a bed half full of huge, overgrown bulbs, eight inches apart and as woody as trees. Poised to evict them with my digging fork, I noticed the part of the bed where they had been harvested. Where each old bulb had been severed from its roots, clusters of baby bulbs had grown. They were juicy, sweet, crunchy, and tender, with a mild flavor. Even at the base of the giant uncut bulbs, these delicious little side ones were forming. Here was a plant determined to have a long season. Among its sprawling, fernlike fronds, now three feet long, umbels of yellow flowers waved, hoping to lure whatever pollinators might still be in the yard.

If your goal is to grow fennel flowers or seeds, both of which are used as seasonings in Italy, plant the herb type. For those who use fennel medicinally, much of the potency lies in the seeds, although the whole plant exerts a benign effect on its particular realm, the intestinal tract. Fennel is said to prevent flatulence, aid digestion, relieve cramping and bloating, calm the stomach, sweeten the breath, and take just enough of an edge off the appetite to keep you from reaching for a brownie.

Sounds like an excellent dessert.

Artichokes for Everyone

The artichoke is a formidable vegetable. Armed like a cactus, its spiny globes are as much a challenge as a temptation. You must peel away many sharply pointed scales to reach what Pablo Neruda called "the peaceable dough of its green heart." But the reward is great. The heart is silky tender when steamed or boiled, sublime when dipped in butter. There are even nuggets of flavor at the base of the scales, to urge you along.

Growing artichokes is a fun project even for eastern gardeners. Most of this country's crop comes from the mild coastal regions of California. The plants, though perennial, do not normally produce the heads (which are actually flower buds) until their second growing season, having survived the winter with their roots in the ground. If the roots are exposed to temperatures below 20 degrees Fahrenheit, the plant usually perishes.

Nevertheless, you can grow them almost anywhere in the United States. Researchers in New York in the 1920s successfully wintered over established plants by cutting them back to a foot tall, gathering in the leaves, and heaping sifted coal ashes over them. In eighteenth-century Virginia, John Randolph overwintered them at Williamsburg with straw as insulation. Thomas Jefferson did something similar at Monticello.

Artichokes can be
grown even in cold
climates.

Some growers dig the roots and pot them up; others store them in the
cellar the way you would dahlia tubers, then divide them once they
sprout in spring.

However, the simplest method today is to grow them from seed as
annuals. This requires a technique called vernalization, by which you
trick the plants into thinking they have been through their first winter,
and thus are ready to set buds. The modern varieties bred by Keith
Mayberry, the green Imperial Star and purple Colorado Star, lend themselves especially well to this practice.

If you're game to try it, here's our routine. We purchase the seeds
in January and sow them in a bright, warm place any time during the
following month or so. Then we transplant them into five-inch pots when
they are about ten days old. Once the plants are six weeks old, we set the
pots out in a cold frame or some other protected space that is closed at
night to protect them from freezing but fully open all day, so that they
experience a few weeks of chilly spring weather—at least as low as
50 degrees Fahrenheit. (You could also set them just outside your door,
where you can cover them for the night if a hard frost threatens.) After

the danger has passed, we plant them in the garden. As far as they're concerned, that chilly spell was "winter," they are now two years old, and it's time to make artichokes. If we lived in a climate where it got down to 50 degrees Fahrenheit but not below 20, we could just grow them outdoors through the winter and let them bear in spring before hot weather sets in.

The varieties that play this game are, in reality, perennial plants whose required chilling period is very brief. With the proper timing, they produce abundant buds of consistent quality that are fine tasting and less prickly to handle. They even have delicious edible stems and less of a "choke"—the nest of fuzzy inedible bracts that sits atop the heart.

Set the plants at least two feet apart in the row. Their long taproots appreciate a well-drained, deeply dug bed, and the more fertile you can make the soil, the more artichokes you will harvest. A plant on average soil might produce five buds, on good soil ten—on a gorgeously rich muck, loaded with organic matter you might get fifteen. Top-dressing with liquid fish fertilizer will supply extra nitrogen and calcium, though I'd go easy in very hot weather, when the plants may enter a stretch of summer dormancy. (In most parts of Italy—true artichoke country—they are a winter crop.) Ample water and a mulch will help keep production going.

The first bud, formed on the central stalk, is the biggest. When you cut that one, the side branches are encouraged to bear. All buds should be harvested while tightly closed, since they toughen as soon as the scales start to flare outward. The smaller you pick them, the more tender and chokeless they will be. With a little trimming of the tips, the tiny ones ("baby" artichokes) can be fried or braised with garlic and olive oil and eaten whole.

The price of fresh artichokes is scarier than their spines. Imagine having all you could eat, for months on end. You could drop the hearts into soup, simmer them and toss them with pasta, layer them in a pungent Mediterranean casserole with capers and anchovies or sardines.

Having said that, I do recall a day when Eliot walked in with a big basket of artichokes and I wailed, "I don't have time!" He dumped them into a big pot of boiling water and cooked them so long that they were

completely falling apart. You could grab and eat several scales at once, then fistfuls at the center, and whole hearts swished in butter. It was quick, it was messy, it was artichoke heaven.

If you can't keep up with the picking, leave some buds and let them bloom. Picture a row of majestic gray-green plants crowned with thistle-like flowers in an intense, almost neon, violet-blue. They'll lure butterflies, pollinating bees, and seed-eating finches, enhancing your garden as much as they do your table.

Peppers Like It Hot

I'm late getting the peppers planted this year, but that's just fine. The longer I wait, the warmer the soil gets, and peppers hate cold soil. The delay will also give me time to spread some compost on the bed and get out my broadfork and loosen the soil deeply. Peppers need that because, while most garden peppers don't grow much farther than two feet tall, their vigorous root systems can go down as far as four feet. Once they're planted, I'll keep them irrigated and pick off the first flowers to keep fruits from forming. Eager as I am, I know they'll be more plentiful later on if I let the plants put their early energy into growing roots.

Delaying gratification is not, normally, the chile lover's strength, and as I learn more about this plant I begin to understand why. If you grow up appreciating spicy food, life is bland without it. How many mothers take their kids to visit the Tabasco sauce factory? Mine did. It's on Avery Island, in Louisiana, a stretch of beautiful marshland with a splendid wildlife refuge. But my southern relations' taste for fire pales next to that of a South American friend who once visited our home for several weeks. As soon as she arrived, she headed straight for the supermarket to buy a big jar of peppers—round green firebombs that she added to everything she was served, from eggs to coq au vin. Adjustment was not an option.

I have long grown sweet peppers too, including a few with the occasional "Russian roulette" habit, where a single "hot" pepper will mysteriously appear. I especially love the mild, wrinkled little shishito peppers, from Asia, some of which are green and some red. But I can fully understand why some people find the hot ones irresistible. Scientists now know that substances called capsaicinoids, found only in hot peppers, lock onto certain human receptors and produce a euphoria not unlike what you'd get from an opiate. A chemical reaction between you and the pepper you've eaten sends a message to the brain that says, "Do something!" Endorphins are released that both deaden the searing sensation and get you a little bit high. Over time, this desensitizes your taste buds, so you need hotter and hotter foods to ignite the burn and start the endorphin flow. Since capsaicinoids do not produce true heat, and are not harmful if eaten in reasonable portions, they have even hit the pharmaceutical trail. They are in topical analgesic ointments that ease the pain of shingles and arthritis, and in nasal sprays that ease congestion and headache. When I flip through the pages of the Redwood City Seed's huge pepper selection, I can just feel my sinuses clear.

As addictions go, the one borne by pepper junkies is supremely benign. Their lives are chained to a health-giving superfood with more vitamin C than in oranges, oodles of protovitamin A, and a wealth of

Peppers grow on compact plants, so it's easy to fit a rainbow of them into the garden.

trace minerals, beta-carotene, lycopene, fiber, and folate. What's more, teaching your mouth to take the heat opens it up to more adventures. Chile peppers vary widely in their flavors, whose richness and subtlety you can only fully enjoy if you consume them in quantity. My Latina friend knew which ones went with certain dishes, an appreciation denied to those for whom they merely taste "hot." We norteamericanos rate pepper heat with various scales such as the American Spice Trade Association's "pungency units" or Wilbur Scoville's Scoville scale, invented in 1912, which ranges from the 1,000 or so units found in the mild Anaheim to over 300,000 in the most incendiary habanero.

I'm working my way up my own little scale based on dishes I love to eat, as in "Poblano: just hot enough for chiles rellenos" or "Jalapeño: great on pizza." I'm training hard with the mysterious little ones you can order on the side in Thai and Indian restaurants. All are members of the genus *Capsicum*, as opposed to *Piper nigrum*, the black Middle Eastern pepper we grind routinely at table.

Capsicum peppers, now a global force, were a South American gift to the world, unknown elsewhere before 1493. It was neither gold nor the fountain of youth that drew Columbus across the sea, but the spices of India, among them black pepper. Imagine the delight in finding a plant with far more zing—whole fields of it, with big red fruits that put the true pepper's little black buckshot to shame. His physician took them back to Europe, and other explorers spread them to the eastern world.

Let's lift a glass to their success—a glass filled with a properly made bloody Mary, generously spiked with Louisiana Tabasco sauce. I remember once reading an article in *New York* magazine about that classic drink, in which the author not only sampled the offerings of the city's bars but also sent them to a lab for chemical analysis. It's hard to cheat on Scoville units, so all packed a decent punch. Most scored well on Worcestershire sauce and lemon. But an appalling number skimped on the vodka and a few contained not one drop. Surely New Yorkers are not so easily fooled. My guess is their thirst was well quenched, they felt happy, and perhaps it was never about the vodka at all.

CHAPTER 25

Garden Fruits

When choosing a shrub, tree, or vine, don't forget to ask yourself whether it could be an edible one. Need a hedge? Plant blueberries or raspberries. Need a small attractive tree? Apples, peaches, and pears all grow to a manageable size. Want more shade in summertime? Put up an arbor with grapevines on it, or hardy kiwis.

Here are my thoughts on some of the most popular fruits to grow, not as orchards, but as family-sized plantings. But don't stop at these. Your particular climate probably contains many fruits that I can't grow, or don't choose to. It's too cool during my Maine summers to ripen pawpaws, a splendid native North American fruit. Persimmons would not survive, nor would lemons—at least not outdoors. I've grown peaches—but just barely. Give a thought to elderberries, quinces, boysenberries, and plums. So rich is the Earth's store of fruits that at this very moment there may be one growing in your yard that I have not even heard of.

Simply Strawberries

Sometimes a box of strawberries will beckon to me from the produce shelf—plump, red, and luscious. I have to remind myself that they were

Grapes and apples fill a tray in fall. The red chokeberries, though technically edible, are there for color.

grown far away and artificially ripened, that their flavor is likely to be bland, that I don't know for sure what substances they might contain. I feel like Sleeping Beauty, being offered the poisoned apple. I decide to wait until strawberry season.

If you look in late spring and early summer, you can find real strawberries grown without pesticides by local farmers. If there's a "pick-your-own" farm nearby it makes a wonderful excuse for a day in the country, especially with kids. But the best are the strawberries grown by you. They're the perfect summer dessert to have steps away from your kitchen—quick to bear, easy to grow, and a natural people pleaser.

Sometimes home gardeners are baffled by the different types of strawberries available and daunted by complex planting schemes that look like some sort of fruit chess. I will try to simplify them for you.

"Early season" varieties such as Earliglow give you one bumper crop in early summer (usually June), great for eating, freezing, and putting up jars of jam. Varieties called "everbearing" produce an early crop, take a break in midsummer, and then bear a second crop in fall. There is also a third category called "day-neutral," which is a form of everbearing that takes less of a pause in midseason; the strawberry's tendency to slow

Day-neutral straw-
berries, mulched
with pine needles

down in response to lengthening days has been thwarted enough to give you a steadier, though less abundant, supply throughout the summer. I like always having enough berries for a few bowls for dessert or to top an ice cream sundae, so I've mostly grown day-neutral varieties such as the reliable Tristar, which gives me exactly that.

Early this summer I planted some day-neutral strawberries in a circle at the center of my herb garden. When they started to bloom, I pinched out the blossoms at the center of each cluster so that the young plants would put most of their energy into putting down roots. These "mother" plants will put out some runners—thin stems with new little strawberry plants at the ends—so that the spaces between them will start to fill in, increasing the berry supply. But there will be fewer runners than there would be with early June bearers, and any that wander outside of my neat circle can be snipped and given away or transplanted somewhere else for extra berries. Meanwhile, they will bear fruit all summer, starting in July. Next year I will refresh the bed with new strawberry plants, or a different crop altogether.

If I were a serious freezing and jam-making gardener, I would plant June bearers that would not produce a big crop until the following June.

These little gems (alpine strawberries) are tiny but delicious. Children love to pick them.

They'd spend their first year growing a good root system and sending out lots of runners with "daughter" plants at their tips. These make next year's berries. (If I conscientiously picked off all blossoms that formed on the mother plants, the whole system would be more vigorous.) The following year, I'd start a second bed, carefully snipping the runners, digging up the daughters, and planting them in Bed 2, while the mothers in Bed 1 bore fruits. I would then continue this system so that I would always have two beds—a growing bed and a picking bed. That might sound like more work but consider this: I would never need to buy new plants.

Still another option is to plant the delightful little alpine strawberries, or *fraises des bois*. These are grown easily from seed, bear the first year, and then keep going for years as hardy perennials. They make tidy, runnerless mounds, perfect for edging a bed of herbs or flowers. They give you mere handfuls of tiny fruit, scarcely bigger than wild strawberries, but their intense woodsy flavor is what a wine lover would call "complex." Varieties tend to be named for Old World royalty: Catherine the Great, Charles V, Baron Solemacher. I've had good luck with Alexandria.

Another strawberry I'm growing again this year is a modern variety called Mara des bois, which is larger than an alpine, but has a flavor almost as sublime. It was hybridized in 1991 by strawberry breeder Jacques Marionnet from four varieties with the goal of achieving intense flavor in a reasonably sized berry. Its season in France is late August into fall, and it is easily stressed by intense heat, humidity, drying winds, and stagnant air. Often it will stop bearing during hot weather but then start up again when it cools down. Though technically an ever-bearing variety, it does put out enough runners to give you a permanent supply of plants.

Caring for strawberries is a matter of keeping the soil moist but not soggy and the bed weeded. Weeding is a delicate maneuver, as you have to try to avoid digging up the new little plants that are forming. So it's tempting to put down a mulch. I have used both straw and pine needles successfully, and the mulch does keep the berries cleaner and less susceptible to soilborne diseases. But it makes it harder for runners to put down roots, if it's runners you're after.

Birds can also be a problem. One year the robins were so fond of my crop that I had to put a floating row cover over it, lifting it only to weed and pick.

What about those cute strawberry jars, with a cuplike opening for each plant? Often they don't keep plants sufficiently moist, though some sort of central column filled with gravel is said to help. I think they're better suited to growing drought-tolerant ornamental plants like sedums.

However you choose to grow strawberries, your summer will be the richer for it. In my family there are several summer birthdays, always celebrated with a cake with cut-up berries between the layers and whole ones on top, set in a whipped cream frosting. Shortcakes appear for other special gatherings. According to my warped logic, I can get away with bakery-made shortcake biscuits if I grow my own berries.

Sometimes in summer people arrive at our home without warning. A salad is quickly gathered, herbs snipped, a dressing made. Something might be grilled on a fire. After that, I tell my guests that the "pick-your-own farm is that-a-way," indicating the strawberry bed. And off they go.

A Fool for Raspberries

In the language of botany, a plant is "armed" if it packs certain defensive gear. A cactus uses sharp spines, which are modified leaves, to protect itself from creatures seeking the water inside its stems. A lemon tree guards its fruit with thorns, which are modified branches. Bramble fruits such as raspberries are armed with prickles, which are modifications of the plant's epidermis (its skin). Birds, which help to spread the seeds, are not deterred. But mammals like us are unwelcome.

The raspberry is a lot like its close cousin, the rose, long described by poets of romantic temperament as a fair prize to be courted and won, a seductive lady desired for her beauty but guarded by sharp thorns. Excuse me, prickles. I'm not sure what perverse part of Nature's plan made raspberries taste so delicious, lip soft, and nearly devoid of tartness when fully ripe, then dangled them on canes that catch on your sweater and lash you like whips.

A raspberry lover will put up with that. She will go out and find them warm from the late afternoon sun, saying "I'll just pick a few." Her eye is drawn to those with the deep red color of ripeness, but her fingers make the final test. If a berry resists a gentle tug, it has a day more to go. If it collapses between her fingers, overripe, she drops it to the ground. Otherwise, she continues to pop them into her mouth, happily spoiling her appetite for dinner.

Of all fruits, raspberries are the most perishable and hard to ship, expensive even while in season. And I, for one, would hate to let a summer go by without my favorite raspberry pie, in which half the berries are cooked and the other half raw, stirred into the filling after it has thickened and cooled. Or a simple dish called raspberry fool, which is just pureed fresh raspberries folded into sweetened whipped cream and served in a wine goblet.

Still, some gardeners think twice about planting raspberries. Their yearly pruning and training may seem daunting but it's not, once you get into the routine.

You'll need to prepare a wide, permanent bed that is well weeded and well fortified with compost. Buy yourself a pair of sturdy leather gauntlet-style gardening gloves to make maintenance painless. (I found a woman-sized pair from a company called Womanswork.) You will also need to buy plants. Raspberries dug from the wild are harder to pick and not as productive. We are often advised to decline offers from berry-growing friends who are pulling out their extras, and to start afresh with certified virus-free stock.

There are two types of red raspberries. The most common bears each summer on canes produced the previous year. After there are no more berries to pick, you cut the canes that have fruited to the ground, being careful to spare some one-year-old canes with no little spent clusters on them. If you are using a row system, during the winter remove any canes that look spindly, and thin the good ones to about one or two per foot in the row. Cut the tips of those to a good picking height—about five feet. During summer, remove any canes that come up between the rows.

The other type is the so-called everbearing raspberry, which bears in fall on first-year canes. If you leave the plants in the ground, trimming back only the part that has fruited, they will bear again the following summer, though the crop will be smaller. Like many gardeners, Eliot and I just cut or mow down the whole row, thus sacrificing the summer crop in favor of one big, bounteous fall one. This is much simpler, and the best option if you are growing an everbearing variety and a regular summer one as well. We have even taken this a step further and are currently growing only an everbearer as a fall crop and no summer one at all, because in our climate the fall ones are always much healthier.

If you set up a good trellising system, your berry rows will not look like the foundation planting around Sleeping Beauty's castle and will be more pleasant to pick. The plants will be less disease-prone because they'll get more sunlight and better air circulation. One technique is to drive in a stout post at both ends of the row, with two cross pieces attached to each, to make a telephone pole shape. Strong wire is then strung from post to post at the ends of the four arms, to make a long enclosure in which the canes must grow. They are held upright and accessible, with a clear demarcation between path and plot. You then boldly don your gloves and dig out, pull out, or mow down any canes that grow outside this defined corridor.

In a variation of this plan, the canes are tied to wires on either side of the row so that they make a V. This lets more sunlight into the center of the row, encouraging new canes to grow there instead of in the paths.

In recent years, Eliot and I have used a different planting scheme altogether, which we find much better suited to the home garden. Instead of planting raspberries evenly spaced in a row, we plant them in hills, meaning clusters, as with a hill of corn, a hill of squash, and a hill of beans. We drove in stout posts six feet apart in a row, with just one plant per post—soon to multiply itself by sending up new canes at soil level. Each fall, after pruning out the canes that have just borne fruit, we select the new ones that will bear the following summer, tying them to the post with heavy-duty twine just tightly enough so that they remain vertical and won't collapse with winter snow and ice. We restrict these to eight of the sturdiest canes, growing as close as possible to the post, and cut off the rest at soil level. The result is a series of tidy thickets, like dense bushes, that we can walk all the way around in comfort instead of having to plunge into the briers.

The more organic matter you spread on the soil around the plants, the healthier they will be and the more berries you will have to gorge on. Rotted manure is ideal, even manure mixed with wood chips—which are too resistant to decay for use on vegetable gardens—will do fine as a mulch for raspberries.

Another important task for the berry gardener is to punch two holes in the rim of a one-quart yogurt container so that you can tie string to it and hang it around your neck. It's handy for berry lovers of any age to use while picking with both hands, nibbling as they go, and still bringing in enough for a pie.

Not all raspberries are red. There are yellow, black, and purple ones (the black, and often the purple, fruit on side shoots and are slightly more

complicated to prune). And not all raspberries will enjoy mild winters and hot summers. If you live in a warm climate, search out varieties with heat resistance.

Or, you can simply grow blackberries instead, which are also delicious and decidedly heat friendly. Some are even thornless. Not that you're afraid of a few prickles.

Pruning Grapes

The days of wine and roses they're not, but the days of mud season offer their own odd pleasures. Putting on rubber boots and poking around the garden. Looking for the emerging tips of spring bulbs. Cleaning up debris that winter's winds have scattered. And pruning the grapes. That could have been done at any time during their dormancy, but now there's a bit of urgency, because it must be done before the buds start to swell. And with the dead leaves all blown off them and the vines' skeletons laid bare, we can see more easily where to cut.

Pruning is a satisfying garden job because you are shaping a plant, working on a scaffolding that, in the mind's eye, will soon be covered with

Hayden gets a snack from the grape arbor.

leaves. The work will direct and promote the season's growth. Paradoxically, you destroy plant tissue so that healthy, well-managed plant tissue will grow.

About twenty years ago I picked out some grape varieties that I knew would ripen in our short growing season: Swenson Red, Worden, and Edelweiss. (We also grow a hardy seedless variety called Canadice.) To support them, our neighbor Mark Kindschi built us an iron arbor that runs the length of the south-facing side of the house. When bare, the vines let the low-angled sun in the windows for solar heat. When leafed out, just like a roll-up awning, they shade the granite terrace I laid, for late summer meals. Eight vertical iron pillars, each with a vine planted at its base, hold up a framework that rises at a slight upward angle and connects to the house.

Grapes produce mighty vines that grow at a heroic rate, so they must be pruned each year, otherwise, they'd become a mass of greenery too weighty and wandering to manage. Sunlight would not reach the ripening fruit. And on our arbor, even the denseness of too many branches would block the winter sun that finds its ways through our windows.

Generally, Eliot does the pruning. The goal is to create a thick cover of foliage but in a controlled way. Using a combination of hand pruners, loppers, and a pruning saw, he cuts back all of last year's long shoots close to the main branches from which they emerge, leaving just one bud on them from which a replacement branch will grow. He takes out or shortens any established branches that are crowded or seem excessive. While he's up there, he anchors the main branches to the overhead supports with self-locking black plastic ties, so that they won't fall or blow around.

Meanwhile, I'm down there on the ground, dragging off the prunings and snipping off the shoots that continually appear on the vertical trunks of the vines, up to the top where they change direction and become part of a leafy, living roof.

The grapes don't bear until October. But there are still a few weeks where you can finish an outdoor meal, then stand on the long wooden table, reach up, and pick dessert.

Making the Must of It

I never knew it had a name. Every year I make a syrup from the deep blue-black Worden grapes on the arbor. This is incredibly simple to do. I pick all the grapes (from our one vine, more than enough to fill a five-gallon bucket), wash them, and then put them in two large stockpots, stems and all. Then I set them on the stove over medium heat and they immediately release their juice.

After an hour or so, the skins have shriveled and much of the liquid has been reduced in volume. I strain out the pomace (the stems, skins, and seeds), first in a colander, then in a fine strainer, pressing with a big spoon to get all the juice out. The pomace goes onto the compost pile, and the juice goes back on the stove to reduce further, until it is thick enough to coat the back of a spoon. Then I freeze or can it in half-pint jars. It's tart, but I leave it unsweetened so that I can adjust the sweetness later, according to the syrup's use. If I'm just dribbling a bit over the apples in an apple pie, for extra flavor, I might leave it as is. But if I'm going to pour it over vanilla ice cream, I'll add some honey or sugar and reduce it a bit more. And that's exactly the way I served it to our friend Max, along with some late everbearing raspberries.

"This is called *mosto d'Uva*!" he exclaimed. "Grape must. It's a specialty of Emilia-Romagna in northern Italy." And so it was. Prowling the image banks on the web, I saw it being boiled, bottled, drizzled over fruit, yogurt, custard, or cheese, sprinkled onto meats, made into murky flour-thickened puddings, sipped in small glasses and—wait a minute—poured into bathtubs, where near-naked women lay barely submerged.

Was I the last person to hear about vinotherapy? This newly popular spa treatment involves immersion in, or slathering with, mashed-up grapes to imbue one's skin with youth-preserving polyphenols.

My idea of vinotherapy is opening a nice bottle of Côtes du Rhône and applying the polyphenols from within. But there are still so many uses for my tasty little home product. I've tried it on lamb chops, and on pork belly. Delicious! Next, I want to dot it on fresh figs.

If I were more ambitious, I might turn it into balsamic vinegar, the way they do in Modena (again, in Emilia-Romagna), allowing it to ferment sequentially in barrels of diminishing size, each made from a different wood. After seventy-five years I'd have something unbelievably special. But *mosto d'Uva*, two hours off the vine, is pretty damn nice. I once bought it in a bottle, under the name of *saba*, but it was not as intense as my home brew—which is always on hand, along with a quart of ice cream, for a sweet ending to a meal.

Blueberries

Apart from the sky, blue is rare in nature, and even more of an oddity on the plate. A delphinium blossom or a huge, iridescent morpho butterfly are both miracles of blueness. But I pass up those Peruvian blue potatoes in favor of golden ones, and the same goes for blue corn chips and turquoise M&Ms. Maybe I mistrust blue because it's the color all food becomes if it sits around too long.

The one crowning exception is the blueberry. Light or medium blue on the bush, deep blue in a pie, this native fruit is one we've grown up with, and after eating that pie we wear our blue smiles proudly. We know what that color is all about. Among a number of studies demonstrating the blueberry's high nutritional value was one by the USDA Human Nutrition Research Center on Aging at Tufts University. It ranked some forty fruits and vegetables for antioxidant activity, a process that protects the body against aging, environmental toxins, and disease. The study put blueberries squarely at the top. It's thought that blue-purple anthocyanins are the source of this power.

Since blueberries are delicious, and a magic health potion to boot, I have always grown at least a few bushes to ensure a yearly crop, and I'd grow them even if I didn't love the fruit. They're handsome, long-lived shrubs, too long ignored as ornamentals and taken for granted, like so many of our natives. The white flowers, if not dazzling, are pretty, and the fall foliage is a spectacular red, orange, or gold. Most varieties are a convenient four to seven feet tall. Since they like moisture, they're often suitable for a pondside planting. They also make a fine informal hedge, combining well with other bird-friendly shrubs like winterberry and viburnum, or in a border of acid-loving plants like mountain laurel and rhododendron. You can even grow them in pots.

There are two important things blueberries need, though: dependable moisture and acid soil. In the wild the highbush type is often found in swamps, not sitting with its roots *in* the swamp but perched on hummocks at least fourteen inches above the water table. They have shallow, fibrous roots that lack the root hairs by which other plants adjust to a range of moisture conditions. In your garden they'll require good drainage and some irrigating in dry weather, especially when fruiting in early summer, or in late summer when they set the fruit buds for next year. Lowbush blueberry, a northern species, and the towering rabbiteye blueberry, a southern one, are both more drought proof.

As for the acidity factor, the ideal pH for blueberries is between 4.2 and 4.8, and if your soil is very alkaline, or is heavy clay, they may not be the crop for you. They may also simply be out of step with your gardening life. Since most edibles prefer a neutral pH (that is, around 6.5 to 7.0), you may have limed your garden's beds from time to time or applied wood ashes to them. Nevertheless, it is possible to acidify a neutral soil to make certain elements available to blueberries, notably iron, zinc, and manganese. Adding acidic organic materials such as peat moss and composted pine bark will increase acidity and at the same time help the soil to retain the moisture the bushes need. If this is still not enough, you can add elemental sulphur. We have used a product called Tiger 90CR Organic Sulphur, made by Arbico Organics, which contains no nitrogen, potassium, or phosphorus, just 90 percent sulphur. A fifty-pound bag covers up to 10,000 square feet. (Sandy soils might need one-third less, and clay might need one-half more.) In general, blueberries don't need a lot of fertilizing, although a sawdust, bark, or pine needle mulch is helpful.

Apart from hungry birds, we have not had any pest issues. Sometimes our plants are attacked by a fungus called witches' broom, which causes

Learn to spot the all-blue color that blueberries have when fully ripe.

dense clusters of reddish, nonproductive twigs to form in the branches and systemically infect the plants. (The presence in our woods of another host, balsam fir, is probably the reason ours persists.) We prune these out whenever they appear and then burn them to kill the spores. So far, the damage has been minimal.

If your chosen site needs some work, it would be best to prepare it in summer or fall, let the soil mellow, then set out the plants early the next spring. Give new plants lots of water and prune off the fat fruiting buds the first year to promote vigorous growth. Shop your local nursery in search of a selection of early, midseason, and late varieties, for a long harvest. Planting more than one will also help insure cross-pollination and hence bigger, more numerous berries.

The fruits are at their peak of flavor and potency after they have been thoroughly blue for several days. Birds know this too. Some people put netting over their bushes—I prefer just to plant enough for everybody. The berries are ripe when they are uniformly blue (check the undersides!) and fall easily into your hand or bucket when touched. To freeze some for year-round eating, spread them on a cookie sheet. When they're frozen hard, collect them into plastic bags. This keeps them nicely separated, and you can do it a little at a time, as they ripen.

The harvest starts in June with early varieties like Duke and Earliblue. There will be a feast of blueberry pancakes, blueberry cobbler, blueberries to sprinkle on cereal and ice cream. Blueberries to bake into muffins and bread pudding. Blueberries in syrup and jam. How about in milk custard? Maybe not. That might be just a little too blue.

The Luxurious Melon

In the garden's festival year of fruits and vegetables, the ripening of the melons is a joyous celebration. In the days preceding we prowl the vines on hands and knees, fondling, inspecting, sniffing. Then, suddenly, the kitchen table is piled with rinds, the floor speckled with seeds, and there we are, munching happily, sweet juice dribbling down our chins. It's a good thing the harvest lasts for many weeks and we all can have our fill, for melons eaten out of season will never compare with this feast.

Everyone has a favorite. For some, watermelons are the ultimate summer food, others like the cool, green sweetness of honeydews. The ones I dream of in winter are the classic orange-fleshed melons we call cantaloupes—though properly speaking they're a broader class called muskmelons. Their flavor has a hint of exotic spiciness that to me evokes their Middle Eastern origins. Growing them has become a grail quest for an ever more intense flavor and scent that merge so completely I can't tell where scent leaves off and taste begins.

So many melons, so few square feet of garden, especially if they're grown in a new spot each year—which is advisable. Take a look at Amy Goldman's exquisite book *Melons for the Passionate Grower* and you'll see the gardener's plight. Seductively photographed, each fruit seems to say, "Grow me, even if I take up half your yard."

In summer, sample melons from local growers to see which you like best and which do well in your area. One winner called Goldstar has succeeded best in our Maine climate, but it's now hard to find, and my heart

The flavor of a ripe Charentais melon is one of the high points of summer.

truly belongs to the little French Charentais, a pale, smooth, gray-green melon that turn slightly yellowish when ripe. When well grown, its rich orange flesh is as tasty and perfumed as any I've tried. In a climate with humid summers your best bet for the Charentais type is one of the disease-resistant varieties like Savor.

Perhaps another French variety, such as Noir des Carmes or Petit Gris de Rennes, could become my new "ultimate." Or the Spanish Piel de Sapo ("Toad's Skin"). Or the British Hero of Lockinge. I'm intrigued by those little Queen Anne pocket melons, not for their flavor but for the scent that led women to wear them in the pockets of their clothing like a dab of Arpège. By trying new ones I discovered the aromatic Vieille France and the heirloom Blackfoot Mountain watermelon—the richest, the reddest ever.

Often a melon somebody has described rhapsodically will taste different when grown in one's own soil. It can take a while to get certain melons right. They need a warm, sunny spot and prefer a light but fertile, slightly alkaline soil. Using plastic mulch to warm up the soil around the plants will get you an earlier harvest, as will starting the seeds indoors several weeks ahead, then setting them out when the soil temperature has reached 65 degrees Fahrenheit. Floating row covers will protect the young plants from pests, such as cucumber beetles, but remove these when the first blossoms form, to let in pollinators. Provide a steady water supply until the new fruits are ripening, then keep them slightly dry (though not to the point of wilting) to intensify the melons' flavor and prevent splitting.

Deciding when to pick a melon is like staring into a crystal ball. Its appearance might give a clue. In a Charentais, for instance, little cracks at the blossom end are a good sign, and skin that's progressed to orange means it's gone too far. With most muskmelons you can check for "full slip"—the stage at which the stem separates from the fruit when gently pushed with your finger. But this doesn't work with honeydews, crenshaws, casabas, and Charentais, which must be cut. With the Charentais, the last leaf on the stem, just before the melon, turns pale when the fruit is ready. Honeydews soften slightly at the blossom end. Growers with perfect pitch can thump a watermelon (as Pop taught me) and distinguish the light ping of "unripe," the dull thud of "gone by," and the melodious resonance of perfection. With the most fragrant types, the nose knows best.

Melons don't improve much once they're picked, and rarely keep for long. Refrigeration dulls their flavor. Better to heap them in the middle of the table and try to eat them right away. In our house, this is never a problem.

Apples for Life

The old saying goes, "An apple a day keeps the doctor away." But why not a peach or a plum? Perhaps because in the old days an apple was one of the few homegrown foods you could eat fresh all winter. A cellar full of these long keepers gave you a daily, living package of fiber and vitamin C right up to the time when the summer fruits were ripe.

The apple tree is a year-round wonder in the ornamental sense too. Few sights are prettier in springtime—even old, gnarled trees, when they flower, look like something out of *Swan Lake*. In summer we appreciate their graceful shapes, the dappled shade they cast, their ripening apples in shades of red or gold. Some of these hang on into fall and winter on the angular branches, outlined in snow. These are small, companionable trees, often the first ones young children learn to climb. They certainly were for me.

Home gardeners, even if they embrace the concept of edible landscaping, are sometimes daunted by apple culture, which is not quite as simple as planting a row of junipers. But it's so much more rewarding. A single standard-sized one will make a fine shade tree someday, though unless you have another apple tree to cross-pollinate it, you'll usually have to rely on the presence of one in the neighborhood with an overlapping bloom time if you want fruit. (Even a crab apple will suffice.) With dwarf or semidwarf trees you might have room for a mini-orchard, one that would include apples for early eating, followed by midseason and late ones. Dwarf trees will also bear at a younger age.

Thousands of apple varieties are available. Among my favorites are the vigorous Spigold and the russet types—so sweet, pest resistant, and long-keeping. Liberty, a tasty all-purpose red apple, is probably the best of the disease-resistant varieties.

When Eliot first started our farm over fifty years ago, he planted a lot of different apple varieties, then waited to see which ones would thrive. That's one way to go about it. It also helps to let local nurserymen and orchardists steer you toward the ones best suited to your area.

Select a sunny spot. Buy one-year-old whips, which will establish better than older trees. Water them abundantly the first year.

Mulch young trees with straw or hay, then keep mulching every year if possible. The great plantsman Liberty Hyde Bailey advocated this in 1886 and numerous studies since then have confirmed its benefits to health and yield. Mulch stops erosion, protects roots in winter, retains moisture in summer, prevents competition from weeds and grasses, conveys slow-release nutrients to the trees, and cushions the fruit when it falls. You might have to pull a little mulch away from the trunks in winter, then exclude voles and borers with fine-mesh collars, anchored at the bottom with circles of crushed stone.

Planting a diverse collection of flowering shrubs and herbaceous plants can help keep apple trees healthy. In the old days, shrubby hedgerows between fields supplied nectar-rich flowers for insects that pollinate apple trees, and also sustained predator insects that preyed on insect pests. Beneficial insects are especially drawn to the Umbelliferae, plants with umbrella-shaped flowers like dill, lovage, cilantro, fennel, and parsley. They love legumes, especially clovers. Buckwheat is a great nectar plant too, as are all the Compositae—daisies, sunflowers, tansy, yarrow, asters.

Don't expect perfect supermarket apples. Gardeners worry a lot about apple pests and diseases, especially scab, which often disfigures leaves and fruits. Most of us just live with it, but it can be partly deterred by raking up fallen apple leaves or by growing resistant varieties. And well-rotted manure and compost spread beneath the trees is a great tonic. It helps them to resist many ills, just as you do when you eat things that are good for you—like apples.

Pruning Apples

Yearly pruning is extremely beneficial for apples. Its most important goal is to let sunshine into the tree so that the fruiting branches will bear, and their fruits will ripen, but it also lightens the tree's load and helps air to circulate through the branches. It's best done in winter, when the tree is dormant, so if it's February and we haven't done it yet, now's the time, before the buds start to open.

Cold nights and warm days start the sap flowing in trees, as anybody in sugar maple country will tell you. The same thing happens metaphorically to people if they've just been through a serious cold stretch. A sunny day gets our juices going. The ground, even if thawed, is too soggy for digging and planting, but out we go in search of a useful job to do.

Pruning apples expertly for maximum yield is an art but even a novice can make life better for a tree. With pruning saw and loppers, you remove any dead wood, then the weak, upright shoots (called water sprouts) that ascend from the branches, and any shoots or branches that droop downward. Cut close to the base of the branch, but without damaging the circle of tissue called the branch collar. Remove any awkward limbs, including ones that head back toward the interior of the tree or crisscross better branches beneath them.

When you are done, the ground will be littered with your prunings, and even these can help fuel that urgent spring need for purposeful activity. If some of those awkward branches have fruiting buds at their tips, bring these inside and stick them in a big vase or bucket of warm water. They will soon sprout dainty white blossoms (or pink ones, with some varieties of crab apple). Even the new green leaves will lighten the mood of indoor rooms.

Branches three or four feet tall can be used for pea brush. Sharpen their ends and set them aside. Later on, you can poke them into the ground a foot or two apart, next to a row where a pea crop is to be planted. Brush is a traditional support for peas, and it is more handsome than wire or string mesh.

The rest of your prunings can go onto the brush pile or be used for firewood if you have a woodstove or fireplace. Applewood is pleasantly aromatic, either alone or in combination with other woods. Spring may be on its way, but after a sunny day with a crisp, cool ending, a fire is just the thing.

Storing Apples

In an age when most fruit was grown at home, the care of it after harvest was not taken lightly. On the old English farm estates, a tree fruit was coddled like a pet. You would not sever it from the tree with the rough shake of the branch, only a gentle twist of the hand, or an assist from a padded basket on a pole. Books such as Susan Campbell's *Charleston Kedding* and Jennifer Davies's *The Victorian Kitchen Garden* give us a glimpse of "fruit rooms" where these culinary gems were stored on slatted shelves. To separate them, writes Campbell, "the finest fruits were laid only on the best writing paper" so that they picked up no unwanted odors. Imagine how they might have viewed the spare fridge where Eliot and I keep our apples for winter eating, in a plastic crate inches away from leftover pizza.

We are, however, mindful of the care that even a backyard apple grower should take with fruits to make them keep well. We sort through the harvest and only keep the ones most free of bruises, which invite decay. Less perfect ones are put up in glass jars as applesauce or pressed into cider.

A root cellar, kept just above freezing, is fine for apples, but the ethylene gas that they give off will cause deterioration in any vegetables that share that space with them. Our spare fridge is hardly His Lordship's fruit room, but it makes a good root cellar substitute. The Golden Russets, Roxbury Russets, and Spigolds we keep there give us months of good eating. They start to soften by spring but, even when a bit mealy or spongy, they can be peeled, cored, and sliced into rings. These I brown very slowly on both sides, in butter, and eat them for breakfast or any meal with bacon, sausage, or other form of cooked pork. They are just sweet enough to be a foil for the meat's fattiness and cook slightly better for not being crisp and young.

Russet apples' firm flesh makes delicious apple rings.

Making Cider

Eliot loves to tell a story about visiting Normandy at apple time. That northern French province is true apple country, and in fall the fruits are piled high around the bases of the trees to "sweat," or mellow, for a few weeks. Then they're made into hard cider. A farmer invited Eliot into his kitchen to try his home brew, made from apples trucked to the cider press the previous year. "Is that far?" Eliot asked. "Of course not," his new acquaintance said. "Doesn't every village have one?" After several glasses they'd become even better friends, and a bottle of Calvados came out, the apple brandy for which Normandy is famous. This too was made from the man's own apples, at the local distillery. "Is that far?" Eliot asked. Again, the reply: "Doesn't every village have one?"

In early America, cider was the beverage of choice, and there was a press not just in every village but on most farms. Your press was as important as your root cellar, or your barn. The word cider then was synonymous with hard cider, as it still is in Europe. Its association with the nonalcoholic "sweet" cider is a post-Prohibition phenomenon.

In our household, more than a cellar of wine, a stash of sweet cider is what we prize, and look forward to making each fall. Our fifty-year-old orchard yields ample fruit, and for a long time our friend Tom Hoey, a professional cidermaker, let us use his press.

Homemade cider, from unsprayed apples, surpasses any you can buy, and the experience of pressing is part of its appeal. Families talk about the fun they have cidering, with the kids washing the apples and tossing them into the hopper, one parent manning the chopper and the other cranking the press. If you need convincing, try to find the recording of "The Cider Song" on the wonderful old album *I'll Take the Hills: Banjo Dan's Songs of Vermont*.

One year we finally bought a press with an electric chopper from Bob Correll at Correll Cider Presses. It's a beautifully made implement, easy to use, that gives great yields. Bob's presses take time to make, so we spent a year and a half on his waiting list before ours arrived. But now on sunny fall weekends, as different apples in the orchard ripen, we're blending varieties together for a good balance of tart and sweet, tasting the rosy-colored juice as it flows down the sluice. Freshly made fall cider, consumed within weeks, is ambrosial, with frozen cider a close second. Lacking the freezer space for that, we can as much as possible in half-gallon jars. (Consult any basic canning guide for tips.)

Our press has created its own little village, as neighbors arrive with their apples to take a turn at it. In fact, a purchase like this might well be shared by a community, since it is costly. Bob once offered, on his website, to take items in trade, such as "freezer meat, firewood, needed services, hardwood lumber." But alas, his village, Elmira, Oregon, was quite some distance away.

Citrus Country

My citrus orchard, as I so grandiosely called it, was like the gang of kids in *Annie*. The calamondin, bearer of tiny, seedy, orange-like fruits, was left in my care when its owner went on a trip and never came back to pick it up. The Valencia orange and the Ponderosa lemon were abandoned on a patio when a neighbor moved away. The twin Meyer lemons had belonged to someone's ex, and the sixth was a mutt of unknown origin and doubtful pedigree. Orphans all.

I am not a houseplant person, but for years this collection would spend the winter in our sunny south-facing living room, occasionally erupting in clusters of divinely scented white flowers, and even making a few fruits. They pressed their foliage up against the glass French doors, sticky with exudates from their yearly scale infestation. Somehow, they survived the spider mite attacks, and even the mealybug plague unleashed by two bargain palms from the Home Depot. Only the barely edible calamondin looked perky no matter what. In spring, just when I thought they could take no more tribulations, I would turn all of them outside and they would thrive.

The terrace behind the house became their summer camp, with plenty of sun to green them up and rain to wash off the black sooty mold. I waited until the temperature was consistently in the sixties to take them out, placing them in full shade for the first week, then dappled shade and finally full sun. In fall, I did all that in reverse. Surrounded by pollinators, they bloomed bounteously and even set fruits, though not all of them matured.

Citrus plants are notoriously temperamental as indoor plants. Rarely will they die, but they don't like change. Sudden increases or decreases in temperature, light, and humidity cause what I call a leaf tantrum. A few leaves fall, then more, and suddenly they litter the floor, leaving the plant denuded. Having made their point, they immediately put out new growth and burst into bloom. Much as they like our sunny windows, though, our living room is not ideal for them in winter because a woodstove keeps it too warm. Sunny and *cool*, they insist. Got it?

Calamondins, though less versatile in the kitchen, tolerate the indoors better than the other citrus fruits.

One year I planted them in a minimally heated farm greenhouse for the winter and their health soared. Lots of pollinating insects flew in the greenhouse doors and roof vents, ensuring good fruit-set. Birds had free access too, and the sparrows made a specialty of keeping them aphid-free.

The worst they ever suffered in that greenhouse was the equivalent of a cold night in Florida. Freed from their pots, their roots luxuriating in deep, compost-rich soil, they had healthy leaves and were heavy with fruit. It is a tradition each year for me to make Eliot a lemon meringue pie for his December birthday. That year the lemons were homegrown.

CHAPTER 26

Herbs

Herb gardens traditionally are tidy, decorative, and self-contained, but herbs themselves are not. Some of them creep (such as thyme), sprawl (like sage), or spread by seed (such as lemon balm). Visit the popular garden herbs in their native habitat—typically the rocky hills of the Mediterranean region—and you may stroll through them with difficulty, as lanky, woody stems grab at your ankles. Inhaling the scent of their resinous leaves, you pay homage to their great culinary and medicinal virtues, but when you see how they grow, you understand why gardeners plant them with discipline in mind. You can grow them in a more natural style—let's say in a well-drained rock garden where boulders are the perfect foil for the various greens, grays, and blues of their foliage—but when space is an issue, geometry is applied.

My own herb garden is the old-fashioned foursquare type, with granite edging, gravel paths, and a circle in the center. That center bed tends to vary its crop each year, from sunflowers to strawberries and beyond. But the corner beds are mostly devoted to perennial herbs of the mint family (Lamiaceae), such as sage, lavender, oregano, marjoram, anise hyssop, and thyme. Besides being essential for cooking, these plants are all beautiful when they bloom, advertising their nectar with blossoms in shades

Lavender, thyme, sage, and cilantro spring into bloom, along with red poppies and yellow sedum.

of blue, purple, dark red, or white. All are premium sources for pollinators such as bees and butterflies and are alive with their motion. But still, the garden depends on the traditional symmetrical aesthetic that goes back to colonial times, medieval times, and ancient Persia before that. And the game plan? Plant, feed, water, contain, and control.

Managing Herbs

In the wild, these herbs are kept low and scrubby by the nibbling of goats and by occasional fires, fueled by the volatile oils from their aromatic leaves. Without either assist, I use hand pruners to keep them from getting too lanky, being careful to leave just enough old wood to generate a lush, compact resprouting.

I also remind myself that they were born to hate the rich soil of our gardens, and sometimes our climate as well. The Mediterranean region is a biome characterized by moist, mild winters and hot, dry summers. Usually when we consider plants for our gardens, we go by the U.S. Department of Agriculture's Winter Hardiness Zone Map, which is based on minimum winter temperature. For these herbs, survival can seem so unpredictable, you'd be better off following the prophecies of Nostradamus. With some, to be sure, winter cold is a factor. Sage seems indestructible, whereas rosemary must be taken indoors for the winter in cold climates. In between are the ones like thyme, tarragon, and lavender, which can be counted on only in the protected corner of our yard where the herb garden is sited, and rarely in the exposed fields of our farm.

It's all about drainage. The roots of Mediterranean plants are adapted to drought, not to flooding. When there is rainy winter weather in the hills of Provence, Greece, or their other haunts, the water drains down the slopes, and percolates through soils aerated by stones and grit. Even the relative poverty of the soil seems to favor success. At the farm we've had good luck planting them on a sunny, south-facing slope. In the home herb garden, those planted next to the gravelly paths are superbly healthy because excess water drains away from their roots. The thyme even migrates into the gravel on purpose. If your site is more sump-like, raised beds might save the day.

Anything you can do to keep the soil well aerated in winter is helpful. It should be loose and fluffy so that water cannot accumulate and fill the air spaces plant roots need in order to breathe. Dig in plenty of organic matter, especially compost. Builder's sand can be added to a heavy soil as well, but depending on how much clay you've started with, you might have to add as much as 50 percent sand to improve the texture, and you will still need to add organic matter as well. Some gardeners add chicken grit (available from feedstores), which is usually composed of ground-up oyster shells or granite meal. It makes a good surface mulch for herbs too, since it helps keep the crowns dry. Crowns are often as prone to winter rot as the roots are, especially in the cases of winter savory and thyme.

When you plant perennial herbs, leave plenty of space between them to let air circulate, though it's best to protect them from icy winds. Mulches help because they moderate the fluctuations of soil temperature that are hard on plants in winter. But don't mulch with flat autumn

leaves, which will mat down and make the ground even soggier. Instead, wait until early winter when people are discarding their Christmas trees and place them over the plants until spring, in time for new growth to begin. Often the worst damage occurs in the dreariest part of mud season, when most of these plants are wishing they were on Corfu or in Portofino. And who could blame them?

But that's not the end of the herb story. Not all popular herbs are perennials. I sometimes think of my herb plot as a playing field with two opposing teams. In summer, amid all those blue and lavender spikes, umbrellas are also hoisted. That is to say, some members of the plant family called Umbelliferae are coming into bloom. They were given their botanical name, derived from the same root as the word umbrella ("little shade"), because their flowers form a parasol-like shape called an umbel. Queen Anne's lace, the wild ancestor of our modern carrot, has a classic umbel, a lush and lacy, slightly concave dome. Look closely at an umbel and you'll see that it's composed of a cluster of stems, each with a smaller umbel at the tip. Dill's yellow flowers show this very clearly. Angelica, a medicinal herb whose stems and flowers are sometimes candied, has umbels that are almost spherical, a ball made up of balls. Other umbellifers include chervil, cilantro, and fennel.

Generally the goal of the herb gardener is to keep cutting and using the herbs' foliage in order to keep them from flowering as long as possible. But I let a lot of them bloom. The umbels are little helipads where bees and other beneficial visitors land and fill up on nectar. The flowers are lovely, too, and make great filler for bouquets. Many of the seeds they bear, such as dill, caraway, cumin, and fennel, are mainstays of cuisines around the world. And they are all annuals that start out as little transplants, or even seeds that are direct sown. How do they hold their own when asked to share a garden with well-established, often woody perennials?

If I need to grow an especially large amount of an annual herb—if, let's say, I want to turn my basil crop into jars of pesto—I give the plants their own row in the vegetable garden, where there's plenty of room for them to get big and bushy. But for average herb use (a snip here, a snip there), I find ways to fit them into the herb plot, which is a few steps from the kitchen where those snips are frequently, and instantly, needed. Another strategy is to allow some of them to go to seed. Dill does so eagerly, covering its spot like a little dill lawn. Some years I don't even bother to start dill plants ahead but rely on its volunteers. The same goes for cilantro and anise hyssop.

So I keep restraining the well-established perennials and make sure there are spaces big enough for the annuals, keeping the soil there loose, fertile, and easy to work. With careful maintenance, this system can work.

The Truth about Mint

When we say that a plant is easy to grow, we usually mean that it takes care of itself. You extend the single kindness of planting it, and it gives you a bounteous harvest even when ignored. By this definition, mint is as easy a food plant as you'll ever find. A hardy perennial, you need only designate a spare corner of the yard for it, in sun or in shade. Damp soil befits it best, but an average soil will do, as long as there's enough organic matter to help retain moisture.

It might seem strange that none of the true mints (*Mentha* genus) share my official herb garden with all of their close relatives such as oregano and thyme. But finding that out-of-the-way corner for mint is essential. Introduce mint into a garden and it will make work for you, year after year. Its aggressive underground stems will creep rapidly among the roots of its neighbors and swamp all but the most aggressive ones. Schemes such as surrounding it with barriers will fail, although planting it in a large freestanding pot can work in the short term if you keep it well watered. Gardeners often give up on mint as a weedy nuisance.

In a place where mint can be mint, it is well worth growing and savoring. Those who know its flavor mainly through Life Savers, toothpaste, and envelope glue should try adding its leaves to cucumbers and onions sliced and stirred into yogurt for an Indian raita, a cool-tasting complement to a hot curry. I love to chop it up and toss it with sliced oranges in summer, spiked with a splash of Cointreau. It gives salads an unexpected fresh flavor, and it's brilliant in beverages, from juleps and mojitos to strong sweet tea, either hot or cold. I sometimes combine mint with lemon verbena and honey for an aromatic summer cooler. And it is a proven tummy tonic, soothing for indigestion.

There are many kinds of mint, from the familiar peppermint and spearmint to more subtle forms such as apple mint and chocolate mint. These flavors are not always very pronounced, and if several kinds are grown together they will cross-pollinate, confusing things further. I've enjoyed growing black mint, a type with very dark green leaves and stems, which yields a fine, strong tea. I make a point of cutting and drying it for a winter supply before it goes to flower and before it gets the rust disease that sometimes strikes in midsummer. Neither the rust nor the cutting-back deters the plants, which grow back bushy and strong.

Mint grown from seed does not come true to type, so it's best to start either with cuttings or divisions of established plants. And surely no gardener who grows mint would ever mind parting with a clump.

One January day I was temporarily mintless and stopped by a local nursery to buy a new plant. The plants they had were spindly and small. Finally, I came upon a friendly woman who was potting up plants in a greenhouse. She offered to rent me their large mother plant so I could take cuttings from it. (A mother plant, or stock plant, is one kept on hand for propagation.) I would not have been more surprised if she'd rented me her own mother. "It's okay to keep it till Monday," she said. "We won't start propagating mint until mid-March." So I took my rent-a-mom home, snipped a few of its stems, and put them in a glass of water. I have also done this with mint bought at the grocery store.

If you've ever put mint stems in water, you've seen how they start to send out roots immediately. After a few weeks, if those roots are a white tangle in need of nourishment, you might transplant some into a container of potting mix.

When the ten-hour day arrives in early February and the sap starts to run in the maple trees, we celebrate with Eliot's Maine Mojito, for which he uses maple syrup (rich in minerals such as manganese and zinc) instead of simple syrup. We add rum, club soda, and fresh-squeezed lime, then toast to the welcome prospect of spring.

Humoring Rosemary

Just as there are indoor and outdoor cats, there are indoor and outdoor rosemary plants. In their natural outdoor state they grow, thrive, and perfume the air on the rocky cliffs and hillsides of Greece and the south of France, where ample sun warms the volatile oils in their needlelike leaves. But in a climate known for relentless snow and ice, followed by cold, oozing mud, it's not a good risk. Many of us find it safer to grow the plants in containers and treat them as houseplants—or make them commuter plants that go outside in spring and retreat to a sunny window in late fall.

This too has its perils. I was once given a large rosemary in a decorated terra-cotta pot by a friend who could no longer house it. The plant then

Rosemary, at home
in a clay pot

moved with me from apartment to apartment and house to house. It became a pet, increasingly ungainly and hard to please. It finally went to herb heaven in 2016 and I learned not to get too attached.

I'm not the only one. Millie Owen, in her delightful book *A Cook's Guide to Growing Herbs, Greens and Aromatics*, wrote, "Shakespeare must have had houseplant rosemary in mind when he said it's for remembrance: remember not to let it get dry, remember to check it for pests, remember to keep it pinched back, remember to keep a constant watch on it—and it may be happy if it's a mind to." Rosemary dislikes dim light and is unforgiving as to moisture. Not enough watering will kill it. Too much watering, especially if the soil is heavy and poorly drained, or the saucer full of water, will kill it just as fast. Owen was right: you have to watch it and sense its needs. In fact, with perennial herbs that tend toward woodiness, like rosemary, sage, and lavender, you actually get the most beautiful, pliant, and flavorful foliage if you start new ones each year, whether from seed, cuttings, or small nursery-grown specimens.

Rosemary dislikes dim light, so choose the sunniest spot you can. If you feed it now and then with a well-diluted liquid seaweed fertilizer or fish emulsion, it will respond quickly with fresh but somewhat spindly new growth, soft enough to be good in salads. The older leaves are more pungent, though, and are the ones I snip to massage into crevices in a leg of lamb before roasting.

The most important thing about rosemary care is the Zen of watering. The standard advice is to water thoroughly, then let the soil dry out, but each step has its limits. Letting the pot sit in a deep saucer of water can rot the plant. (If water floods any saucer, it's best to empty it into the pot of a neighboring plant that looks thirsty.) Letting it get too dry can also kill the plant quickly.

The balance between too much water and too little is the discipline you must master. Like the "wax on, wax off" technique taught to the young pupil in the film *The Karate Kid*, it is a meditation that might spill over into the rest of your life. Go, respect the rosemary, and be mindful.

In Love with Lemon Verbena

Nature's chemistry set has a multitude of flavors, and she loves to mix them. Even those that stand out as the signatures of specific plants, such as lemon or lavender, are complex formulations. Parts of those formulations reappear in different plants, and never in quite the same way. We are always sensing subtle taste echoes as we munch our way through the plant kingdom. Just think of the flavors that trained palates discern in wine.

The flavor we call "lemon" is a case in point. It's unmistakable in the fruit itself, and a clear presence in other plants with the word in their names. Of these, the tropical lemongrass (*Cymbopogon citratus*), whose delicious stems are used in Asian cooking, is the most lemony, but there are also lemon verbena, lemon basil, lemon thyme, lemon bergamot, and lemon balm. Others are prized for lemony aromas, such as lemon eucalyptus, *Pelargonium crispum* (an annual "geranium"), and marigold Lemon Gem. Some of these have strong chemical personalities in which the lemon part is really just a hint.

Lemon verbena is my favorite. A relative newcomer to the pantheon of classic culinary herbs, it originated not in the Mediterranean region where many herbs are found but in South America. There are no legends in which Greek nymphs are chased by lustful gods and transformed into lemon verbena plants just in the nick of time. Nor is there as much familiar medicinal lore. The plant was not known to the European apothecaries until the late eighteenth century when it was imported to Spain for perfumery. Yet it does have some repute as a calmer of the stomach and the nerves. The adjective most often used for it is "soothing."

I find it lemony, but barely so, and certainly not a lemon substitute as recipe writers repeatedly claim. With none of lemon's astringency, its clean, grassy taste is springlike—powerful with no hard edges. Order an herbal tea in France (a "tisane") and you'll usually get one made with lemon verbena. Pour boiling water over a few leaves and you'll have an aromatic cup, delicate yellow-green in color and decidedly relaxing. Try dropping a leaf into a glass of white wine, sangria, or champagne.

Tea made from lemon verbena is a summer delight.

When the leaves are young and tender, they can be chopped into a tossed salad or a fruit cup. If older and stiffer, they are best steeped in a warmed liquid, such as the milk that goes into a pudding, ice cream, or sorbet, and then removed. Use it sparingly. Enough to turn a custard green would make the flavor too strong. I love experimenting with it. Once I made a *beurre noisette*—simmering butter until it was nut-brown— then added lemon verbena off the heat for flavor. Poured over potatoes and Tuscan kale it made the dish an instant favorite.

The plant itself is too lanky and awkward ever to have pledged the sorority of cute garden herbs. It doesn't even bloom consistently outside its native tropics, where it grows to ten feet or more. Even in a zone 7 garden it might grow to five feet, sprawling like a forsythia. That's fine with me. Having it intrude upon a path allows you to rustle it, bruise it, and stir up the aroma of its slender, slightly sticky leaves. It needn't be ungainly in a tidy garden. Snipping back the tips early in the season will make it branch and keep it more compact.

Lemon verbena is hard to grow from seed, but a small plant purchased in spring will make an impressive woody-stemmed bush by midsummer. It will survive a Washington, D.C., winter if mulched, but not a Maine one. It may die back to the ground, but will resprout late in the spring, just when you are about to give up and dig it out. It also makes a good container herb, especially if your outdoor soil is heavy clay, which it abhors. Bring it into a bright but sheltered spot in wintertime, but don't be insulted if it rewards this good deed by dropping all its leaves. It is evergreen only in very warm climates. I'd exclude it from your living quarters unless you think spider mites and whiteflies make great house-hold pets. For kitchen use, cut the stems before frost and dry the leaves in a warm, dark place. Unlike most dried herbs, they do not lose flavor over time. They're also good for "strewing," an old-fashioned practice I think of as the lazy person's potpourri. Set a few branches over a heating vent. Sprinkle some leaves in your bath. For garden variety tension, it's better than Prozac.

The Modesty of Tarragon

I look at the robust stand of tarragon in my herb garden and marvel that this useful and well-behaved plant bears the species name *dracunculus*, or "little dragon." *Artemisia dracunculus* is neither winged, serpentine, nor scaly, and while its flavor is assertive, it certainly does not breathe fire. A history of use as an antivenom is one oft-cited explanation. Another is its root system, which consists of underground rhizomes snaking through the ground.

The distinctive taste that tarragon imparts is mildly licorice-like, a quality it shares with anise, chervil, and fennel. Despite this commonality, you could not mistake it for anything else, and one of its best uses is to add dimension to a green salad. Since it neither dries nor freezes well, it is often preserved in white wine vinegar, a pairing that is splendid in salads. A few chopped leaves make a celebration out of a scrambled egg, and sprigs tucked under the skin of a chicken before roasting both scent it and flavor it beautifully. The herb is also the magic ingredient in béarnaise sauce, a buttery potion powered by tarragon, shallots, egg yolk, and reduced white wine and vinegar. Since Julia Child taught Americans to pull off this tricky recipe, the humble steak has never been the same.

Once you acquire a tarragon plant, you will not find it difficult or fussy to grow, given a reasonably fertile, well-drained soil. It does better in the ground than in a pot, and better outdoors than in. Those addicted to fresh tarragon can try bringing it into the house, but don't expect it to overwinter gracefully. The decline of the light in winter makes it shut down and die back, even in a warm room. If you expose it to freezing before bringing it in, that will prompt it to put out new growth. (This trick also works with chives.) Or just wait for fresh green shoots to emerge outdoors in spring, a moment that gardener-cooks impatiently await each year. At our farm, the winters are just a bit too cold for tarragon to survive them, but I have a stalwart, very permanent patch of it in the herb garden, in the corner closest to the house and thus well protected from cold winds. As for spreading by means of rhizomes, its efforts have been modest at best.

To grow tarragon, it's important to know the difference between two kinds, the French and the Russian. Russian tarragon is a vigorous plant easily grown from seed, and if you see tarragon seed for sale, it is probably this one. Though the flavor is mildly tarragon-like, it will disappoint you if you're expecting the real thing. The French kind, on the other hand, rarely flowers, and any seed produced by the plant would not breed true. Its characteristics are the result of human selection over the course of the years, with the goal of concentrating the flavor. Plants sold are divisions from a bona fide clone—or so one hopes. Now and then the Russian type is labeled "tarragon" and pawned off on an unsuspecting gardener hell-bent on flavoring her sole meunière. She rejoices in the plant's eager growth habit, but soon realizes she has been sold a bland imposter. Now there's a creature likely to breathe fire.

The Honorable Bay

Summer still has a way to go yet. It won't be officially over until I bring the bay plant indoors. As ceremonies go, that's a bit of a comedown for this ancient Mediterranean plant, also known as laurel, bay laurel, or sweet bay. In classical times it was formed into garlands to adorn the brows of the worthy—preeminent poets, distinguished scholars, victorious athletes, conquering heroes, and heads of state—as testimony to their merit or their triumphs. ("Baccalaureate" translates as "laurel berries.") The words "laurel" and "bay" have been used to denote fame or honor itself, as in "resting on one's laurels," and the botanical name, *Laurus nobilis*, reflects this heritage.

According to Greek myth, the sun god Apollo crowned himself with bay after Daphne, a nymph who fled from his ardor, had herself turned into a tree—not, as you might guess, the ornamental shrub we now call daphne. The leaves Apollo plucked from the erstwhile nymph were *Laurus nobilis*, the bay on your spice rack, a standard ingredient along with thyme and parsley in the traditional bouquet garni.

It is important to get the name right because other plants are confused with the true bay, none of them edible and some quite toxic. Cherry laurel (*Prunus laurocerasus*), mountain laurel (*Kalmia latifolia*), sheep laurel (*Kalmia angustifolia*), California bay (*Umbellularia californica*), and bay rum tree (*Pimenta racemosa*) are not what you want for cooking.

It is high time this wonderful seasoning was given its due. Bay is perfunctory for most cooks—a leaf tossed into the stew as a background flavoring to impart a subtle note of woodsy richness. This it does well, of course, but there's a lot of culinary mythology when it comes to bay. Why just one leaf, or even a tiny piece of a leaf as some people advise? Perhaps rumors of bay's toxicity persist, by mistaken association with some of its cousins. Chemically it does possess powers, as do most highly aromatic plants. As a uterine stimulant it is best not consumed in large quantities if you are pregnant. I have seen a few references to it as a mild narcotic. The Delphic oracles, Apollo's chosen, were said to have nibbled the leaves to enhance their visions. Its reputation as a tummy tonic and appetite stimulant may well be deserved. I feel hungry just smelling its delicious aroma in the pot—I find that two or three leaves are usually about right.

I wonder why bay is seldom treated as a flavor in its own right. I'll sometimes season a dish with bay alone—a white bean soup, for example. Or I'll make slits in potatoes before roasting them and insert the leaves—best removed before eating since, once dried, they never entirely soften.

Most of bay's problem is that few diners ever eat it fresh. In order to do that you need to grow your own. Bay is a shrubby tree that normally does not survive north of zone 8, though there are likely hardier varieties if you shop around. You can also grow bay perfectly well in a container, moving it outdoors after danger of frost. Tricky to grow from seed or cuttings, it is best bought as a young plant. It likes sun or part shade—I give it filtered light when I first set it outside. Feeding it from spring through late summer will produce plenty of new growth. I use the leaves when they turn from pale to medium green but before they become hard and leathery. Bay is said to be immune to pests but this too, alas, is mythology.

I've seen indoor bay plants plagued with scale and even with spider mites and mealybugs if all the other houseplants have these too. All can be scrubbed off, or treated with horticultural oil, alcohol, or insecticidal soap if they persist. It's a rugged plant, but one that needs excellent drainage. Letting it sit in a puddle of water will bring it to a sad end.

Bay inspires topiary, and you often see it clipped in a lollipop shape. But a bay lollipop in my house would always have huge bites taken out of it, since I use it often. When you discover how good it is in custard, broths, poached fish, pot roast, and curry you probably will too. You might even feel the urge to reward a kindergarten teacher laureate, a nurse laureate, an ambulance driver laureate, or someone else worthy of special honor—maybe someone who has succeeded in growing laurel indoors without it getting scale. Maybe buy three plants while you're about it.

Cilantro

"You're not going to put cilantro in that, are you?"

Eliot gets nervous just seeing cilantro enter our home. I've tried to sneak it into a pot of chili or a Thai curry, along with other flavors, but he always knows it's there. People often describe its unique pungency as an acquired taste, but Eliot will never acquire it. You either love cilantro or you view it as a culinary assault weapon.

In the former category you'll find most of the people on this planet. Cilantro is one of the world's most ancient and ubiquitous seasonings. It only started to appear on American tables in the last few decades, along with other flavors of Mexican and Southwestern cooking, then in Thai dishes that seemed to cry out for its presence. It is central to all the cuisines of Southeast Asia, as well as India, the Middle East, Spain, Greece, South America, China—in fact, one of its common names is "Chinese parsley."

Oddly enough, cilantro seed—known as coriander—has long been part of our own homey repertoire. It is often a main ingredient in curry powder, where it serves as a thickening agent as well as a seasoning. We are used to finding it in breads, cakes, puddings. Though all parts of the plant (whose botanical name is *Coriandrum sativum*) have the same distinctive flavor, it is so mellowed in the dried seed form that even Eliot will eat it.

Those of us who love the taste of the fresh leaves look forward to the seasons when we can snip them fresh. I make sure to have them in my garden every year. They keep little of their flavor when dried, so some cooks freeze the foliage, or even grow a plant on the windowsill in wintertime. In China the flavorful tough white roots are ground up and made into a pickled condiment for year-round use.

Cilantro in bloom

In appearance the plant resembles parsley, except that the leaves are thinner and more rounded. But if you expect it to grow like parsley, you'll only be frustrated. Cilantro has its own program. Instead of forming hearty clumps that produce all season, it begins to go to seed as soon as the summer days lengthen and warm weather sets in. The foliage turns lacy, almost dill-like, as it sends up a tall seed stalk, topped with umbrellas of frothy white or mauve-white blossoms. These are beautiful in the garden or as cut flowers and attract favored pollinators like bees and butterflies. If you let them remain, they'll form tasty, round green seed pods that can be pickled in vinegar and used just as you would capers— another way to extend the cilantro season. (Southwestern cook Lucinda Hutson, author of *The Herb Garden Cookbook*, adds them to deviled eggs and seafood salads.) Left on the plant, they will eventually turn brown and can be harvested for coriander. Simply dry them upside down over a container to catch the seeds as they fall. Since the seeds have husks, most people grind them to a powder with a spice or coffee grinder before using them in cooking. They'll be more savory if you toast them first in a dry pan, then grind them just as needed for each dish.

In spring you can start cilantro ahead, but it is best sown directly, rather thickly, in a sunny, well-drained bed as soon as you can prepare the soil. Start cutting the foliage when plants are about six inches tall. It's worth looking for a bolt-resistant variety such as Santo but I find that, even after it bolts to seed, a single plant will still yield at least a cupful of foliage. Though the basal leaves will have yellowed, the upper ones will be tender and slightly sweet. I keep most of mine going as long as I can, then let them scatter their seeds. Next year one of the most delightful moments in spring weeding will be the discovery of little seedlings. My nose finds them long before my eyes do, as my hands move through the garden.

A serious cilantro addict will make successive sowings every two weeks throughout the summer, then plant a fall crop as well. You might even find some seedlings for sale at a local garden center. In the shortening, cooling days of late summer they will grow vigorously without bolting, and you'll have plenty of leaves for salsas, shrimp and fish marinades, corn relishes, chutneys, guacamole. Frost won't kill the plants, but their flavor will start to weaken, and you'll soon be reaching for the true cool weather herbs, like chervil, sage, and, of course, parsley.

Meanwhile, gather your cilantro while ye may. If nonaficionados will be present, and the odds are good, just chop it and pass it separately in a bowl to sprinkle or decline. All the more for the rest of us.

In Praise of Parsley

In the 1989 film *The Fabulous Baker Boys*, Michelle Pfeiffer's character is trying to demonstrate the utter banality of the song "Feelings." "It's like parsley," she says, holding up a sprig from her plate. "Take it away and no one would know the difference." That's certainly the common view of parsley—a frilly tuft stuck in between the steak and the peas.

Once upon a time, parsley had much more clout. For the ancient Greeks it was the herb of death, worn in garlands by mourners and placed on tombs. The Romans believed it could stop an advancing army and—even more miraculously—purge the fumes of onions, garlic, and wine from the breath. In other lore it could arouse desire, or make you bear the devil's child. In herbal medicine it's been used for numerous complaints and is universally praised for its rich stores of iron, vitamins A and C, folate, potassium, and calcium. Maybe it was the old breath-freshening trick that typecast it as the preeminent garnish, a role it then kept because of its good looks. But parsley is a real food, with its own culinary virtues, and it's so rewarding to grow—easy and abundant—that there is no impediment to having plenty of it on hand, all year.

The one thing that might frustrate you initially is that the seeds germinate slowly. While you can sow them directly in the garden very early in spring, I find that they sprout more quickly indoors, with some warmth. Since there's a long taproot, soil blocks are the most foolproof method because they reduce transplanting shock. But any system will work if you move the seedlings on carefully to bigger containers, while they are still small. Once outdoors, treat parsley as you would carrots, giving it a stone-free bed with loose, fertile soil, well supplied with organic matter that is consistently moist but well drained. Unlike its cousins chervil, cilantro, and dill, it will not bolt and go to seed quickly but will triumphantly soldier on through fall and early winter, until the heaviest freezes beat it down. Usually, the roots will overwinter and regrow in spring. Since it's a biennial that sets seed the second year, the lengthening days of late spring will make it bolt, but you'll still have some to snip while you're waiting for the new spring crop. Sowing another crop in midsummer in the protection of a cold frame will give you a winter-long supply.

Another option is to pot up a few plants and bring them indoors or into a partly protected spot like a sunny shed. Use a deep pot to accommodate as much of the taproot as possible, filled with a loose soilless mix. Water plants right away and keep them consistently moist. Fish emulsion will keep them green.

Whether you grow curly parsley or the flat Italian kind is a matter of taste. I like both. The mossy, curled varieties such as Forest Green are so beautiful that you can edge a flower border or patio planter with them. They're good in dishes where you want to lighten or fluff up the texture, such as rice salad, or tabbouleh—concocted with soaked bulgur wheat, lemon juice, olive oil, parsley, mint, and fresh tomato if it's in season. Curly parsley is also more cold hardy. But the flat kind is a cook's choice, easier to chop and, to many palates, more pleasant tasting, less scratchy in the mouth. We grow a tasty small-leaved variety called Titan. There is

Flat-leaf parsley
growing

also a type known as Hamburg or turnip-rooted parsley, or parsley root, grown for its carrot-shaped, parsley-flavored root. It can even be dug up, stored, and resprouted indoors in a pot for a winter harvest of coarse leaves, to season soups and stews.

The important thing is to use parsley with conviction and passion. You must say, "I want this dish to taste of parsley." Add so much to the vichyssoise that it turns grass green. Make a creamy parsley soup with a chicken broth base. Try parsley pesto—a brighter color than the basil kind—or a parsley risotto.

Parsley dries poorly, with little flavor. It freezes somewhat better but is best used fresh. I keep a just-picked bunch in water on the kitchen counter. To use it as a garnish, make it irresistible by deep-frying it in oil for a second or two, then sprinkle it with salt. Or get into the habit of making gremolata, that excellent Italian mixture of chopped parsley, garlic, and lemon zest, traditional in osso bucco but equally good tucked under the skin of chicken before roasting, or on top of fish. If you have a good winter supply growing, you can even make a hearty Cornish parsley pie, filled with eggs, cream, and cubes of bacon. You can construct that like a quiche with a pastry bottom, like a pot pie with a pastry lid, or like a half-moon pastry turnover. It'll set just the right mood on a cold night.

I happen to think "Feelings" is like instant vanilla pudding. But let's give a big hand for parsley.

Basil Makes the Big Time

It didn't make the front page, but sometime toward the end of the second millennium basil replaced parsley as America's most popular herb. Much of the thanks goes to pesto, the gloriously green Italian pasta sauce that set the nation's food processors humming back in the '80s and is now as much a household word as marinara.

Thanks also goes to our ongoing adventure with ethnic cuisines. We have learned that for true Thai and authentic Vietnamese meals we need basil, and the only way we can get enough of this rather perishable herb is to grow it in our gardens. So we do.

Basil is in many ways an herb of great power. Its name in Greek signifies royalty. Italians deem it an herb of love. Hindus hold it sacred. In France it was traditionally considered a plant with a contrary nature, that must be sown with ranting and curses in order to make it grow.

The flavor is strong too—a bit like that of mint, to which it is related (you can tell by the square stem) but with an unmistakable character of its own. The scent is so volatile that you need only brush up against basil to know it is there. It's a good "pathway" herb, planted where feet go, to release fragrance. Medicinally, it has the power to calm both the nerves and the stomach.

Recently basil has gained fame as an ornamental plant as well. Dark Opal was the first purple basil of note, followed by Purple Ruffles and others. Those that are low in chlorophyll are less vigorous than green basil, but all are beautiful both in the garden and on the plate, and I have found "Red Rubin" a quite satisfactory performer. All are prized as a flavoring and coloring for white wine vinegar. Some basils are merely purple-tinted or, like cinnamon basil, purple-stemmed.

Some, like the lettuce leaf types (used for salads), are huge. Others, like Spicy Globe, are small-leaved, and grow on tiny plants like topiary balls.

Green basils have white flowers, which gardeners assiduously remove to keep leaf production going. This is very hard to do with the purple types, whose pink blossoms are so gorgeously set off by the dark leaves that it's a crime to discard them. It is also good form to let some of your basil bloom for the bees, which love its nectar.

Flavors also vary, according to which essential oils predominate in a given strain. I'm partial to "Genovese" for all-around cooking, a classic, large-leaved sweet Italian variety named after Genoa, the basil capital of Europe. My other favorite is lemon basil, of which there are several varieties, with its delicious lemony edge. Other varieties named for flavor overtones include anise and cinnamon (a Mexican type). The Thai basils,

in which some detect a clove taste, are especially pungent. It is easy to become a basil collector in order to savor these nuances, and some catalogs offer a long list of cultivars.

Basil is an herb for summer. Given plenty of sun, heat, regular water, and a fertile, well-drained soil, it grows abundantly. Perennial in the tropics, it's an annual everywhere else, blackening at the first hint of frost. And in a cold, wet spring it shows its contrary nature. In such a season, my basil will sulk outside the kitchen door, "palely loitering," as Keats would say, despite all the French swear words I might hurl at it. Whether I start it ahead or sow directly, I'm best off waiting till the soil has warmed up, though planting in a raised bed or a container sometimes helps. A shot of liquid seaweed will nudge it along once the weather is more to its liking.

During the summer I'll use it in eggplant casseroles, and with my favorite chopped-yellow-summer-squash-with-onions dish. For a quick showstopper, the classic plate of heirloom tomatoes with fresh mozzarella and whole basil leaves never goes out of style.

But pesto will always be my favorite, made with tons of basil, pine nuts, garlic, real Parmigiano-Reggiano cheese, and enough good olive oil to make the Cuisinart churn. (Sometimes I add it to pasta with the leaves and the nuts left whole.) When the frost apocalypse threatens, I gather great armloads and make pesto to freeze in ice cube trays. The green power cubes then go into plastic bags in the freezer, for pasta with summer's taste, or to give a soup instant personality.

Sometimes when I make pesto I combine basil with other herbs, or substitute a different one altogether, such as chervil or cilantro. But my favorite alternate pesto is made with Italian parsley—tons of it. That might even be grounds for a parsley comeback.

Drying Herbs

There's just enough time to dry some herbs before winter. It was a great year for the mint, which is still green and unspotted in the wet ditch where it resides. The oregano's flowers have faded, but the foliage is in good shape, as is that of the culinary thyme. And the sage? Glorious, as it always is in fall, and even into early winter.

Cutting and preparing herbs for drying is one of the simplest acts of garden husbandry. It took me only about half an hour to pick ample bunches of mint, oregano, thyme, and sage with stems as long and sturdy as possible. In a mere fifteen minutes I removed any brown or yellow leaves, stripped the bottom few inches of the stems, and bundled them separately, since their drying times vary. I always secure the ends with a rubber band instead of string, because the stems will contract as they dry and would therefore slip out of tied string that would not contract along with them. Ten more minutes to loop a string through each rubber band and hang the bunches up.

I've sometimes fantasized about having a kitchen with rustic wooden beams in the ceiling from which to hang my drying herbs, along with a few harvest baskets. It would look great, but in truth, the herbs would gather the dust stirred up by our active household, not to mention the vapors released in cooking. So off they go to the utility room, where the air is still and the freezer gives off a bit of dry heat. The end of a wooden shelf unit that holds the tomato puree and other stored items like jam and dried beans is a good spot. It's easy to loop the strings over it, so that

Herbs hanging from shelves, to dry

the herbs hang upside down for successful drying. The shelves are out of direct sunlight too—another plus.

There are other ways to dry food, in a dehydrator, or an oven set to "warm," for example. But hanging them is simple and effective. The herbs I've chosen to dry are easy ones. Their leaves have a firm structure, without excessive moisture—even the water-loving mint. The ideal drying herb is one like bay, which holds onto its shape, its color, and its flavor when dried. The opposite would be basil, whose soft, tender leaves are quick to wilt, and even turn black, soon after picking. Better to crush or pulverize it with olive oil and freeze it right away. You can then pry off chunks of it as needed for pesto, with the tip of a sharp knife. Tarragon is also fragile and tricky to dry.

Herbs that don't keep their flavor well enough for me to bother with include dill, cilantro, and, to some extent, parsley, which is so winter hardy that I can keep a bed of it alive through the winter in a greenhouse or cold frame and enjoy it fresh-picked. Rosemary, which I find a little too stiff when dried, is also easy to have fresh, provided I bring a pot of it indoors in time.

CHAPTER 27

Looking Forward

The urge to grow your own food runs in circles, in many and varying ways. It can come and go as a matter of importance to a civilization. It might beckon to a person at one point in life, then fade, only to return later on. And it has its seasons of planting and harvesting, renewed again—and sometimes transformed—each year.

I'm not ready to predict that we will return to being Jefferson's "nation of farmers," wholesome as that might be. If it does, I hope it does not happen because of some terrible disaster, but because of the recurrent bursts of enthusiasm I see, often in the very young, and because of the contagious joy I see in the plants themselves, as their seeds sprout, their leaves are lifted to meet the sun, and their edible parts beguile us. When my Italian honey fig started making fruits so full of sweet nectar that they would plop into my outstretched hand, I was quick to tell the greedy rooted tree, "Go ahead. Take over my little greenhouse. Take over my life." That could happen with a tomato. Or a melon.

Heidi, the early
bird, grazes in the
blueberries before
anyone else is up.

Right: Patrick and
Ella

Small Feet

Eliot and I met too late in life to raise children together, but we have
both loved giving our own the run of our gardens, just as my Louisiana
grandparents turned me loose in theirs. Something draws kids to gardens.
Eliot tells me a story about his firstborn, Melissa, when she was still
a toddler. He had planted a long line of flats with seedlings, set up on
benches beneath a row of sunny windows. One day when he was checking on them, he noted a row of tiny footprints, where Melissa had simply
marched down the row, flat by flat, enjoying the feel of the soil on her feet
and between her toes. Far from being irked, he was deeply moved by the
sight of those little prints.

Melissa's younger sister, Clara, got her nickname, the Fruit Vacuum,
from being an especially eager grazer, but it might also apply to her sons,
Bode and Hayden, and to all of us, for that matter. In fact, Melissa's twin
daughters, Emily and Heidi, are grazing legends. All kids love to pull
up our sweet young carrots and nibble on them, much to our delight,
but those two would sample any vegetable we grew. How often do you

see small children walk into a garden and stuff kale into their mouths? Those two did.

At some point, my grandchildren Patrick and Ella must have decided that gardening chores were some special adult privilege—or else that they were just fun to do with Granny. When they'd arrive for a visit, Ella would first check on the chickens, then start making a flower bouquet to take home to her mom. They liked to pick spinach together, with Patrick cutting the leaves and handing them to Ella to put in a bag. Patrick would eagerly join in with any job that was on my agenda. From an early age he was a genuine help, and both of them still are.

I know that a childhood love of gardening is sometimes sidetracked by adolescence, when other activities, and the peer group, come first. But it can return, often when they start to have a home of their own, children of their own, and little footsteps in the ground.

The Garden Year, and the One After

Along about mid-August the garden can be hard to love. Even if it's bountiful and full of good food, some weeds, spent crops, and the odd mark of disease can spoil the nubile, pristine beauty it had in June. Nevertheless, even just a small cleanup can help. Haul away the dead peavines, the wilted potato plants, and the dead foliage at the bottom of your trellised tomato array. Your tomatoes may have a touch of late blight, but so do everybody else's, and there are plenty of nice healthy tomatoes farther up the stem. Right? Get out the scuffle hoe and weed the paths. That will instantly make a huge difference.

The great thing about a vegetable garden is its yearly cycle. Every spring there's a do-over that lets you profit from all your mistakes. This time, you say, the garden will be gorgeous, and every crop productive. But somehow there is never time to do everything. You can count on distractions, interruptions, and promises of help that never quite come through.

Gardeners should have their own customized version of the famous Serenity Prayer, which begins, "God, grant me the serenity to accept the things I cannot change." In fall, especially, we ought to acknowledge all the tasks not performed in our gardens and just let them go. If there are vegetables or fruits we've had no time to dry, freeze, or can before their time was up, we must just say, with serenity, "That's okay. I'll do better next year." Easy to say?

In my case, this past summer, something distracted me from the Italian beans and sweet corn I'd vowed to put up for winter meals. It's surprising that I was even able to can some tomato puree and to freeze those ten pounds of English peas. I haven't picked the winter's apple supply yet, let alone made cider and applesauce but, hey, I can still do it all if I hurry up. Or maybe not. That's where the Serenity Prayer comes in.

My biggest regret is that I can't dry any lemon verbena leaves this year. Even fresh, it's a little too firm to chew unless the leaves are very young, but it does dry very well, curling at the edges and then expanding into an exquisite, perfumed tea when it encounters hot water. The reason I can't dry it is that I never planted it. But I'm okay with that. I'm serene. I'll just wait for next spring.

Dammit.

INDEX

PHOTOGRAPH AND ILLUSTRATION CREDITS

All photographs are by the author, except for the following:

Robert L. Anderson, USDA Forest Service, Bugwood.org; p. 198

Justine Appel, p. 32

Matt Benson, p. 5 (upper left)

Rob Cardillo, pp. 196, 269

Eleanor Damrosch, pp. 11, 12

Fritz-Martin Engel, *Creatures of the Earth's Crust*, p 112; p. 41

Stanley Joseph, p. 35

Lynn Karlin Photography, pp. 17, 66

Library of Congress Prints and Photographs Division Washington, D.C. 20540 USA. Reproduction Number: LC-USEG-D-009050; p. 18

Sherry Streeter, p. 72

Illustrations:

Radishes, p. 8: Francis C. Stokes & Co., Henry G. Gilbert Nursery and Seed Trade Catalog Collection, Biodiversity Heritage Library, public domain

Beet, p. 38: U.S. Dept. of Agriculture, National Agricultural Library, Biodiversity Heritage Library, public domain

Beans, p. 92: Francis C. Stokes & Co., Henry G. Gilbert Nursery and Seed Trade Catalog Collection, Wikimedia, CC0 1.0 Universal/public domain

Lettuce, p. 144: Francis C. Stokes & Co., Henry G. Gilbert Nursery and Seed Trade Catalog Collection, Biodiversity Heritage Library, public domain

Tomatoes, p. 188: Francis C. Stokes & Co., Henry G. Gilbert Nursery and Seed Trade Catalog Collection, Biodiversity Heritage Library, public domain

About the Author

LYNN KARLIN PHOTOGRAPHY

BARBARA DAMROSCH has worked profession-
ally in the field of horticulture since 1977. She writes,
consults, and lectures on gardening, and is co-owner,
with her husband, Eliot Coleman, of Four Season
Farm, an experimental market garden in Harborside,
Maine. From May 2003 to September 2017 she wrote
a weekly column for *The Washington Post* called
"A Cook's Garden." She is the author of several books,
The Garden Primer, *Theme Gardens*, and *The Four Season Farm Gardener's Cookbook*, co-authored with Eliot,
which won the American Horticultural Society's Book Award in 2014.
Her writing has also been published extensively in national magazines.
From 1979 to 1992 she operated her own firm, Barbara Damrosch Landscape Design, in Washington, Connecticut. Her projects since then have
included display food gardens for The Stone Barns Center for Food and
Agriculture in Pocantico Hills, New York, and an award-winning kitchen
garden she designed for Alitex Limited at the 2001 Chelsea Flower Show
in London. During the 1991 and 1992 seasons she appeared as a regular
correspondent on the PBS series *The Victory Garden*. She co-hosted, with
Eliot, the series *Gardening Naturally* for The Learning Channel, airing
from 1993 to 2003.